Motorbooks International books are also available at discounts in bulk quantity for industrial or sales-promotional use. For details write to Special Sales Manager at the Publisher's address

Library of Congress Cataloging-in-Publication Data
Norbye, Jan P.
    [Oldsmobile]
    Oldsmobile, 1946-1980 : the classic postwar years / Jan P. Norbye, Jim Dunne.
        p.   cm.
    Originally published: Oldsmobile. 1981.
    Includes index.
    ISBN 0-87938-731-9
    1. Oldsmobile automobile—History.   I. Dunne, Jim.   II. Title.
TL215.04N67   1993
629.222'0973'09045—dc20   92-33784

On the front cover: The 1950 Oldsmobile 88 Convertible Coupe owned by Bud Juneau. *Bud Juneau*

Printed and bound in the United States of America

Oldsmobile 1946-1980

The Classic Postwar Years

Jan P. Norbye and Jim Dunne

Motorbooks International
Publishers & Wholesalers

Table of Contents

CHAPTER 1

Old Cars In New Dress

AS SHERROD E. SKINNER SAT down to breakfast in his home in Lansing, Michigan, on June 6, 1944, he listened to the news on the radio. The Allies were invading France, and he knew the end of the war was in sight.

That meant it was time to activate his plan. For nearly a year he had been having meetings with superiors and subordinates to discuss preparations for a return to peacetime activities. By this time, plans were well defined and in certain regards, quite firm. Skinner had a busy year ahead of him.

As general manager of Oldsmobile Division of General Motors, Skinner had to formulate, direct and supervise the changeover from war materiel production to making Oldsmobiles again — shiny, new cars painted in all sorts of seductive colors.

Detailed planning of the postwar activity had begun in earnest in the fall of 1943, with a high degree of coordination between the corporate management and the divisional heads.

"Reconversion after World War II," explained Alfred P. Sloan, Jr., in his book *My Years with General Motors* (Doubleday and Company, Inc., 1964), "did not simply mean getting plants back into the shape they had been in before the war. The postwar program was carefully planned for expansion and improvement. It included the organizing and balancing of existing production facilities, new machines and equipment, and some completely new plants." Sloan was chairman of the corporation and realistically settled on a $500-million budget for this program.

For Oldsmobile, there could be no question of making basic changes in the product. The only tooling that did exist was that for the 1942 models, and the division did not have the means to develop anything new even if there had been time to undertake full redesign of, say, an engine or a front suspension system. There was little question, therefore, of *what* to build when the war ended, but considerable problems had to be faced with respect to *how* it was going to be built. It was not just a matter of installing the car-making machinery in its old place, pushing the button and starting a flow of new Oldsmobiles from the assembly lines. For one thing, there was a shortage of many essential raw materials, such as chrome, aluminum, rubber and the chemicals needed for certain paints.

In addition, the work force was no longer the same. A lot of Oldsmobile personnel had gone into military service or civilian assignments related to warfare, and not all would return. Oldsmobile lost fifty-two of its employees on military duty, out of a total of 2,255 who were in the service. Others had reached retirement age during the years that car production was suspended. Consequently, there was a need to 1) hire new workers and 2) train them to carry out specific automotive tasks.

These were the biggest and most obvious problems for Oldsmobile's management in the 1943-45 period. Despite the many uncertainties with regard to timing, the postwar market, the labor situation and material cost and availability, Oldsmobile's planning came very close to the target.

To get an idea of the scope and magnitude of the industrial aspect of the situation, it helps to know something about how the Oldsmobile plants were occupied during the war.

Sherrod E. Skinner (center) with Marvin E. Coyle (left) and 'Engine Charlie' Wilson (right) on the assembly line in Lansing as car production was resumed in 1945.

Several years before the war, Oldsmobile had taken over the former Durant factory in Lansing, adding twenty-one buildings on forty-eight acres not far from Oldsmobile's main plant and headquarters. Having the use of the former Durant facilities enabled Oldsmobile to move its engine and axle production, the stamping plant and the final assembly into what had been a Fisher Body plant up to that time.

Then, in 1940, Oldsmobile acquired a fifty-acre site for a new stamping plant to produce heavy steel pressings. At the time of the outbreak of war, Oldsmobile had a production capacity of 250,000 to 300,000 cars a year. Both Buick and Pontiac had greater capacity, but the expansion of Oldsmobile from 1935 to 1941 represents the rise of the Lansing-based division to take its place on an equal footing with those located in Flint and Pontiac, Michigan.

Oldsmobile car production was abruptly halted in February 1942, and by the end of the war, Oldsmobile had produced forty-eight million rounds of artillery ammunition, 140,000 aircraft machine guns and tank cannon, nearly 350,000 high-precision parts for aircraft engines and 175 million pounds of forgings for military trucks, tanks, guns and aircraft.

Christy Borth reports in his book *Masters of Mass Production* (Bobbs-Merrill, 1945) that Oldsmobile was the first car company to be associated with the production in the U.S. of the Hispano automatic cannon. "It was an automatic weapon of a type with which not even standard United States arsenals were familiar. Designed originally by the French for use by aircraft, it had been adopted and improved by the British, and a set of plans had been flown to the United States in an effort to augment production of the gun by the use of American arsenals during the Battle of Britain.

"Because no plans for this weapon were complete when the British succeeded in getting them out of France, the Americans' attempts to manufacture it were to a large degree experimental. Most of this early work was done by the Oldsmobile Division of General Motors, in Lansing, Michigan. In developing methods for production of this unfamiliar weapon, Oldsmobile workers, under the direction of Sherrod E. Skinner, wrought so many improvements that both British and United States air forces insisted that automotive plants become major sources of the guns. Awarded its first contract at the end of July 1941, Oldsmobile Division immediately subcontracted scores of little tool and automobile-accessory plants to manufacture all but the three most difficult of the cannon's hundreds of parts.

"Although the contract stipulated delivery of the first gun thirty days after all machine tools had been obtained, the first gun parts were being finished a month after the contract was signed, and the first gun was completed, mainly on makeshift machinery, two months later. By February 1942 when the necessary machine tools had finally arrived, the Lansing gunmakers were turning out more than sixty guns daily." The Olds-built automatic cannon was the model that was mounted in the wings of the Curtiss Helldiver.

The two-millionth Oldsmobile car was produced in 1941. In April of that year, and long before the U.S. entry into the war, Oldsmobile began production of 75 mm and 105 mm howitzer shells for the U.S. Army. Most of the aircraft-engine parts manufactured by Oldsmobile were used by Pratt & Whitney.

At the peak of the war-production programs, Oldsmobile had a payroll of 11,218 persons.

In recognition of their wartime performance, Oldsmobile plants were awarded the Army-Navy E pennant with three stars.

Oldsmobile resumed car production on October 15, 1945, a relative late-comer, despite thorough preparations. Ford had been first, getting back into car production on July 6, 1945. Next was Willys-Overland, with a civilian version of the Jeep, on July 17. In third place came Hudson, making its first postwar car on August 15. Most of the GM divisions followed before the end of the year.

Skinner and his assistants at Oldsmobile felt that it was more important to build the highest production volume than to offer a wide choice of models. Consequently, the product line was simplified to include four series on three different wheelbases:

Series	Wheelbase
Special 66	119 inches
Dynamic Cruiser 76	125
Dynamic Cruiser 78	125
Custom Cruiser 98	127

The 1942 model lineup had included a Special 68, whose return Skinner postponed till the 1947 model year. He gave priority to the higher-priced models, Series 70 and Series 90; the first one off the line in 1945 was a Dynamic Cruiser 78 club sedan. Production of the low-priced 66 was held up until June 19, 1946.

Starting in 1939, Oldsmobile borrowed some elements of its numbering system from Buick, which had long ranked its models on a decametric scale, originally based on horsepower ratings. Up to that time, Oldsmobile had used its own model identification code, using a double-digit number to indicate the model year (36 for 1936), and a single letter to denote engine type (F for the six-cylinder and L for the eight-cylinder).

In the Buick-inspired code, Series 60 was the low-line car with a reduced-displacement six-cylinder engine, representing an attempt to get back into the low-priced field and challenge Chrysler's Plymouth.

Series 70 was Oldsmobile's standard six, priced to compete with the Dodge, Nash, Hudson, Pontiac and Studebaker. Series 80 was the Oldsmobile Eight, aimed at the Buick market, where it also met head-on with the new Mercury, Packard One-Twenty, Chrysler Imperial and Nash Ambassador Eight. It was renamed Series 90 for 1940, and Oldsmobile then let the 80-number go out of use.

The new code did not replace the old one, which was retained in parallel—Series 60 was identified as F-39, Series 70 as G-39 and Series 80 as L-39. The same letters were carried over into 1940, the L-40 then representing the new Series 90. Increasingly, the old code was reserved for internal use, while publicity and advertising material stressed the 60, 70 and 90 identification by series.

It got more complicated in 1941. The letter code was expanded to differentiate between the series as well as the engines, so that E-41 meant an eight-cylinder car in Series 60 and F-41 was the equivalent six. Also, J-41 meant an eight-cylinder car in Series 70, whose six-cylinder counterpart was known as the G-41. Series 90 was expanded downward to include six-cylinder models (H-41) as well as continuing the eight (L-41).

Simultaneously, the series code was modified to include engine identification, the G-41 being called '76' and the L-41, '98.' And there, for those who had been wondering, is the origin of Oldsmobile's famous Ninety-Eight appellation. It's not a meaningless number, but one which grew out of a code.

For marketing purposes, the 1941 models were also given names. Series 60 became Special, Series 70 was given the title Dynamic Cruiser and Series 90 was designated Custom Cruiser. Thus, Oldsmobile's use of the term Dynamic dates back to 1941. Also it should be noted that the Cruiser name in those days covered the whole series, from convertible coupe to limousine, and had no special attachment to station wagons (as it now has).

Oldsmobile announced its 1942 models as a lineup of five series on three wheelbases:

Name	Series	Code	Wheelbase
Special (six)	66	F-42	119 inches
Special (eight)	68	E-42	119
Dynamic Cruiser (six)	76	G-42	125
Dynamic Cruiser (eight)	78	J-42	125
Custom Cruiser (eight)	98	L-42	127

These are, in essence, the cars that were dusted off, given some trim and decor changes, and put on the market as 1946 models.

Oldsmobile's exterior design had evolved as a close parallel to the cars of its sister divisions under the direction and coordination of Styling Vice President Harley J. Earl. Throughout the late thirties, Oldsmobile shared the Fisher B-body with the Buick Special, Buick Super and La Salle.

Elements of modern styling began appearing with the launching of the 1933 models, which were the first with fender skirts. Windshields were flat through the 1934 model year, a split V-design being adopted for 1935. That year the headlamps were moved up from fender props to brackets on the sides of the radiator grille. The grille changed from a concave shield design in 1933-34 to a convex, protruding nose in 1935-36. The theme was strictly vertical—just wide enough to enclose the radiator, while running the full height from bumper level to hood ornament. Built-in trunks became available on the 1936 models.

Up to 1936, the Art and Colour Section worked as a single staff with responsibility for the bodies of all car divisions vested in the same personnel. Inherent in this arrangement were great risks of doing harm to the marque image of the divisions, by lack of protection for the exclusive rights of one division to a specific design feature, for instance, and by the system's failure to promote continuity in the evolution of a styling theme associated with one particular division, such as

The last styling stage before the 1941-42 models was the 1940 body, which hints at things to come. The grille was being transformed from a vertical to a horizontal shape, and the headlamps were becoming integral with the front sheet metal.

Oldsmobile. Thus there was a threat of increasing sameness and similarity directed against all GM car makes, which Harley Earl finally perceived as being contrary to the interests of his own department, the car divisions and the corporation as a whole.

The solution was to divide the Art and Colour Section into divisional studios, each one subject to the same overall direction and coordination from above, but working independently of the other studios. From 1936 onward, all but Earl himself and his two top assistants, Howard O'Leary and Stanford Landell, were assigned to one studio handling only one make of car. The studios were separated by walls, and doors were kept locked so that stylists working on Buick or Pontiac designs would not be able to see what was going on with Oldsmobile—and vice versa.

George Snyder was made chief designer of the Oldsmobile studio, and he directed the restyling for 1937 and 1938. On the 1937 models, the grille was pulled down and the sheet metal extended above it. Headlamp fairings became longer, fender lines were raised (and cut off abruptly to avoid extending into the door panels). For 1938, the grille reached higher again, and its lower part was flanked by louvered panels blending into the fender lines. Headlamps were moved into depressions formed for that purpose on top of the fenders.

A thorough restyling for 1939 brought a lower grille, and the grille pattern was extended to the louvered panels below the headlamps, which had been moved inboard of the fenders. Bumpers were very simple, straight bars with two overriders, and the cars still had running boards.

Snyder was head of the Oldsmobile studio when the 1940 models were designed. It was Lewis Simon, working under Snyder, who actually did the 1940 front end.

Front fender lines tapered off into the cowl sheet metal on the 1940 models, which had a horizontal-theme grille, lowered from the 1939 version, and widened to incorporate the louvered panels below the headlamps. Running boards were enclosed on the 1941 models, and a lot of horizontal chrome strips showed up on the fenders.

The headlights were actually incorporated in the fender profile. Below each headlamp was a vertical chrome ribbon with seven ribs, each forming a column that framed the grille on the sides. Grille design and decor became bolder and windshield angles faster, though the V-front design with two-piece flat glass was retained. Trunks were fully integrated with the body profile, and used as a styling device to balance the overall design.

Much of the credit for the cohesiveness of the 1941 models belongs to Edmund E. Anderson, who became chief designer for the Oldsmobile studio in 1938, when design and modeling work was just starting on the 1941 models.

The production-model 1942 grille was trend-setting in that it integrated the bumper with the decorative design elements of the grille assembly. The two bumper overriders carried a three-part horizontal wing, whose center section was surmounted by a separate split grille, completing a pyramidal theme for the overall composition. The main grille spread out behind the bumper overriders, ending with parking lights below the headlamps. It was a busy and confused design, developed by Roy Brown, who later created the front end of the 1957 Edsel for Ford.

In his preliminary sketches, triple horizontal wings extended along the upper edge of the grille and around the fenders to the wheel openings, an idea that was close to Chrysler/DeSoto decor. The grille itself was an assembly of horizontal wires, the center section protruding to form a base for the hood lines. The headlamps remained in their inboard position, with fairings half submerged into the fender surface.

One of Brown's sketches showed a bumper with three overriders—one central, and one in line with each headlamp. The actual 1942 model had only two, positioned closer together, forming part of the grille.

The 1946-model sheet metal was basically unchanged from 1942, but the new models had a new grille of striking simplicity, consisting of four horizontal bars, all bent down at the outer ends while maintaining their spacing, so as to form a layered image. It was modern, it was original, and it was to serve as an identification mark for Oldsmobile for a long time.

Because of the way styling sketches and models were moved around—one design often being shown to several divisions—it is often difficult to trace the origin of a new idea. But, we believe the 1946 Oldsmobile grille design came from George Snyder, who worked on camouflage and other military projects that GM handled during the war and had a hand in many postwar facelifts at GM Styling.

Sherrod Skinner had a good relationship with his bosses at the head of the corporation, and Oldsmobile was regarded with benevolence from above. The president, Charles E. Wilson, had no strong ties to any other car division, and therefore no biased loyalty to a particular make of GM car. The executive vice president, Marvin E. Coyle, had spent most of his earlier career at Chevrolet, and while it is true that Chevrolet continued to gain strength while Coyle held positions of high power in the corporation, there is no indication that its growth was gained at the expense of Oldsmobile or any other division.

And remember, it was Sloan himself, as chairman, who approved all plans, whether it concerned plant expansions or what cars would have which body. Sloan was trained as an engineer, but found his energy channeled toward management at an early age. He became famous, of course, as the quintessential administrator and the architect of GM's rise to its predominant position in the world's motor industry.

Wilson was an engineer with wide-ranging experience, and it was perhaps logical that Sloan should balance his appointment by naming an executive vice president who was basically an accountant.

Marvin Coyle was mainly self-taught, having been born on a farm in Crawford County, Pennsylvania, but having grown up in Fairmount, Indiana, where his formal schooling ended before he reached the age of twenty. He went to work for a cooperage firm in Louisville, Kentucky, and in 1911, three years later, he moved to Detroit in answer to a job advertisement. The job was at Cartercar, a moribund General Motors division which was liquidated in 1915. Coyle was transferred to Oakland, and early in 1917 came to Chevrolet where he was to make his reputation for managerial talent. He became controller of Chevrolet and then assistant to the president, as the general manager was called then. William S. Knudsen held that office from 1922 to 1933, making Coyle vice president of Chevrolet in 1930, and general manager when Knudsen was promoted to the post of executive vice president.

Coyle was to follow in his footsteps, for after running Chevrolet for thirteen years, he succeeded to the office of executive vice president of GM in 1946.

Charlie Wilson had come up another route entirely. He was born in Minerva, Ohio, but his family moved to Pittsburgh when the boy was fourteen. He went to the Carnegie Institute of Technology where he proved to be a brilliant student and graduated with a degree in electrical engineering before his nineteenth birthday. His first job was with Westinghouse, and his first experience with cars came in 1912 when he helped design starter motors. By 1916 he was in charge of all electrical-equipment engineering at Westinghouse.

Three years later he left Westinghouse to become chief engineer and sales manager of the automotive division of Remy Electric Company. This firm belonged to General Motors, and was eventually merged with Delco. By 1926 Wilson was president and general manager of Delco-Remy. Sloan was so impressed with Wilson's performance at Delco-Remy that he made him a GM vice president in 1939 and included Wilson in the policy and administrative committees.

Wilson became acting president of GM in 1941, when Knudsen resigned to go to Washington and direct the industrial programs for defense production. It was under Wilson's leadership that GM produced $12 billion worth of armaments during World War II. In 1946 Sloan formalized his position and made Wilson president of General Motors.

Wilson (whose middle name was Erwin) was colloquially known as 'Engine Charlie,' not because he worked like an engine or resembled one in any way. It was a nickname invented on Wall Street to distinguish him from another C. E. Wilson (whose given name was Charles Edward), long-time president of the General Electric Company—hence his handle of 'Electric Charlie.'

Engine Charlie proved himself as a master of corporate planning and industrial achievement during the postwar expansion. He was also smart enough to know when to stay out and not meddle. It was his confidence in Skinner that gave Oldsmobile the advantage of a relatively free hand and an opportunity for taking initiatives that might nave been denied to a less trusted (and less profitable) division.

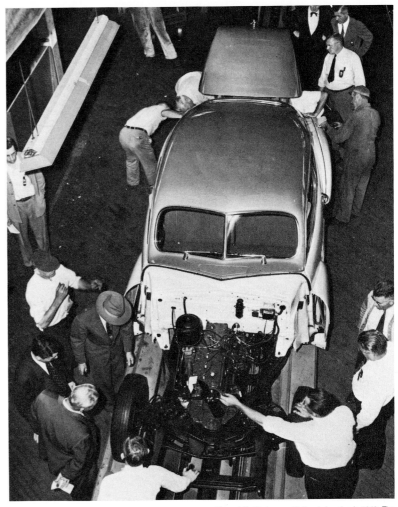

View of the final assembly line in Lansing in 1946. The main part of the body was 'dropped' on the chassis in one operation, while the front end sheet metal was added later.

CHAPTER
2

The Ballast of Things Past

PRODUCT ENGINEERING TOOK a back seat to production engineering in the 1944-46 period. The pressure from Skinner was on the need to produce what they had, and not to complicate the production by finding new and different things to make. Sherrod E. Skinner was an engineer, but he was not an automobile man in the sense of having drawn cars as a kid, repaired cars or hopped them up as a teenager, or being destined for the auto industry to the exclusion of all other career choices.

His appointment as general manager of Oldsmobile was in no way presaged by his personal inclinations, previous experience or visions of future Oldsmobiles (if he had any). He had never worked for a car company until August 5, 1940, when he succeeded Charles L. McCuen in the top spot at Olds Motor Works (as it was still called up to January 1, 1942, when it became Oldsmobile Division).

Who and what was this man, then? Sherrod E. Skinner was born in New Britain, Connecticut, in 1896, attended local schools and graduated from Rensselaer Polytechnic Institute in Troy, New York, in 1920, armed with a degree in mechanical engineering.

His first job, apart from working as a machinist's mate while serving in the United States Navy during World War I, was as a production engineer for the general engineering firm of Landers, Frary and Clark Company in New Britain. In his ten years with this company, he rose to the position of assistant general superintendent, which was somewhat short of his ambitions.

He began to look around for a position with a more promising future, and in 1930 he joined Ternstedt Manufacturing Company, which had been a division of General Motors since 1919. The company produced metal trim, various body hardware and auto accessories.

As chief engineer of Ternstedt, Skinner was responsible not only for production and quality, but also for new product development. On December 1, 1935, he was promoted to general manager of Ternstedt. The division prospered under Skinner; and the big bosses of the corporation, William S. Knudsen and Alfred P. Sloan, Jr., regarded him as a potential candidate for the highest office. But traditionally, no one gets to be chief executive officer of GM without successfully having led a car division for some time. That's why Skinner was transferred to Oldsmobile—to round out his qualifications for further promotions. Of course, his performance at Oldsmobile would come under the closest scrutiny, not only by his superiors, but from rivals at similar levels of executive rank.

Before we delve into an analysis of Skinner's leadership and contributions to Oldsmobile, we must look in some detail at the cars the division was building during that period.

The engines were of prewar origin, one six-cylinder and one eight-cylinder—not very modern examples of engine design even at the time of their introduction.

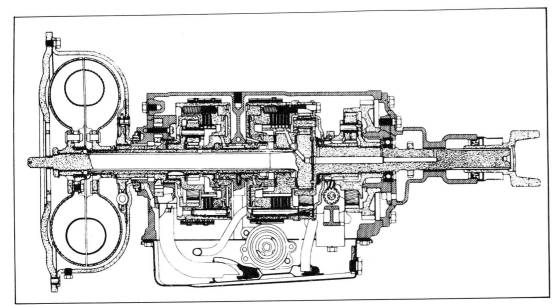

In its 1946 version (left), the Hydra-matic transmission consisted of a fluid coupling (in place of the clutch) and a four-speed planetary gear set, replacing the three-speed synchromesh transmission. Automatic shifts were made by hydraulic servos. The first production-model transmission (right) with automatic shifts became available on Oldsmobiles in 1940. Fluid coupling was much larger in diameter than the gear system.

The standard transmission was a three-speed column-shift with synchromesh on second and top, while Hydra-matic was optional on all models.

The 1946 chassis was basically unchanged from 1942 specifications. There was the same X-braced frame and the same quadri-coil springing, with anti-sway bars both front and rear, and double-acting hydraulic shock absorbers at all wheels. The steering system was called 'dual center-control,' and used worm and double-roller steering gear. Hydraulic four-wheel brakes were standard, with a pistol-grip handbrake offering cable-actuation of the rear wheel brake shoes.

Both the six- and eight-cylinder Oldsmobile engines were of the L-head type, with side valves arranged in one row on the same side of the block. If that seems primitive to the eyes of today's drivers and mechanics, it's useful to remember that the L-head was still the industry standard in 1946. Among its proponents were Packard, Chrysler, Hudson, Pontiac and Continental for in-line engines; plus Ford, Mercury, Lincoln and Cadillac for V-type engines.

L-head engines were easy to manufacture, and production costs were low. Maintenance, such as valve adjustment, and repairs, such as valve-grinding and decoking of the head, were simple operations. If they were not among the most efficient, L-head engines tended to run quietly and reliably, with long life.

The 1946-model engines had the following key specifications:

Type	Bore × Stroke	Cu. in.	Hp @ rpm	Torque @ rpm
L-6	3.50×4.125	238.1	100 @ 3400	190 @ 1400
L-8	3.25×3.875	257.1	110 @ 3600	210 @ 2000

Both had a single, one-barrel Carter carburetor and a compression ratio of 6.5:1.

The eight ran faster because the stroke was shorter and the pistons lighter. The six had a fatter torque curve in the low range because of its longer stroke. Both engines had a considerable background, with direct ancestors dating back to the twenties.

The original Oldsmobile six was new in 1923, a 40-hp unit with its cylinders cast *en bloc*. With a bore and stroke of 2.75x4.75 inches, and a displacement of 169 cubic inches, it got the reputation of being a pretty weak engine, not just in horsepower terms, but also with regard to wear and reliability. Boring it out to 2.875 inches (and 185 cubic inches) for 1927 gave it a little more power but no more stamina.

A completely new engine was designed for 1928 by a team led by the young Charles L. McCuen, who had joined the Olds engineering staff in 1926, with recent experience from Rickenbacker and Packard.

The new six had a shorter stroke of 4.125 inches, while the bore was expanded to 3.1875 inches, which gave a 197.5-cubic-inch displacement. In 1928 tune with a compression ratio of 5.0:1, it was rated at 62 hp. This engine was kept in production through 1933 without basic alterations. Power output was raised to 84 hp for 1934 by boring it out to 3.38 inches (213.5 cubic inches). Two years later the cast-iron pistons gave way to aluminum ones, and power output climbed to 90 hp.

A complete redesign followed, in which the six was brought in line with a new straight-eight then on the drawing board. These engines were designed for manufacturing on the same machining lines, and for more rational production, with a high degree of parts commonality. For historical reasons, due to the differences in origin and evolution, the pre-1937 six- and eight-cylinder Olds engines had no interchangeable parts and did not share tooling.

The 4.125-inch stroke was retained in the new six, and the bore increased to 3.44 inches, which raised displacement to 229.6 cubic inches. With a compression ratio of 6.1:1, the engine delivered 95 hp at 3400 rpm. Maximum torque was a substantial 180 pounds-feet at 1600 rpm.

The new engine program began in 1934 when Harold T. Youngren became chief engineer (succeeding Charles L. McCuen, who had been promoted to general manager the year before). Youngren had wide-ranging experience in engine design, chassis engineering and complete vehicle development, from Allis-Chalmers, Westinghouse, Falls Motor Company, Harley-Davidson, Fergus, Pierce-Arrow, Studebaker and Buick. Though he had never before held the title of chief engineer, he was the best-qualified engineer Oldsmobile had ever had.

It was Youngren who laid out the new engines, avoiding any revolutionary break with Oldsmobile's traditions in power unit design. He was able to improve the engines in terms of sturdiness and lightness, while simultaneously achieving gains in power, performance and smoothness.

An experimental engineer named Jack Wolfram made important contributions to the development of the new engines. He had come to Oldsmobile in 1928, after seven years with Chandler Motor Car Company in Cleveland, and became assistant chief engineer in 1940.

Before we get into a detailed description of the engines, it is necessary to look at the background of the eight-cylinder unit.

Oldsmobile introduced its first in-line eight-cylinder engine in a new, higher-priced car line—the L-32—in the 1932 model year. It was a long-stroke unit, with 3.00-inch bore and 4.25-inch stroke, giving 240 cubic inches of displacement and a rated output of 90 hp. Youngren had a particular dislike for this engine, and began laying out a new one shortly after his arrival in Lansing. It went into production for the 1937 models, with a short 3.875-inch stroke and a bore widened to 3.25 inches, which raised the displacement to 257 cubic inches.

Both engines continued using the same construction materials, such as cast iron for cylinder heads as well as the blocks. The L-head concept was retained, and the new engines did not look all that different from their predecessors when seen with all their accessories installed under the open hood of the car. The vital differences were internal.

For example, Youngren had insisted upon the use of full-length water jackets completely surrounding each cylinder. By achieving more uniform temperatures throughout the engine, distortion was averted and bore wear reduced, which meant longer life between overhauls as well as reduced oil consumption.

Due to the small difference in cylinder displacement, it was not logical to have the same cylinder spacing for the eight as in the six. That would have resulted in a longer and heavier eight, and invited a whole rash of problems from crankshaft vibration to installation space.

The engines were, however, designed to share connecting rods. The rod was a steel forging, with the big end split on the centerline and bolted together. Rod length was considerable, 7.8125 inches, in the interest of reducing side thrust on the piston and thereby limiting bore wear and restricting oil consumption as the miles began to tell.

The two engines also had the same valves, with head diameters of 1.5625 for the intakes and 1.422 for the exhausts. The eight had a different camshaft with higher lift—0.314 inch compared with 0.298 inch for the six.

Coil-type valve springs were used, having 9½ coils inside a free length of 2.625 inches. Valve stems ran in copper-alloy guides, and the lifters were 3.09 inches high for the six-cylinder intake valves, 3.10 inches for the exhausts. The respective figures for the eight were 3.09-3.10 and 3.12-3.13 inches.

Camshafts were chain-driven from the crankshafts. Both engines used the same timing chain, a forty-seven-link design of one-inch width and a total length of 23.5 inches.

Because of its smaller bore, the eight-cylinder engine had lighter pistons (twenty-four ounces compared with twenty-seven ounces in the six). In both engines, all pistons carried two compression rings and two oil-control rings. The eight-cylinder had capacity for six quarts of oil, five quarts in the six-cylinder.

The six-cylinder crankshaft ran in four main bearings, curiously non-standard in their dimensions. Journal diameters gradually got bigger toward the back of the engine, starting with 2.478 to 2.479 inches for the front main, with intermediate steps of 2.54 and 2.666 before reaching maximum at 2.686 for the rearmost.

The rearmost bearing was also the widest at 1.625 inches, compared with 1.53 for the front main and 1.375 for the two in the middle. This may have facilitated some aspects of assembly, but the number of different bearing shells must have been a headache for the engine fitter as well as for the spare parts department.

Crankpin bearings were all the same: 1.25 inches wide and 2.123 to 2.124 inches in diameter. Thus, the crankpin-to-main-journal overlap varied from 0.2375 to 0.3375 inch, which must be considered ample in a slow-running, low stressed engine such as the Olds six.

The shaft was 33.125 inches long from end to end and weighed 84.3 pounds. The eight-cylinder crankshaft had a weight of 95.8 pounds and measured 38.875 inches in overall length.

Both crankshafts were steel forgings, having hardened bearing journals and integral counterweights: seven for the six-cylinder and eight for the eight-cylinder shaft.

The eight-cylinder crankshaft was carried in five main bearings. Bearing dimensions were similar to those in the six, following the same taper pattern toward the front. In the eight-cylinder engine, in fact, bearings were narrower in some cases; right down to 1.1875 for the second and fourth mains. Crankpin bearing sizes were identical, however.

Carter carburetors were used on all Oldsmobile engines for many years. The six was equipped with Model 481-S which had a throat diameter of 1.375 inches. On the eight, Oldsmobile mounted a Model 503-S with a 1.1875-inch throat.

Apart from boring out the six to a full 3.50 inches for 1939 and raising displacement to 238.1 cubic inches, neither engine was subject to redesign as long as it remained in production. Running modifications were made, however, to modernize the engine whenever technically and commercially feasible. For instance, Oldsmobile adopted electro-hardened aluminum pistons for both sixes and eights for the 1946-model engines.

Oldsmobile's 1946 models had a three-speed synchromesh gearbox with column-shift as standard, with a dry, single-plate clutch and an open, one-piece propeller shaft taking the drive to the hypoid-bevel rear axle. The shaft was tubular, with a universal joint at each end and a front needle bearing just ahead of the knot in the frame X-bracing. Automatic transmission—Hydra-matic—was optional on all models at an extra cost of $134.24.

While the manual transmission had hardly evolved at all since the adoption of synchromesh (by Cadillac in 1928, followed by Oldsmobile three years later), the replacement of the floor-mounted lever by a long linkage to the steering column cannot be regarded as an improvement in transmission design. The change came about from a desire to offer room for three abreast on the front bench seat (for which most cars of the thirties were really too narrow, anyway).

Attention focused instead on the automatic transmission, where Oldsmobile had indeed become a leader, though it was not part of the project at the outset.

Alfred P. Sloan, Jr., recounts in his book *My Years with General Motors:* ''By 1928 the Research Laboratories had reached a consensus on an automatic-transmission form that might be satisfactory. This was an infinitely-variable type using a steel-on-steel friction drive employing a mechanical principle like that of a ball bearing.

The Oldsmobile six-cylinder engine in 1938 version, with the Automatic Safety Transmission attached. It's a test engine, put on a wooden tabletop stand after removal of the oil pan, awaiting inspection.

''The Buick Division was assigned the job of developing this transmission, since we had no general engineering staff at the time. Many units were built and tests conducted, and it was finally determined to produce this type of transmission in 1932. However, despite our best efforts, we never managed to solve all the problems involved, and this transmission was never put in any General Motors car sold to the public.

''By 1934 a group of engineers in the Cadillac Division were finally on the road that was to lead to the first mass-production automatic transmission for passenger cars, the Hydra-matic. This special group was transferred to the corporation's Engineering Staff at the end of 1934 to become the Transmission Development Group. A set of pilot models were built, tested and turned over to the Oldsmobile engineers. During 1935 and 1936 thousands of test miles were run on different experimental units from one end of the United States to the other.''

Before Oldsmobile got involved, the principal engineers on the project were Earl Thompson, the father of synchromesh, and his top assistant, Oliver K. Kelley.

The outcome of Oldsmobile's work on this project was the first successful automatic gear changer used on an American-made car. A four-speed unit, Oldsmobile called it the Automatic Safety Transmission and made it available as an option for certain models.

The Automatic Safety Transmission was first offered for the Oldsmobile Eight only, as an eighty-dollar option, starting in May 1937. The following year Oldsmobile made it available also on the six-cylinder models (and even offered it to Buick, who listed it as an option for the Special).

It was called Automatic Safety Transmission not because there was anything unsafe about the standard gearbox, but because it enabled the driver to keep both hands on the wheel even when shifting, which was assumed to be a possible safety factor.

Despite the name, it was not truly automatic, but only semi-automatic. It did not have two-pedal control, but relied on the use of a clutch pedal that was used for moving off from standstill.

The selector lever had two forward-drive positions, L for low and H for high, plus N for neutral and R for reverse. The driver had to select L or H before pushing in the clutch pedal and releasing it. If left in low, the car would not upshift beyond second gear. In H position, the car would start in first, then skip second, and operate thereafter with automatic shifts between third and fourth only. Automatic shift points were determined by car speed and engine load (as registered from the throttle opening).

The gearing consisted of two sets of planetary gears, with a brake band and an overrunning clutch for each gear set. The bands and clutches were controlled by hydraulic servos actuated by pressured oil whose flow was directed (a) by the selector mechanism and (b) by speed and load-sensing devices.

Tests with the eight-cylinder Oldsmobile at the GM proving grounds showed that the Automatic Safety Transmission gave fifteen percent better average fuel mileage than the standard three-speed transmission.

This was largely explained by the change in axle ratio that accompanied the automatic's installation. Since it had four speeds rather than three, it also gave a twelve-percent improvement in acceleration times.

The step from semi-automatic to fully automatic operation involved considerable technical innovation, but Oldsmobile accomplished it in a remarkably short time.

O. K. Kelley was an expert on hydraulics, and had long been familiar with the hydraulic coupling, originally patented in 1905 by Dr. Hermann Föttinger. It was commonly used in ships during the 1920's, and in 1926 Harold Sinclair began developing a motor-vehicle version. The chief engineer of Daimler in Coventry became interested, and through their collaboration, Sinclair's Vulcan 'fluid flywheel' was combined with the Wilson four-speed planetary transmission and used for the 1930-model Daimler cars. The Daimler example was not the only input that led Kelley to a hydraulic solution.

There was also the Lysholm-Smith torque-convertor transmission, invented by Alf Lysholm in Sweden, first used by Leyland for its big buses in 1931 and standardized in 1934.

General Motors began experimenting with Lysholm-Smith transmissions on Yellow Coach (later GMC) vehicles in collaboration with the Twin Disc Clutch Company which held the American rights to the Lysholm-Smith system. Spicer Model 90 and 91 torque-converter transmissions went into production for GMC coaches in 1938.

Because of the torque-converter's higher slip losses and the greater experimental ingredient in its behavior, Kelley preferred the fluid coupling when he developed the Hydra-matic. Later, when he created the Dynaflow for Buick, he took the torque converter approach.

The first Hydra-matic was essentially a combination of the Automatic Safety Transmission with more elaborate automatic shift devices and the addition of a fluid coupling in place of the clutch.

Much of the development work performed by Oldsmobile was carried out by a young engineer named Harold N. Metzel, who had started out as a test driver at the proving grounds when he joined Oldsmobile in 1928. His contributions were deemed so valuable that by 1937, Youngren appointed him transmission engineer, with responsibility for all transmission work within the division.

The Hydra-matic was introduced on the 1940-model Oldsmobile, and by the end of the 1941 model year, over 130,000 Oldsmobiles equipped with automatic transmission had been built.

Cars equipped with Hydra-matic used a 3.63:1 axle ratio, whereas the cars having synchromesh gearboxes had axles with a 4.30:1 final drive ratio. This change in overall gearing enabled Oldsmobile to claim that the Hydra-matic actually saved ten to fifteen percent gasoline.

To give credit where credit is due, it should be pointed out here that Chrysler had been the first in America to offer a fluid coupling. It was part of the three-speed Fluidrive transmission (with manual shifts) that was first made optional on the 1939 Chrysler Imperial Eight.

On the original Hydra-matic, the shift lever had four positions: neutral, hi, lo and reverse. With the level in hi position, the transmission made all shifts automatically between first, second, third and fourth gear ratios in accordance with torque requirement at the wheels. With the lever in lo position, the car could operate only in first and second gear ratios. Manual use of lo was intended for emergencies, extremely steep grades or for engine-braking.

The transmission was made up of four basic units: the fluid coupling, two forward-drive planetary gear sets and one reverse planetary gear set. Each gear set comprised a central sun gear, an outer ring gear (annulus) with internal teeth, and three planetary pinions in mesh with both the ring gear and the sun gear.

Gears were engaged or disengaged by applying or releasing a front clutch and sets of brake bands working against the outer faces of the ring gears. The bands were actuated by hydraulic servos controlled via a hydraulic governor linked to the propeller shaft and a hydraulic valve body connected to the throttle linkage, with manual override.

Theoretically, the output shaft turned at 0.694 times crankshaft speed in third gear. In second gear, output rpm was reduced to 0.395 of crankshaft speed; in first gear, 0.274.

With the throttle fully open, the shift from first to second occurred at 15 mph. At 30 mph, it would go from second to third. The upshift into direct-drive top would follow at about 65 mph. At light throttle, the shifts would occur in quick succession, with fourth-gear engagement at about 20 mph. Stepping on the gas had a kickdown effect, capable of downshifting to third at any speed between 20 and 60 mph.

In 1940, Oldsmobile asked a mere $57 for the Hydra-matic option, which was a long way from recouping the real costs. It meant that General Motors was selling the automatic transmission below cost in order to achieve a major expansion of the total car market. Lack of skill in gear-shifting would no longer be a block to anyone who wanted to buy a car.

Maurice Platt, who had joined Vauxhall about 1937 and made his first visit to Detroit the following year, remembers meeting O. K. Kelley and driving prototype cars with hydra-matic transmissions. Writing in *Motor*'s (London) issue of April 9, 1966, Platt made this interesting comment: "Going back for a moment to the decisions which preceded putting the Hydra-matic into production, I think it is worth emphasizing that the top management of General Motors knew quite well that the extra cost would be excessive unless tremendous efforts were made both by the designers and by the production engineers. They also had to have sufficient faith in eventual sales to authorize the heavy capital investment in highly productive machine tools needed to achieve minimum piece costs."

The 1946-model Hydra-matic had one important advance over the prewar version. It introduced the internal-gear type of oil pump for continuous circulation of the fluid in the coupling.

While bodies were usually renewed on a three-year cycle, engines could have a production life of fifteen to twenty years without basic change and the chassis

The Oldsmobile eight-cylinder engine in 1948 version was practically unchanged from prewar specifications. It had a bore of 3.25 inches and a stroke of 3.875 inches, giving a 257.1-cubic-inch displacement.

was also not subject to annual alterations. Major elements were replaced at spaced-out intervals, all in accordance with the division's overall engineering and manufacturing programs, and coordinated with corporate planning to an ever-increasing extent. In trying to analyze the anatomy of the 1946-model Oldsmobile, we find that all the main components were developed well before the war.

View of the Oldsmobile manufacturing complex in Lansing in 1946. The administration building is near the center, right of the parking lot. Shipping department had its own railhead.

The prewar Oldsmobile chassis was developed under the direction of Maurice A. Thorne, who had been a development engineer with Studebaker for some years before he was placed in charge of the company's proving grounds outside South Bend. When Pierce-Arrow came under Studebaker control in 1929,

Thorne was sent to Buffalo as an experimental engineer to help the company develop new and modern products. Thorne lost faith in Studebaker's management when the corporation fell into receivership in 1933, and began to look around for a better job—no simple thing in the middle of the Depression years.

But Thorne had a reputation, and Oldsmobile was glad to get him. He went to Lansing in 1934 with the title of project engineer. Within a year he was in charge of chassis design, and in 1940 he became assistant chief engineer for body, chassis, electrical and accessories, working closely with Youngren and serving as his right-hand man.

The X-braced frame of the 1946 Oldsmobile was wide-based, with its side-members running as close to the rear wheels as possible, and keeping the same width close to the cowl area, where they were bent inward to make room for the front wheels to steer. Cross-members carried engine mounts, and the engine was set well back in the chassis—only the front cover and accessories coming forward of the wheel axis. This engine position tended to provide even weight distribution, a better-balanced ride, faster steering response, reduced understeer and lighter steering effort.

This frame had been created for the 1941 models, which was directly based on the 1937 frame design. Prior to 1937, Oldsmobile had used ladder-type frames with a plurality of cross-members running straight across between the two side-members. For 1937, Oldsmobile had a new frame, with a rigid central X-bracing, and a reduced number of cross-members. The new frame was lighter than the 1936 version, and yet it had far greater strength and torsional stiffness.

The rear axle was located by long, diagonal torque arms whose forward ends were pivoted in brackets on the X-member, just aft of the knot. A track bar located the axle laterally. The coil springs were mounted slightly behind the axle housing, with hydraulic shock absorbers mounted separately. The rear anti-sway bar ran across the chassis below the differential nosepiece. This design stemmed from 1937 when Oldsmobile first adopted coil-spring rear suspension for the 1938 models.

Earlier models had used Hotchkiss drive, with semi-elliptic leaf springs to take up the driving thrust as well as to carry the load and provide a flexible ride.

At the front end, Oldsmobile had independently sprung wheels with upper and lower A-frame control arms, and coil springs standing on the lower arm. Shock absorbers were hydraulic, and an anti-sway bar was standard on all models.

When Oldsmobile first adopted 'knee-action' for the 1934 models, the design was a copy of Cadillac's, engineered by the great Maurice Olley.

Thorne altered the geometry to suit the Oldsmobile's shorter wheelbase and lighter weight. For the 1937 models he revised the complete front suspension system, using lower control arms of I-beam-section forged steel in preference to the former arm which was fabricated from box-section steel members. Further modifications were made for 1939, and then—for manufacturing reasons—there was a complete redesign for 1941. This became the version used for the 1946 model cars.

Oldsmobile's brakes had progressed in detail at irregular intervals since the division first adopted hydraulic brakes on the 1934 models.

All 1946 models had eleven-inch drums on all wheels, with wider linings for the eight-cylinder models. On sixes, front linings were 2.0 inches wide; and rear ones, 1.75 inches wide. On the eight-cylinder cars, front linings had a 2.5-inch width; the rear ones, an even 2.0 inches. These dimensions gave total lining areas of 159.8 and 181.1 square inches, respectively.

Brake shoes were arranged in duo-servo fashion, to get some measure of self-energization in both trailing and leading shoes. Power brakes, of course, were still a thing of the future.

CHAPTER
3
Opportunities and Constraints

WHAT THE AUTO INDUSTRY had going for it in 1945 was the hungriest car market ever. It was due to the cumulative effects of a 3½-year production stoppage, following a decade of economic recession. The national market had risen to 3.88 million cars in 1929 and hit a low of 1.1 million in 1932. The four-million mark was never approached before the war, for after reaching 3.4 million cars in 1936 and 3.5 million in 1937, the market fell below two million cars in 1938.

There was a pent-up demand, estimated at between twelve and twenty million cars, which meant that the industry would have to work to capacity for up to five years before it could be filled, and before the scrappage rate could begin its return to normal levels.

No company with the ability to produce cars had anything to fear from competition. The need for advertising and sales promotion was at zero. Cars sold themselves as soon as they were unloaded at the dealership. For the factories, the only headache was to assure fair and profitable distribution.

Oldsmobile sales executives did not need to worry about Henry J. Kaiser going into the automobile business, offering the Kaiser car at the price of an average Oldsmobile. Nor did the presence of DeSoto, Mercury, Studebaker, Dodge, Nash or Hudson in the same price bracket constitute the slightest germ of worry for the men in charge of Oldsmobile. Every company, every division, had a ready buyer for every car that could be built. Their sales performance was dependent purely and exclusively on the factor's production capacity.

Into this seller's market jumped Oldsmobile with its slimmed-down model range, best illustrated in comparison with the last of the prewar four-door sedan offerings:

| Series | Baseline Price (suggested retail) | |
	1942	1946
66	$ 984	$1,407
68	1,026	suspended
76	1,086	1,497
78	1,128	1,584
98	1,307	1,762

The 66 was built on a 119-inch wheelbase, available as a four-door sedan, club sedan and club coupe. It was painted in the division's standard colors in solid or two-tone combinations.

In June 1946, Skinner said that a 66 convertible coupe and a 66 station wagon would follow as soon as possible, perhaps by August. They were added as 1947 models.

The Dynamic Cruiser (Series 76 and 78) was built as a club sedan and four-door sedan only, while the Custom Cruiser (Series 98) had a convertible coupe in addition to the four-door sedan and club sedan. The four-door sedan was a

1948 Oldsmobile 98 Futuramic club sedan introduced spectacular new styling. It was built on a 122-inch wheelbase and used curved glass in the windshield and backlight.

notchback, while the club sedan had a fastback roofline. A fastback version of the four-door B-body sedan was available as a no-cost option. All of Oldsmobile's 1946-model bodies were completely 'bonderized' and finished with six coats of lacquer.

Body engineering was, as before the war, the responsibility of John Oswald, who also served as the division's director of styling. That does not mean he took part in the body design at the concept stage. It means that his opinions were the division's guidelines in their considerations of proposals from GM Styling.

The Oldsmobile styling studio was part of the corporate Styling Staff, and the division was its customer, in the sense that it had the right to turn down anything the stylists came up with. On the other hand, the division was not allowed to go to outside styling consultants, but had to cooperate with the Styling Staff until an acceptable proposal had been worked out.

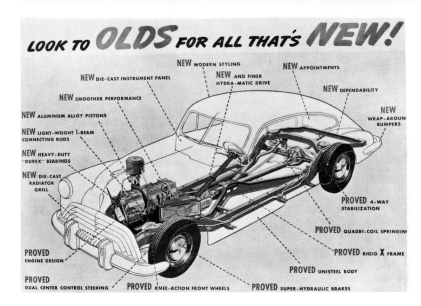

1946 Oldsmobile Custom Cruiser 98 club sedan carried rear fender spats. Fake whitewalls were plastic inserts, fixed to the rims. The car stood on a 127-inch wheelbase, and was powered by a 110-hp straight-eight.

Sales literature for the 1946 models stressed the main difference between postwar and prewar models.

Oswald had to evaluate and pronounce on the manufacturability, quality and durability aspects of all Oldsmobile bodies considered for future production. For this he was well qualified. He was an old pro who had worked in the drafting rooms of the Columbus Buggy Company and the U.S. Carriage Company during his high school vacations, and was familiar with the techniques of high-grade coachbuilding as used in the world of horse-drawn vehicles.

His education was completed with studies at the Alexander Hamilton Institute, the Andrew F. Johnson School and the Washington School of Arts. From 1922 to 1924 he served as chief body engineer of the Emil Body Company, and in the following two years he held the same title with the Phillip Body Company. Auburn Automobile Company hired Oswald as chief designer in 1925, and he stayed with Auburn for four years, leaving in 1929 for a post with Oldsmobile. By 1933 he was Oldsmobile's chief body engineer, working closely with P. J. Mauck, his counterpart at Fisher Body, over the years. His preparation of the first postwar models was to be his last job for Oldsmobile, however.

There were many changes in the exterior sheet metal. For instance, the fenders had been pulled out of their 'suitcase' shape and stretched halfway into the front doors, which called for substantial tooling alterations. Oswald also had to work in liaison with the production engineers, especially with John Dykstra, the general manufacturing manager.

John Dykstra was born in Holland but came to the U.S. as a boy and was apprenticed to a tool-and-die maker in the Detroit area. After World War I he joined a company that was later taken over by Hudson Motor Car Company. Hudson made him a manufacturing specialist, and he played a key role in setting up its new steel-body plant. He was named plant manager for all the sheet metal operations and body fabrication and assembly. Because of this experience he was able to apply for a production job with Oldsmobile in 1934—and get it.

Soon, Oldsmobile would have a new man in this post, also. What happened? The story began when Harold T. Youngren left his position as chief engineer of Oldsmobile in 1944 to take over as engineering director of Borg-Warner. His successor? Thorne did not get the appointment, for he was chief of product engineering at the Fisher Tank Plant at the time, and the corporation considered him essential in that job.

Instead, Skinner appointed Jack Wolfram as chief engineer, and we'll get better acquainted with him later. But Youngren was to have considerable influence on Oldsmobile affairs for years to come; for in mid-summer 1947, he left Borg-Warner to take over the highest technical office at Ford Motor Company and develop that company's first true postwar line of automobiles.

To do that, and to do it his own way, right in the Ford camp, staffed with people who had worked under old Henry for most of their lives, he figured he had better bring in his own team. Where from? From Oldsmobile.

Youngren talked to Oswald, and Oswald talked to George Snyder, the stylist. They both went to Ford in 1947. Neil Blume, who had been on the Oldsmobile engineering staff since 1931, got wind of what Youngren was up to and offered his services, which were promptly accepted. Blume later served as chief engineer on the Edsel program. Youngren also persuaded John Dykstra to come to Ford and handle part of the production side (which he did to great effect), setting himself off on a new career that brought him right to the presidency of the Ford Motor Company.

This exodus of high-ranking Oldsmobile men may have rankled Skinner, but he did not show it. He knew the strength of the Oldsmobile organization, and filled the vacant posts mainly by promoting from within, occasionally getting a transfer from another division or one of the corporate staffs. Among examples of the former, we can cite Lowell Kintigh, who had joined Oldsmobile in 1930 as a dynamometer operator, and now was placed in charge of experimental engineering. An example in the latter category can be found in the young Pete Estes, who came to Oldsmobile from the Research Laboratories. Kintigh was to become chief engineer of Buick, and Pete Estes would be Oldsmobile-trained as a future president of General Motors.

The Oldsmobile studio was placed under a new chief designer, Art Ross, who had joined GM Art and Colour in 1936, and worked with Bill Mitchell on the 1939, 1940 and 1941 Cadillac designs. His influence on Oldsmobile styling was to show up in the Futuramic 98 of 1948, but more about that later.

As far as new-product planning was concerned, Oldsmobile had in 1945 the freest hand it would ever have again. With the degree of autonomy the division had at that time, it could have gone off in any direction and pursued an idea to any length, limited only by the basic constraints imposed by its role and rank within the General Motors organization. In those days those constraints had a great deal of flexibility. Any car division that was operating with healthy profits carried a lot of self-determination. It had the power to influence major decisions at the corporate level. And it could steer its product development the way it wanted to. Oldsmobile had a long and enviable record of making money for GM, which assured it generous latitude in its dispositions.

Of course, this does not mean that Oldsmobile could introduce a brand-new car without telling the corporation about it. But all divisions were expected to originate new-car projects. They designed and built their own prototypes in complete independence of one another. There was little or no interdivisional communication on the subject of experimental cars. They were each division's private property.

Only when production was definitely planned did a new-car project come up for corporate consideration. Production of any new and different car meant investments in new manufacturing facilities, which had to be carefully coordinated at the level of corporate management.

1946 Oldsmobile Dynamic 76 club sedan had the Fisher A-body fastback in two-tone color scheme. It was built on a 119-inch wheelbase; the flathead-six was rated at 100 hp.

Oldsmobile had a reputation as GM's 'experimental' division. It had pioneered the development of automatic transmissions, for instance. Oldsmobile was reputed to have a daring attitude with regard to innovation—and an ability to pull it off well, without running into quality and reliability problems. Its later work on engines will testify to Oldsmobile's capacity for advances in engineering.

But new car concepts were rare at Oldsmobile. Different types of cars were not created that broke with Oldsmobile's established market position in terms of size and price, nor vehicles that were fundamentally different in layout or construction from the Oldsmobiles of current or recent production.

When Chevrolet started its small-car project, the Cadet, in the middle of the war, Oldsmobile did nothing of the kind. Oldsmobile knew about the Cadet at a fairly early date, but regarded it as a down-market car relative to the existing Chevrolet, and no such car could have been successfully offered to the Oldsmobile clientele of that time. Thus there were marketing considerations behind Oldsmobile's failure to look into light-car engineering and design at the outset of the postwar era. The outcome was a postponement of the day of the domestic compact. Light-car engineering at GM was allowed to lapse, so that when the need for small

1946 Oldsmobile Dynamic Cruiser Series 70 convertible. The same chassis and body were able to accommodate six- or eight-cylinder engines with minimal alterations.

1946 Oldsmobile 60 Special station wagon. It was a genuine 'woodie' with van-type (vertical-split) tailgate. The roof was made of four separate steel pressings.

cars became urgent, the corporation was unprepared, even at Chevrolet's end of the market.

Oldsmobile engineers did not try to rethink their concept of the car that would be the right one for Olds buyers five years and more into the future, except in a purely conventional scope.

Perhaps there was no way Oldsmobile could develop a car as radical as the Tucker Torpedo and entertain any hopes of getting it into production. But why not? Because of the interdependency among the divisions, which had its roots in Sloan's organization plan from 1923-24 and was formalized by the creation of the GM Engineering Staff under Ormond E. Hunt as vice president in 1929.

Alfred P. Sloan, Jr., explained: ''Mr. Hunt then succeeded me as chairman of the General Technical Committee and took on the task of coordinating the advanced engineering work of the whole corporation. Under Mr. Hunt's guidance, the advanced engineering in the divisions became a corporation staff responsibility.''

The corporation plainly did not intend for Oldsmobile, or any other car division, to get too far ahead in advanced studies on its own. Distant-future projects were reserved for the Research Laboratories and the Engineering Staff, which would subsequently make their work available to the car divisions in much the same manner as the relationship between the divisions and the Styling Staff developed.

Even when no new research was involved, the divisions could not undertake sweeping changes in the product line. That's because the manufacturing setup had to be coordinated among the divisions. And no car division was free to act on good ideas involving different engineering principles until decisions could be made at the corporate level. This could have been detrimental to progress and put all the GM car divisions at a disadvantage vis-a-vis their smaller and more flexible rivals. Consider Oldsmobile's situation in particular:

Highly conscious of its need to share basic bodies with Buick and Pontiac, as well as its position in the market place, filling the gap between the other two, with some overlap downward with Pontiac and upward with Buick, Oldsmobile's management did not feel free to explore the possibilities of unit body construction, for instance, the way Chrysler (Airflow), Lincoln (Zephyr) and Nash (600) had done. Nor could Oldsmobile undertake research in aerodynamics with the intent of applying the lessons learned from the wind tunnel to future production cars, because of the interlocking body programs with the other car divisions (and Fisher Body). Oldsmobile did not have more than marginal independence with regard to body design and construction.

''In those days, though, we built nearly everything else ourselves,'' recalls a former Olds engineer. But Oldsmobile bought frames from A. O. Smith, manual transmissions and axles from Chevrolet (or Detroit Gear, another GM division), automatic transmissions from what was to become Hydra-matic Division, steering gears and linkages from Saginaw, clutches from Borg & Beck, brakes from Bendix, radiators and heaters from Harrison, electrical equipment and instruments from AC and Delco, and various body hardware from Ternstedt. There was not much more than the engine, front and rear springs, suspension arms and miscellaneous small parts that Oldsmobile actually produced itself.

Still, the division's engineering staff, reporting to the general manager, was the deciding factor with regard to product specifications. An Oldsmobile designed and assembled in Lansing was indisputably a genuine Oldsmobile, regardless of the variety of outside sources for the components going into it. In fact, it must be regarded as just as genuine, even when built at other locations. Using GM branch factories near important market concentrations for local assembly of the products of several divisions had started under Knudsen's direction in the mid-thirties.

Production of Oldsmobiles began in the GM plants at Linden, New Jersey, and South Gate, California, in 1936. Oldsmobile assembly was added to the functions of the Buick-Oldsmobile-Pontiac (B-O-P) plant in Kansas City, Kansas, in 1946. The following year, the B-O-P plant at Wilmington, Delaware, began assembling Oldsmobiles. Framingham, Massachusetts, and Atlanta, Georgia, were new assembly points added during 1948.

The Oldsmobile car hardly changed at all during the 1945-48 period, and the product range did not expand beyond the three wheelbases inherited from the 1942 models, nor outside the five basic body styles. In fact, the production was simplified for 1948, when the 98-series wheelbase was brought down to share the 124-inch wheelbase of the 70-series.

Here is the 1948 series lineup and list prices:

1946 Oldsmobile 60 Special club coupe. The 60-series included a club sedan, convertible, four-door sedan, and station wagon. Panel vans were not revived after the war.

Body Type	66	68	76	78	98
Chassis only	$1,050	$1,105	$1,180	$1,235	$1,335
Club coupe	1,385	1,440			
Deluxe club coupe	1,520	1,575			
Club sedan	1,410	1,465	1,475	1,530	1,790
Deluxe club sedan	1,545	1,600	1,615	1,670	1,890
Four-door sedan	1,450	1,505	1,545	1,600	1,860
Deluxe four-door sedan	1,585	1,640	1,685	1,740	1,960
Convertible coupe	1,725	1,780			2,310
Station wagon	2,305	2,360			

An interesting sidelight on Skinner's (and probably that of his general sales manager, D. E. Ralston's) humanitarian attitude, is provided by the Valiant program. In 1946 Oldsmobile built 12,891 cars with a Valiant label, which were delivered to handicapped servicemen. The following year Oldsmobile delivered 26,344 Valiant cars. The Valiant label meant the car was specially equipped to be driven by a disabled person. Oldsmobile had been a leader in developing controls for the handicapped, with the Hydra-matic drive as a key feature of the system.

The success of the Hydra-matic also calls for some comment. First, the facts: Hydra-matic transmissions were installed in eighty percent of all 1947-model Oldsmobiles built for domestic sale. The following year, Hydra-matic was made standard on the 98 (with a 3.90:1 axle ratio). Demand for the automatic transmission was tremendous, for Oldsmobile equipped 93.7 percent of the cars it produced in 1948 with Hydra-matic. In 1950, Oldsmobile produced its one-millionth car equipped with Hydra-matic transmission (The half-million mark had been passed in 1948.)

It was no longer a cheap option, but the remark was only rarely heard that "I can do a lot of shiftin' for a hundred and fifty bucks!" And yet, ease of driving is an inadequate explanation for the customers' readiness to pay extra for the automatic transmission. There was also the novelty value, and associated with that, a peculiar American tendency to equate innovation with improvement, without serious or critical assessment. Having an automatic transmission became fashionable. It was the newest thing, and many drivers were made to feel less expert for *not* having it,

1947 Series 70 Dynamic Cruiser club sedan. Combined with the long 125-inch wheelbase, the fastback styling gave a sleek, extravagant look to the whole car. Whitewalls are plastic snap-ons.

At the wheel of the 1948-model 78 club coupe, the driver was comfortably seated, with plenty of legroom, headroom and elbow room. The eighteen-inch steering wheel had three spokes in T-formation and a full-circle horn ring, and had a nice feel. The worm-and-double-roller steering gear was fairly slow-geared, but a good grip on the wheel was important for making tight turns. At low speed, considerable effort had to be exercised to turn the wheel, for there was a lot of friction in the 6.50-16 low-pressure balloon tires.

The big speedometer dominated the instrument panel, which included an indicator for the Hydra-matic, giving the driver visual confirmation of his selection. While 98 drivers had a starter button on the dashboard for fingertip operation, the lower series continued the old system of combining the starter switch with the gas pedal movement. Pushing the pedal to full-throttle position would set the automatic choke, and further pressure on the pedal would bring the starter motor to life.

The eight-cylinder Olds was very quiet, whether running at full power or idling. The six was equally smooth, however, and free of vibration. But the Oldsmobile engines were not made for performance. Even with the eight-cylinder, acceleration was sluggish. It could not keep up with a Buick, for instance, and would even have to bite the dust in comparison with a six-cylinder Hudson. But the Oldsmobile gave better gasoline mileage, and was perhaps a more trouble-free car than its speedier rivals.

"Oldsmobile's vision of its car was safe, reliable transportation for the middle-class American family," is how a veteran colleague in New York expressed his view of the first postwar cars. "They were heavy, but surprisingly handy and maneuverable. Comfort was a big thing at Olds, it always was. I believe they spent more on outfitting their interiors than Buick did, and there's no doubt that the Oldsmobile was the quieter car."

High-speed handling or roadholding was not what Oldsmobile was famous for, but the 1948 78-series could be forced to corner quite quickly, with no abnormal vagueness in the steering, and a generally good road feel, free of kickback and shake. Body roll was quite moderate, which helped keep the front wheels more or less upright during cornering, as well as keeping the driver more securely seated—an important thing in those pre-seatbelt days.

The springs were soft, and the car had a tendency to 'float' on certain road surfaces at about 30 mph. Speeding up or slowing down would cure this. Small bumps were swallowed up by the tires and springs in combined action, but big bumps could upset the whole car. Even on a straight road, a serious washboard surface would start the rear axle hopping and pulling to one side, usually toward the ditch. Despite the long wheelbase, the ride was not free of pitch when the going got rough; and stopping the car on anything but a smooth road called for expert modulation of the brake pedal.

though it was *they* who had the skill to operate a manual gearbox. (Not that we should make too much of this skill.)

Synchromesh had taken the need for careful timing out of gear-shifting duties, along with the need to match engine speed to car speed for the next-wanted gear. No muscle was called for, neither in moving the lever, nor in pushing the clutch pedal. Finding the gears was no mystery, and the engine gave audible indications of when up- or down-shifts were necessary. All in all, it is tempting to conclude, with the benefit of hindsight, that the automatic transmission sold itself more because of its image of progressive engineering than on the strength of tangible advantages.

The Hydra-matic transmission proved very satisfactory for acceleration and cruising. But in heavy traffic, and in hilly country, the lack of engine braking would bother many drivers who were in the habit of downshifting to slow down the car, and being ready for renewed acceleration, rather than using the brakes, and delaying the downshift till the moment power was again needed (as was in fact the Hydra-matic's manner).

Automatic shifts were not always smooth, but people accepted that without grumbling. How many drivers never botched a shift with clutch and gearbox? The automatic transmission, on average, did better than the average driver.

Seat adjustment of the front bench was arranged so that the seat was lowered as it slid backward on its runners, allowing for the fact that people with long legs also have a longer torso and need more headroom. Despite the high and long hood, the driver had a generally satisfactory view of the road ahead. At the time, buyers were not critical of visibility having been sacrificed on the altar of Detroit's new omnipresent deity, Styling. They learned to park even if the right front fender was out of sight—many aimed by the hood ornament. As far as backing up was concerned, few people relied on mirrors. Many copied the truck driver's way of opening the door and leaning out, with one hand on the wheel. Mirrors were small, and not always well placed, though rear window size had been growing fast since 1939.

Big changes were to come, in engineering as well as in styling, as Oldsmobile got its real postwar cars ready. These changes were not always for the better, but the world was waiting for Oldsmobiles that were new and different—and that's what it got.

CHAPTER
4

The Rocket V-8 Engine

GETTING A NEW ENGINE into production was one of the top priorities for Oldsmobile after the war. That was the case for all GM car divisions, and preliminary studies had been under way for years—at Cadillac, for instance, since 1936. Buick and Pontiac also had new engine programs, delving deep into fundamental research. But it was Oldsmobile that was to be first on the market with a modern engine.

Its origins can be traced to research work undertaken shortly after the end of World War I, more than twenty-five years before the introduction of the Rocket V-8.

This research work was undertaken because of the detonation problem auto engines were having in the early twenties. It started when Alfred P. Sloan, Jr., of GM asked Charles F. Kettering of the Dayton Engineering Laboratories (the organization that later formed the nucleus of the GM Research Laboratories) to look into the whole business of knock, compression and fuel composition.

Kettering allied himself with Thomas J. Midgley, Jr., of the Ethyl Corporation. Midgley had studied Helmholtz's works on the laws of radiation. He also referred to Professor Callender's findings from experiments made in 1907, proving that a non-luminous flame may cause heat loss during and after combustion. Midgley and Kettering initiated a comprehensive search for chemical additives that would improve the knock resistance of gasoline. They tried additives from aniline to tellurium ethyl, and as a result of their reports, the oil companies began offering gasoline containing tetra-ethyl-lead.

That solved the problems for the time being, and compression ratios rose steadily from 4.5:1 in 1924 to 6.5:1 ten years later. About 1938, Kettering ordered a new look at high compression. His assistants designed and built a thirty-cubic-inch single-cylinder test engine with a choice of pistons, giving a range of compression ratios from 6.2:1 to 15:1.

Kettering learned from the test results that there was little to gain in torque or horsepower, on one hand, and specific fuel consumption, on the other, by raising compression ratios much beyond 12:1. He therefore recommended a target of 12.5:1 for possible future engine designs.

Next, Kettering's group designed and built a heavy diesel-like six-cylinder test engine. It was so big and heavy that it would not have been practical in a passenger car. It was built that way so that the limits of normal combustion could be explored without risk of mechanical damage when going beyond the limits. And in that sense it was a very useful engine.

As it turned out, a stack of test reports also indicated that combustion pressures, bearing stress levels and friction losses were far from being as critical as had been feared. On the strength of this evidence, Kettering began to design a new

Cross section of the Rocket V-8. Obvious features are extra-strength connecting rods, hefty bearing dimensions, crossflow cylinder heads and wedge-shaped combustion chambers. Chrysler hemi-head V-8 engine (smaller photo) forms an interesting basis for comparison with the Rocket. Chrysler's splayed valve needed a double set of rocker arms and shafts. It was heavier than the Olds engine, as well as more expensive to produce.

Before the Rocket name was adopted for the Oldsmobile V-8, it was promoted as the Kettering engine in honor of the research engineer who explored the limits and benefits of high compression.

The young Gil Burrell (nearest the engine) with Production Chief John Dykstra in New York for the presentation of the V-8 engine to the Oldsmobile dealers.

high-compression (12.5:1) six that would be no heavier than the production-model sixes of the time.

The 181-cubic-inch test engine developed comparable power and torque with the 238-cubic-inch Oldsmobile side-valve six, and was road-tested in the same vehicle. Fuel consumption was about forty percent lower, on the average, while acceleration was quicker. The test engine was an in-line six also, with a seven-main-bearing crankshaft, having a bore and stroke of 3.375 x 3.375 inches and bathtub-type combustion chambers with parallel overhead valves.

Complete test engines were also sent to the fuel companies so that they could formulate the right kind of gasoline for it. The Oldsmobile test cars ran on aviation fuel. GM Research Laboratories even had its own mix, known as Triptane. GM operated a pilot plant in Detroit for its own use, and it cost about $10 a gallon. Triptane was rated at about 200 Octane, and could accept compression ratios in the area of 16 or 18:1 without detonation.

The test car weighed 4,100 pounds and had a 3.63:1 rear axle. At a constant 40 mph, it returned 18.5 mpg with the side-valve production-model six. With the experimental 12.5:1 compression six, the gas mileage figure climbed dramatically to 26.5 mpg. The engine was free of detonation and roughness problems—Kettering declared it ready for development as a production engine.

But the high-compression six was never developed for production. Instead, Oldsmobile went to the V-8 configuration. This was not done just to irritate Cadillac, but for absolutely sound technical reasons.

Six cylinders would perhaps not be enough to develop the kind of power the industry expected its future cars to require. And even if a six that was big enough and powerful enough could be designed, it would have vibration problems due to the length of its crankshaft. Only a V-8 configuration could provide a short enough crankshaft to avoid torsional vibration problems with the kind of forces that were at play in high-compression cylinders.

Nothing but a V-8 offered the same advantages. For instance, the V-8 offered a fairly economical way of getting the desired structural stiffness into the crankline, without adding extra weight. In addition, the V-8 block had to be long enough to hold space for five main bearings, thereby providing room also for big cylinder bores within compact dimensions.

Oldsmobile had built a V-8 in the years 1915-20, and used one in the 1929-31 Viking that was probably made by Northway. But as we have seen, in-line sixes and eights were the mainstay of Olds engine production during the thirties and forties. Cadillac, on the other hand, had been in continuous production with V-8's since 1914. But the Cadillac V-8 was a side-valve engine—slow-revving, super-silent, but not very efficient nor very powerful.

Preliminary studies for the new engine began in 1946. Many engines were designed and evaluated before Oldsmobile settled on a ninety-degree V-8. "It's the ninety-degree angle that is best for balance," stated Gil Burrell, who was in charge of the experimental engine department at the time.

Gilbert J. Burrell was born in Lansing in 1905 and graduated from Michigan State University in 1928 with a degree in electrical engineering. That same year he joined Oldsmobile and was put to work building and tearing down experimental engines in the company's dynamometer laboratory.

After a thorough analysis of the basic ninety-degree V-8 cylinder dimensions, Burrell went for a big bore and short stroke. The big bore gave a lot of piston area, which was excellent for acceleration. The short stroke extended the rpm range upward. Both these factors worked in favor of higher performance. Structurally, the big-bore, short-stroke layout made for a compact block, short connecting rods and ample crankpin overlap; all of which contributed to lightness and rigidity.

Though Kettering had used overhead valves in his experimental high-compression engine, the use of a similar cylinder-head-and-valve operation was no foregone conclusion. Burrell took nothing for granted, and looked at all sides of every question, basing every choice on sound engineering principles.

"We could see that as compression ratio went up, it was going to be a problem making an L-head engine breathe properly," Gil Burrell said. "That was another reason we went to overhead valves and the V-8 design."

The basic V-8 design was approved in October 1947. While development work continued apace, the production engineers went to work and, before long, tooling orders began to go out. V-8 engine production began on November 3, 1948.

The public got to know it as the Rocket engine. "The name was picked by a guy on the sales staff," we were told, "who was forever after known as 'Rocket' Jones." (G. R. Jones became general sales manager of Oldsmobile in 1949 and served for many years in that post.) "The Rocket name has been good for us," said an Oldsmobile sales official. "We still use the emblem."

The Rocket was a new kind of engine. Americans were used to V-8's, mainly Ford's rather than Cadillac's, but this was the first they had seen with twin rocker covers, topping each bank and towering above the spark plugs whose leads flowed over them.

Thus, Oldsmobile beat Cadillac by over two months. The two divisions had been doing parallel studies, based on Kettering's research work, and Cadillac started production of its own high-compression overhead-valve V-8 in January 1949.

Both were designed and developed independently. "The Rocket was strictly an Oldsmobile project," said Gil Burrell. "I've been brought up to compete violently with other divisions."

Sherrod E. Skinner (left) and Charles F. Kettering pose with the Oldsmobile V-8.

As chief engineer of Oldsmobile, Jack Wolfram had laid down five ground rules for the engine that must be regarded as inviolable. First, the engine must have the structural strength to run reliably with very high compression ratios, and run smoothly even after long mileage and normal carbon buildup on the combustion chamber surfaces.

Second, it had to have overhead valves in order to breathe properly, but the exact valve configuration was not spelled out.

Third, the engine should be designed for lower intake manifold temperatures, to assure improved cylinder filling and adequate valve cooling to avoid detonation.

When it became the Rocket engine, Oldsmobile was quick to use supersonic-flight symbols for its exhibits. Gil Burrell stands closest to the engine. With him is Lowell Kintigh, who was connected with the development of the Rocket V-8. Kintigh later became chief engineer of Buick.

Fourth, the compression ratio was to be the highest possible, consistent with fuel availability at the gas station pump at the time of production startup.

Fifth, the engine designs should allow compression ratio increases up to 12:1 with minimal tooling changes, so as to take full advantage of the engine's potential as soon as commercial fuel quality improved, and at minimal extra cost in production.

In 1948, the octane rating of premium fuel was only about 88 (Research method), and that set a limit for compression ratios far below what was possible with aviation or test fuels. Cadillac stopped at 7.5:1; Oldsmobile, at 7.25:1.

"We were shooting for a 9:1 compression ratio in the 287-cubic-inch V-8," reminisced Gil Burrell. "Well we didn't get the octane we wanted, so we had to settle for a lower compression, about 7.25:1, I think it was."

Both Oldsmobile and Cadillac were ceaselessly demanding higher-octane fuels from the petroleum companies. "We had meetings with a lot of oil people," Gil Burrell remembered. "We'd tell them we needed higher octane so we could increase the compression and efficiency of our engines, and they would tell us it was going to cost a lot more money."

When Oldsmobile had to accept a lower compression ratio, it became necessary to increase the engine size in order to maintain the planned power output. Gil Burrell: "We didn't want to give up performance, so we increased the displacement to 303 cubic inches. When Cadillac found out what we were doing, they scrambled to increase the displacement in their own engine. They didn't want anybody that close to them."

The Oldsmobile engine had been planned for a displacement of 287 cubic inches, and Cadillac's for 309. In 1947 the Cadillac was redesigned with a 331-cubic-inch displacement.

The 1949 Cadillac V-8 was 4¼ inches shorter, three inches lower and about 200 pounds lighter than the 1948 side-valve V-8. It had a 3.8125-inch bore and a 3.625-inch stroke. Maximum output was 160 hp (more than ten up on the 1948 L-head) on a 7.5:1 compression ratio, and the car would go from standstill to 60 mph in 13.4 seconds. Oldsmobile chose a similar (0.92) stroke/bore ratio, with a 3.65-inch bore and a 3.4375-inch stroke.

Using gasoline of 79 ASTM and 86 Research octane rating, the Rocket V-8 delivered 135 hp at 3600 rpm in stripped form (bare engine, in Society of Automotive Engineers parlance). With standard accessories (water pump and fan, air cleaner, muffler, starter, generator and fuel pump), maximum output was 129 hp at 3600 rpm. The bare-engine torque was 263 pounds-feet at 1800 rpm, which slipped to 255 pounds-feet with all standard accessories fitted.

The cylinder block was a single casting that comprised both banks, the upper crankcase and the upper half of the flywheel housing. A lightweight casting and ease of assembly were obtained by ending the block on the crankshaft centerline.

Valve lifter bosses were part of the block casting. Openings were provided below these bosses to allow oil thrown off the valve gear to splash onto the water jackets. This had nothing to do with lubrication, but made use of the oil flow as part of the cooling system.

Sectioned Rocket engine comes under the gaze of 'Engine Charlie' Wilson (nearest engine) and Charles L. McCuen, director of the GM Engineering Staff and a former general manager of Oldsmobile.

Production version of the Rocket V-8 from 1949. It was standard in all 88 and 98 models. It started out with a modest compression ratio of 7.25:1 but soon demonstrated its performance potential.

Under severe operating conditions, peak oil temperatures in the V-8 stayed about twenty-five degrees Fahrenheit cooler than in the side-valve in-line eight, which meant that less energy was going to waste. Faster warmup was also obtained this way, because some of the combustion heat went into the oil, which speeded up the heat buildup throughout the oil system to normal operating temperature, as well as serving to slow down sludge formation in the oil.

All cylinders had complete water jackets, and the minimum space of 0.3125 inch between barrel walls assured unrestricted flow through those gaps. Cylinder-head bolt bosses were tied into the block walls, completely separated from the cylinder walls, with less risk of cylinder distortion during tightening of the head bolts. The crankshaft, made of SAE 1145 MOD steel, weighed exactly sixty pounds. It carried a vibration damper at the front end. The crankshaft was only 25.4 inches long, compared with 38.875 inches for the former eight-in-line engine.

Centerline distance between the main bearings had been brought down from 8.1 inches to 4.625 inches, and the average overlap between main bearing and crankpin journals increased from 0.4 to 0.69 inch. The crankshaft carried six counterweights in an unusual pattern that eliminated counterweights on the fillets on either side of the central main bearing.

Connecting rods were I-section steel forgings and quite short, only 6.7 inches center-to-center in order to obtain the minimum block height. Crankpin journals were 0.875 inch wide, and 2.25 inches in diameter. Bearing shells were steel-backed with a Durex matrix and Babbitt overlay.

Oil-feed holes to the bearing journals were offset so as to get the oil into the bearing ahead of the maximum-load position and let the oil build up a wedge to protect the bearing and increase bearing life.

A clever device was found to spray oil on the cylinder walls at low speeds: A hole was drilled at the split line of the rod bearing, i.e. at ninety degrees to the rod axis. At a given angle, near bottom dead center, this hole would index with the crankpin journal oil-feed hole and spit oil—perfectly aimed into the corresponding cylinder of the opposite bank, where the piston was then near top dead center, and the walls bared to the fullest extent possible. Naturally, this was in effect at all speeds, but more important at low piston speeds, particularly under high load.

Pistons were aluminum castings with a steel-strut insert and full-floating wrist pins. Piston skirts were cut away at both front and rear to provide clearance for the crankshaft counterweights. The steel-strut insert helped stabilize the aluminum and prevent thermal distortion of the piston, as well as preventing wide variations in piston-to-bore clearances.

Piston weights were equalized for each engine by drilling into the crankpin bosses of any piston that was heavier than the standard for that individual engine. Nominal weight for the standard piston was twenty ounces.

Two compression rings and one oil-control ring were fitted on each piston. Both compression rings were taper-faced and inside-beveled, while the oil-control ring was of a wide-slot, narrow-land design.

A single central camshaft was chosen, with hydraulic lifters in two rows, each bank having its own rocker arm shaft with push rods and rockers. The valves were slanted at eighteen degrees from the cylinder axis, tilted at twenty-seven degrees from vertical.

The valve angle was chosen partly in order to obtain a short rocker arm, and partly for reasons of gas flow characteristics. Lube oil for the rocker arms was delivered through holes in the camshaft bearing journals.

The spark plug was located at the high end of the wedge-type combustion chamber, opposite the quench area which was intended to guard against detonation.

Combustion chamber surfaces in the cylinder head were not machined, and Oldsmobile engineers claimed that cylinder-to-cylinder variations in displacement were no more than plus-or-minus 1 cc.

Exhaust valves were made of XCR steel, with intake valves of SAE 3140 steel. Exhaust valve materials are more critical, since those are the valves that must resist heat. Intake valves run cool. Exhaust valve stems were $1/16$-inch thicker than on the intake valves, to assist heat dissipation. Exhaust valve stems were also undercut at the lower end to prevent sticking.

The exhaust system had a single pipe leading to the muffler and tail pipe, as the gases from the left-side manifold were ducted to a union on the front on the right-side exhaust pipe, below the manifold flange.

The left-side manifold also had a heat valve at the outlet, which was open during normal operation but closed for cold starts and during the warmup period. When closed, it directed the gases through a crossover passage in the center of the cylinder head and into the heat box of the intake manifold, from where it escaped into the right-side exhaust ports. This system preheated the charge to facilitate ignition and burning, permit shorter choking durations and save fuel.

The downdraft carburetor was mounted on a two-level intake manifold, developed for uniform mixture distribution and reliable cold-starting in low ambient temperatures. The exhaust manifolds were bolted onto the heads at a minimum distance from the exhaust ports, thereby assuring a short path for the exhaust gas through water-jacketed areas and minimizing heat rejection to the coolant. That, of course, lightened the burden on the cooling system, but the muffler had to accept hotter gases.

The carburetor was of the side-entrance type, designed to cause the least air flow restriction in combination with the cross-mounted air cleaner and silencer assembly. The ignition distributor was mounted at the rear of the engine, below air-cleaner level, very well protected, but not in a position of ideal servicing accessibility.

The generator was bolted on at the front, above the intake manifold, and driven by a separate belt from the fan pulley. The water pump was of the single-impeller type, contained in the front cover, which had cast-in water inlet and outlet passages.

Oil filler tube and crankcase breather were located on top of the front cover. The AC mechanical fuel pump was installed low down on the right-hand side of the engine, next to the front cover.

The engine mounting system had a single front mount and two widely spaced ones at the back. The front motor mount bracket was bolted to the engine's front cover, centrally located below the water pump.

During tests at the GM Proving Grounds the Rocket engine proved to give better fuel economy as well as far superior performance than the side-valve eight. The Olds 98 with the in-line eight got 16 mpg at 50 mph. With the new and more powerful engine, the 1949-model 98 did 17 mpg at 50 mph.

In performance tests of the 1949-model 98 against the 1948 Olds 98, the newer car had a top speed of 96 mph compared with 88 mph for the older one. The older car climbed a seven-percent-grade hill at 55 mph in third gear and 44 mph in fourth (both with Hydra-matic). With the V-8 engine, those speeds rose to 64.5 and 59 mph, respectively. Third-gear acceleration from 10 to 60 mph under wide-open throttle gave the following times: 13.5 seconds for the V-8, 18.1 seconds for the 1948 model.

What made the Olds different from other V-8's? To Gil Burrell, "there was no one thing about it that was really unusual. We just tried to make it as smooth and quiet as possible."

Oldsmobile spent over $10 million to erect and equip a new engine plant for the Rocket V-8. It was remarkably advanced in terms of automation, with transfer lines handling up to eighteen engine blocks at one time. Electronic control panels showed progress in the materials flow and kept operations on schedule. Inspection and checking equipment was installed at special stations to catch inaccuracies before they had gone too far. Electronic measurement techniques were used to check tolerances.

And each and every engine was given a forty-minute dynamometer test, with full instrumentation, immediately on completion. The test data would determine if the engine was cleared for installation in a car, or had to go in for rectification of one sort or another.

Early in 1949 the engine plant reached its initial production rate of thirty engines per hour. By the end of the year, output had been doubled to sixty engines per hour. "The V-8 cost $200 more than the six when it was introduced," Gil Burrell remembered, "and it was a great sales tool... By the middle of the summer, sales of the V-8 were up to where it cost us less than the six." During the mid-sixties, the plant was producing 150 engines an hour.

Demonstration cars with transparent plastic hoods were sent out in the field to get customers to look under the hood without opening it. Built-in lighting kit served to illuminate the engine compartment at night. Over 2,000 such demonstrators were built. In the initial installation, the Rocket V-8 was mounted entirely aft of the front wheel axis, providing more even weight distribution but not allowing the most efficient space utilization.

CHAPTER 5

Power Play

A CHANGE OF CHARACTER took place in the Oldsmobile because of the Rocket engine. It became a hot car, and it wasn't long before Oldsmobile began appearing in stock car races—something unheard of in the days of the L-head eights. The Oldsmobile six continued in production through 1950, with its displacement increased to 257 cubic inches. From the start of the 1951 model year, all Oldsmobiles had V-8 engines.

"The Rocket engine was originally developed for the 98," Burrell said. "But Skinner wanted it in the smaller cars, too. So the 88 was introduced.

"The better power-to-weight ratio really made the 88 a hot performer. It was the pace car at Indy in 1949."

Reviving the 80-series was an idea from the marketing staff, and Skinner was quick to approve it. The idea for the vehicle specifications was Skinner's own. He may not have realized exactly what sort of a car he was creating by jamming the powerful V-8 into the shortest-wheelbase car Oldsmobile made, but the result was a sensation.

The 88 was built on the same 119.5-inch wheelbase as the 1949-model 76 and shared the same Fisher A-body (which was also used by Chevrolet and Pontiac). It was about four hundred pounds lighter than the 98 and was geared for higher speed, with a 3.23:1 axle ratio (compared with 3.64:1 for the 98). Installed in the 88, the Rocket V-8 gave 18.75 mpg at 50 mph.

The 1949 models were completely restyled. They were postwar creations, made to fit on existing frames. These bodies were part of a corporation-wide program, with piecemeal renewal of the whole range of A-, B- and C-bodies. As far as Oldsmobile is concerned, the rejuvenation process began when the division sprang its Futuramic 98 on an unsuspecting public in the early summer of 1948.

Remember, the Rocket V-8 was still top secret, and the profile of the typical Oldsmobile owner was a sedentary professional man of forty-five to fifty-five years of age, with some college education, an income that would have allowed him to own a Cadillac, a house in the suburbs, an overweight wife who picked the color of the car but did not much care for driving and two sons whose only ambition was to have cars of their own—not Oldsmobiles, but Ford V-8's. That profile did not change between 1945 and the late fall of 1948, when the Rocket burst on the scene.

Sales performance during that period was somewhat lackluster. Of course, the 1946 figures are invalidated by the effect of the long strike which interrupted Oldsmobile's production from November 1945 to April 1946. But the division was not running at capacity in 1947 or 1948, either!

	1946	1947	1948
Total market (millions)	1.815	3.167	3.49
Olds sales (domestic)	93,094	180,078	175,531
Olds rank in sales race	7th	7th	7th
Olds market share	5.13%	5.69%	5.03%
GM market share	37.8%	41.9%	40.6%

1950 Oldsmobile Futuramic 98 convertible coupe. The main structure was the same as on the Holiday coupe. The wheelbase was 122 inches, and the car weighed 4,112 pounds.

At the top was Chevrolet with a twenty-percent market share. Ford's share dropped from eighteen in 1946 to seventeen the following year, and then to fourteen percent. Plymouth held on to a steady ten percent of the market. Oldsmobile was not competing against the low-priced three. But it was frustrating for the men in Lansing to see Buick, Pontiac and Dodge lead Oldsmobile by varying margins.

It was particularly galling that Buick, with its higher prices, should be in front. But Buick had an image: It was known as a powerful car, with its legendary valve-in-head straight-eight; and Buick's styling was more daring, more flamboyant, than Oldsmobile's. Pontiac had lower prices, overlapping Chevrolet's, but an image problem just like Oldsmobile: Pontiac was known as an old-fashioned car, made for long life, but utterly dull. Skinner had the courage to face the facts, and the ability to implement his plans for remedial action. This ability depended in part on his good relations with Wilson and Coyle, who were easily convinced of Oldsmobile's needs and usually approved Skinner's proposals. Two such proposals got him the Futuramic and the 88—two important strategic weapons in Oldsmobile's arsenal.

"The Futuramic heralds the dawn of a new Golden Era for America's oldest motor car manufacturer," proclaimed Oldsmobile sales literature. The division was

in fact celebrating its fiftieth anniversary of car-making, and in the process of completing a new final assembly line at the Lansing works.

But what was the Futuramic? It was a marketing name for a whole new styling concept. All the GM car divisions were to share it for the 1949 model year, but Oldsmobile was able to jump the gun and start production late in the 1948 model year. Harley Earl directed the restyling for all divisions, and Art Ross was responsible for the Oldsmobile adaptation. He was able to carry over the 1946-48 grille theme, modified by tasteful simplification and a great sureness of line. Two of the horizontal bars were eliminated; the remaining two were made bolder, and integrated with the bumper design.

Oldsmobile's old heraldic emblem, which had survived in stylized form as a colored badge centered above the grille on the 1946-48 models, yielded to a new and bigger design featuring a globe representing the world (planet Earth) garnished with a chrome-finish orbital ring. This became a new identification mark for

1949 Oldsmobile 98 Futuramic Holiday coupe was the division's first two-door hardtop, with wraparound rear window. The engine was a 135-hp, 303 cubic-inch high-compression V-8.

On the Lansing assembly line in 1949, the complete car was timed to come off the line 2½ hours after the body had been received and written in. Despite such speed, Oldsmobile quality was maintained.

Oldsmobile, and was repeated on the trunk lid. The heraldic shield was not lost or forgotten, however, for it was reproduced on the hub caps.

At first, Futuramic styling was restricted to the 98-series (still using the L-head eight-cylinder engine), built as a four-door sedan, club sedan and convertible coupe only. Front fenders were blended completely into the main body, so that the continuation of the fender line became the car's belt line. In that, the Futuramic resembled the Darrin-designed slab-sided Kaiser and Frazer, Frank Spring's 'step-down' Hudson and Ed Macauley's modernized Packard. But in contrast with those cars, the GM design retained separate rear fenders, bulging boldly from the tapering midriff of the body.

It gave a muscular look to the rear quarters, like the hind legs of a tiger crouched for attack. Because the belt line was lowered, it became possible to increase the glass area, and thereby achieve an airier, more cheerful and inviting look in the interior. Curved-glass single-sheet windshields were adopted, while the side glass remained straight. Chrome was used sparsely, with a discreet accent line along the rear fender as the only side decoration.

To capitalize on being first with this look, Oldsmobile's sales department decided they needed a name for the new style, to emphasize the break with anything left over from prewar days and impress customers with its future-oriented product. It did not take long for someone to suggest the name Futuramic, and it was instantly approved by management and adopted as a slogan. It was an Oldsmobile exclusive. The other GM car divisions had the same bodies, but not the name.

The Futuramic 98 was unchanged with regard to wheelbase, continuing the 125-inch spacing of the front and rear wheels. For the 1949 model year, the 76 got the Futuramic A-body, its wheelbase was stretched to 119.5 inches and its tire size increased to 7.10-15 (7.60-15 on the convertible and the station wagon).

Because the car got heavier, Jack Wolfram felt it needed more power, and Lowell Kintigh redesigned the six, raising its displacement to 257 cubic inches. The cylinders could not safely be bored out beyond 2.53124 inches, so it became necessary to lengthen the stroke, which meant going to a new crankshaft. There were limitations to how much the stroke could be stretched; for a longer stroke meant a wider swing of the crankpins and rods, colliding with the crankcase walls if overdone. With a stroke of 4.375 inches, no modification of the block casting was necessary, and Wolfram was satisfied to see the six come up to equal the displacement of the side-valve straight-eight, which had been taken out of production.

The big six delivered 105 hp at 3400 rpm, with a maximum torque of 200 pounds-feet generated at the amazingly low speed of 1250 rpm. As a result, the new 76 had excellent top-gear flexibility, which made for smoother driving in traffic and on difficult roads by reducing the need for gear-shifting.

It also gave excellent fuel economy, doing eighteen miles to the gallon at a steady 50 mph. The three-speed column-shift synchromesh transmission was standard, with Hydra-matic as an extra-cost option. The solenoid starter with the pushbutton on the dash, formerly reserved for the 98, was adopted across the board.

The model lineup was revised for 1949, the old names, Special and Dynamic Cruiser being replaced by the Futuramic label. The 60-series was discontinued, and the 78 gave way to the 88. Inevitably, prices went up:

1949 Models	76	88	98
Club coupe	$1,630	$2,025	
Deluxe club coupe	1,765	2,150	
Club sedan	1,655	2,050	$2,290
Deluxe club sedan	1,790	2,175	2,380
Town sedan	1,715	2,110	
Deluxe town sedan	1,850	2,235	
Sedan	1,725	2,120	2,360
Deluxe sedan	1,860	2,245	2,450
Convertible coupe	2,025	2,420	2,810
Deluxe station wagon	2,735	3,120	

Skinner's motivation in creating the 88 was not due to a transfusion of hot-rodding blood, nor a simple merchandizing trick of upgrading a car and charging a higher price. On the contrary, his decision was based on manufacturing considerations. He wanted to close the six-cylinder engine plant and retool it for other machining work, and standardize V-8 power in all Oldsmobiles. The economics of streamlining engine production can be regarded as his ace in the hole, giving Skinner an irrefutable argument when seeking Coyle's approval for his 88 project.

There was some talk of building two versions of the V-8, going back to the originally planned 287-cubic-inch displacement for the 88 while reserving the full 303.7-cubic-inch V-8 for the 98. But Skinner was able to persuade both Coyle and Wilson that this would complicate the production setup, introduce additional parts and slow down the assembly process. Production of the 88 started in February 1949, two months behind the rest of the 1949 models. It was an instant success.

In July 1949, the 88 became available with a new body style, the Holiday hardtop, a two-door sedan on which the B-post had been eliminated. The B-post was the roof pillar behind the front door in Fisher Body language; the A-posts being the pillars on each side of the windshield; and the C-posts, the rear corners.

Ned Nickles, long-time chief designer of the Buick studio, had built a scale model of such a design back in 1945, and Fisher Body worked with Buick's body engineer, Edward T. Ragsdale, to develop it for production. Buick had it first, of course, for the 1949 Roadmaster Riviera. Later in the year, it was offered to the other divisions. 'Rocket' Jones, who was a whiz at picking clever names, suggested calling the hardtop Holiday, believing that that label captured a feeling of freedom, leisure and fun, which he discerned in the car's appearance. So, Holiday it was.

Over 200,000 racegoers watched Wilbur Shaw drive the 1949 convertible 88 in front of the thirty-three-car field for the pace lap at Indianapolis on Memorial Day.

1950 Oldsmobile Futuramic 88 four-door sedan. With the Fisher B-body on the short wheelbase from the 76-series and the powerful V-8 from the 98-series, the Rocket 88 became a symbol of speed.

Even before that date, many minds had been toying with thoughts of the Rocket V-8's potential as a racing-car engine.

A race promoter in Florida, Bill France, sensing the attraction of having new cars on the racetrack, introduced a new late-model class in stock-car racing. As head of the fledgling National Association of Stock Car Auto Racing (NASCAR), Bill France thus opened the door for Oldsmobile's entry into the world of oval-track racing.

Among the first to race-tune the Rocket V-8 was a California speed-shop wizard named Ak Miller. Born in Denmark, he came to the United States as a boy of three and grew up in California. His friend and former drag-racer Pete Coltrin told us: ''He cut his teeth at places like El Mirage with backyard hot-rods using Chevy sixes and Ford V-8's with overhead-valve heads. His brothers and Whittier colleagues were dyed-in-the-wool flat-head Ford fans, but from boyhood, Akton reckoned that overhead valves was the way to go.

''One first thing that Miller did with the Olds V-8 was to 'sink' the hydraulic valve lifters. He disposed of the ball check and *innards* of the basic cam follower piston, and with a sturdy steel push rod topped with a locknut valve adjustment cap, got away from valve float and added many more rpm's and horses. It was a simple device and tappet adjustments needed only two open-end wrenches and a feeler guage, and you had more than another 500-plus revs without valve float. All at a very

1950 Oldsmobile Futuramic 88 Deluxe Holiday coupe.
This model introduced the one-piece curved windshield on
Oldsmobiles. Hood ornament stressed the Rocket theme.

modest price. You didn't want to overdo things but the Olds V-8's were mighty forgiving.

"Next to Kettering I think Ak was the one who best realized the potential of the Olds V-8. He shaved the heads and came close to reaching Kettering's 12:1 compression ratio. He fitted bigger valves and enlarged the inlet and exhaust ports. All this without intruding on water passages or causing hot spots."

It is interesting to reflect that Cadillac's V-8, though lighter in weight and having higher horsepower, was not greeted with the same enthusiasm by the racing fraternity. Briggs Cunningham entered two Cadillacs in the twenty-four-hour race at Le Mans in 1950: one four-door sedan and one special-bodied open two-seater which the French immediately dubbed 'Le Monstre.' They ran with uneventful reliability and finished tenth and eleventh—the sedan in front of the roadster. The following year, Cunningham returned with new cars using Chrysler power.

Nor did Cadillac engines make a big hit with drag racers; and Cadillacs were never seen in stock-car racing. Peter Coltrin thinks the Oldsmobile engine was tougher, while "the Caddy engines were more delicate and much more expensive to repair. The Olds V-8 had more 'meat' and more *honest* horsepower. They were better suited for boring out to get more cubic inches, and the heads had more meat for widening the ports."

"To add cubic inches by 'stroking' was not considered the way to go," explained Pete Coltrin. "The stock crankshaft never gave trouble and it was best left alone. Some guys tried it and some guys cried. There again the internal bits and pieces were better than big brother Cadillac. Little details were better than the Cad. Some people at Lansing were keeping the faith.

"Another thing about the Olds engine was *torque*. It would pull just about any axle ratio without complaint. Here, again, the Olds V-8 was more flexible than Cadillac's V-8. While the Cadillac got much praise, the Oldsmobile V-8 was really the better engine."

In stock-car racing, the Olds 88 had it all its own way in 1949, winning six out of nine Grand National events (Lincoln scored two wins and Plymouth, one). The leading Oldsmobile drivers were Robert 'Red' Baron and Bob Flock, ranking first and second on points in their NASCAR division. Though Hydra-matic was standard equipment in the 88, the factory would cooperate by fitting synchromesh gearboxes on special order (presaging the so-called 'delete option') and giving a choice of seven different axle ratios from the standard 3.23:1 up to a super-short 4.55:1.

Reporting in *Special-Interest Autos* (October 1970), Francis G. Hitchcock wrote: "Among the highlights of the 1949 season was Curtis Turner's win at a Langhorne Speedway in an Olds 88 before 20,000 wildly cheering spectators. It was the biggest crowd at the Pennsylvania 200-miler since World War II. Bob Flock and 'Red' Baron placed second and third in their 88s, but the wildest action of all involved a woman from Atlanta, Sara Christian, who moved from 17th starting position to place sixth overall. Broken wheels and suspension pieces from all makes of cars—strewn over the various tracks—cost Olds drivers the lead on several occasions."

The following season saw Oldsmobile triumphant on oval tracks all over the southeastern states, winning ten out of nineteen Grand National events. It was a memorable day during the annual Speed Week at Daytona Beach in 1950, when Joe Littlejohn drove an Olds 88 club sedan up and down the measured mile on the beach for a two-way average of 100.28 mph. This performance toppled a fifteen-year-old record, set back in 1936 by a Hudson Eight with a speed of 93.88 mph.

Oldsmobile made its mark in international sports-car racing by an outright win in the first of the famous Carrera Panamericana in Mexico in May 1950. Herschell McGriff and Ray Elliott shared the driving in a notchback 88 two-door sedan. "Punctured the oil sump about a thousand yards from the Tuxtla Gutierrez finish line and staggered home *first*," recalled Pete Coltrin.

In June 1950, Paul Frere drove a four-door 88 sedan to victory in a production-car race at the Francorchamps circuit in the Belgian region of Ardennes—a performance which he repeated in 1951 and 1952.

In NASCAR racing, Oldsmobile was unbeatable in 1951, with twenty wins out of a total of forty-one Grand National events. Bob Flock, with his brothers Tim and Fonty, collected most of the trophies. But Oldsmobile domination ended in 1952, when the 88's were eclipsed by the six-cylinder L-head Hudson Hornets. Thanks to the spirited driving of Fonty Flock and Bill Blair, Oldsmobile still enjoyed some moments of glory that season, such as when Blair trounced all opponents in the

Atlanta 500, and when Flock ran home in first place in a 150-mile race at Occoneechee in North Carolina.

Ak Miller's attempt in the Carrera Panamericana ended in failure. Pete Coltrin remembered: "He got about mid-way along the nineteen-hundred-mile distance, at Leon Guanajuato, to be exact, when the diff (I think) gave up. One happy side effect was that his co-driver, Doug Harrison, met and later married a pretty local lass."

High hopes dawned at the start of the 1953 NASCAR season, when Blair led Fonty Flock to a one-two victory at Daytona; but aside from Buck Baker's win at Darlington, the rest of the year was very disappointing for Oldsmobile drivers.

Ak Miller decided to have another go at the Mexican road race and made a sports car, powered by an Olds V-8 rebuilt and tuned by himself. The body was based on a 1927 Model T Ford. The chassis was strengthened and modern brakes fitted. "The gearbox was from a 1939 La Salle," Pete Coltrin read from his notebook, "with a Nash overdrive unit attached at the tail of the gearbox housing. A Lincoln differential was used. The Caballo de Hierro [Iron Horse] was ready in time for the 1954 race."

The details of what happened are best told in Pete Coltrin's words: "To avoid carburetor fuel surging, Miller made his own manifold and 'siamesed' two (four, really) Holley carbs mating them front to back. The only trouble he had with these was north of Mexico City early one morning, some thousands of feet above sea level, when the 'Caballo' started to stumble. A quick look revealed that, like airplanes, automobile carburetors are subject to icing conditions. Miller diagnosed the situation right away, and he and Harrison carefully chipped away the ethyl-red-tinted ice out of the carb chokes and continued on their way. They made it home to

Ciudad Juarez ahead of some Ferraris." The race was won by Juan Manuel Fangio driving a Lancia D-24 with a four-cam 3.3-liter V-6 engine.

Meanwhile, back at Lansing, Oldsmobile had been doing some hot-rodding. Bob Dorshimer, an engineer who had joined Oldsmobile in 1950, was assigned to develop heavy-duty parts, both engine and chassis, to assist the division's racing clientele.

Out of this project came the J-2 option, with 8.5:1 compression, solid valve lifters, high-lift camshaft and adjustable rocker arms. Also included were a reinforced rear axle, stronger springs, beefed-up steering linkage and high-strength engine mounts. Final drive ratios down to 3.08:1 and up to 4.55:1 were offered.

Due to the large number of racing drivers who remained faithful to Oldsmobile, the 88's made up a majority in most fields; and though spectacular successes became rarer and rarer, so many Oldsmobiles figured in the results that as late as 1955, Oldsmobile drivers amassed enough points to place the make second in the NASCAR championship.

At Daytona in 1956, Lee Petty's J-2-equipped 88 was timed at 144.928 mph over the flying mile. The mark was raised to 146.52 mph the following year by Major J. A. Robinson (a member of the U.S. Air Force Thunderbird aerobatics team) driving his own J-2-equipped Oldsmobile 88. Fleets of 88's were engaged in NASCAR

1950 Oldsmobile Futuramic 76 club coupe. As trunk capacity of the sedans increased, the popularity of the club coupe waned. Well-proportioned body design kept the coupe alive, however.

1950 Oldsmobile Futuramic 98 club sedan. The 98-series shared the B-body fastback with Cadillac, and had its own specific rear fenders. This body also had the one-piece curved windshield from the Holiday.

model year, the 88 accounted for better than one-third of Oldsmobile's total output:

88 four-door sedan	46,386
88 club sedan	38,707
88 town sedan	5,833
88 club coupe	11,561
88 convertible coupe	5,434
88 station wagon	1,355
Total 88	109,276
Total Oldsmobile	288,310

events through the 1959 season, but that was the final season for Olds participation in stock-car racing. As if to celebrate the closing of an era with a fitting climax, Lee Petty won the Daytona 500 of 1959 in a photo finish from Johnny Beauchamp's Ford Thunderbird after a hard-fought race-long duel in the opening event staged on the tri-oval speedway.

Looking back on Oldsmobile's days in stock-car racing, Bob Dorshimer recalled that ''it was a hell of a lot of fun. We got into it because Olds did not, up to then, have the image we wanted to have. I learned a lot from it. But I can't say it led to any big differences in our product. Things they say, like 'racing improves the breed' is baloney, for those machines are really and truly special cars. But you *do* learn something about engines.''

After this review of the 88's racing career, its performance in the market place calls for our attention. From the date of production startup till the end of the 1949

The thrill of driving the 88 was condensed in the action under the driver's right foot. Throttle response was instant, and the car seemed to leap ahead almost without effort, so smooth and quiet was its performance. The speedometer was a big semicircle with a scale of about half-an-inch per 10-mph increment. Watching the needle sweep across the dial toward higher numbers became a favorite pastime.

Springs were softer than on the former 78-series, and smooth-road ride comfort was noticeably improved. But on bumpy road surfaces, the body movements tended to exaggerate the initial disturbance; the car bouncing along in low-frequency undulation, while the wheels themselves were hammering the tires against the roadway in the rapid cycle of a pneumatic riveter.

On curves, there was more body roll than in earlier models, despite the new car's lower center of gravity; but the steering remained quite responsive, free of vagueness and yet well cushioned against road shock. It was not unreasonably slow-geared, but there were a few complaints of excessively high steering effort.

Seats were wider and roomier, and though one sat lower down, the view down the road was actually improved, for the cowl was lower, too, and the hood shorter, with a helpful slope toward the fenders, which came more easily into view. Glass area was considerably increased, improving rear vision as well as serving to brighten the whole interior. The hump in the rear floor had been raised somewhat, for the need for ground clearance did not permit further lowering of the propeller shaft; but there was still ample legroom, even for sitting three abreast.

For 1950, Oldsmobile shortened the 98's wheelbase to 122 inches and gave it a leaf-spring rear axle suspension. This was a strange step after so many years of all-coil suspension, and the reasons for it are not evident. "The way I remember it," said an Oldsmobile engineer, "we were pushed into changing our rear suspension because the corporation was changing to a new B-body where our coil-spring design didn't fit. We also had to stiffen the frame and develop a whole new bodymount system."

At that time, Buick also had coil-spring suspension for the rear axle, but managed to adapt its design to the new B-body, while Oldsmobile's chassis engineers, Jim Lewis and Andy Watt, figured out that the quickest solution to the problem was to look at Cadillac's rear end and do something similar.

Cadillac's Hotchkiss drive, with semi-elliptic leaf springs, had given entire satisfaction since the switch to high-compression overhead-valve engines. It was clear that, with adequate leaf width and enough leaves in each spring assembly, leaf springs could handle the axle-locating and thrust-carrying forces that were put on them, without folding up, twisting or breaking. Each spring was made up of five leaves, 2½ inches wide and fifty-eight inches long.

It was a low-cost solution, which eliminated many parts and several assembly operations, and whose drawbacks were easily covered up. Theoretical drawbacks, such as wheel hop under hard acceleration, ride discomfort and noise due to torque reactions, proved not to be very serious.

Some comments by Pete Coltrin throw an interesting sidelight on the rear-suspension situation by pointing out that all was not well with the existing coil-spring design (which continued for the 76- and 88-series): "It was common to replace the factory shock absorbers with Gabriels. I did this on my 1949-model 88, and filled the rear coil springs with inflateable air bags. That made for a stiff ride, but proved a good investment."

The long leaf springs selected for the Oldsmobile 98 had lower rates than the coil springs they replaced, and to balance the car, the front coil springs were softened also. At the same time, suitable changes were made in the calibration of the shock absorber valves to provide more damping.

The worm-and-double-roller steering gear was replaced by a Saginaw recirculating-ball system on the 98. This change was accompanied by raising the overall steering ratio to 27:1, which made it necessary to crank the wheel more for any given turn. In return, the steering effort was diminished. On the 88, which

1950 Oldsmobile Futuramic 88 station wagon. As fender lines came up toward the belt line, the wood panels receded to a small area around and below the windows. Horizontal-split tailgate had been adopted.

continued with worm-and-double-roller steering, the ratio was raised to 25:1.

The Hydra-matic transmission had been improved in two ways. The first change was a modification in the hydraulic control system, affecting servo action so as to assure smoother shifts. The second alteration consisted of reducing the number of shifts when starting off in drive by making second-gear starts (2.63:1 rather than 3.82:1) for the 88 and 98. The 3.82:1 ratio was still in there, but would only come into play in low.

Automatic transmission was made optional for all series (at $158.50), while a higher-capacity three-speed synchromesh gearbox was adopted as standard for all 1950 Oldsmobiles.

Body styles for the 76 and 88 did not change, and the new 98-series included the following types: four-door notchback sedan, two-door fastback sedan, Holiday two-door hardtop and convertible coupe. The 76 and 88 shared the A-body with Chevrolet and Pontiac, while the 98 used the B-body in common with Buick and Cadillac.

During 1950 the Lansing assembly plant attained its planned schedule of eighty cars per hour, and the division produced its three-millionth car.

The editors of *Motor Trend* tested a 1950-model Olds 88 and found its top speed to be 92.11 mph. It ran the standing-start quarter-mile in 19.86 seconds, and

1951 Oldsmobile 98 Deluxe four-door sedan. Aiming for hardtop look but needing to open the back doors, the stylists filled in the gap with chrome. Tire size was increased to 7.60-15, and the axle ratio lowered to 3.90:1.

What could not have been so well planned, however, was the purpose to which the engine plant would next be turned. It was retooled for production of 3.5-inch bazooka rockets, needed in great quantities for the United Nations's police action in Korea. In addition, a new steel storage building was tooled up to manufacture 90-mm tank cannon.

By the end of the war in Korea, Oldsmobile produced more than eight million bazooka rockets and over seven thousand tank cannon. In fact, Oldsmobile was cited as being the lowest-cost producer of these rockets.

Because of the strategic-materials shortage, Oldsmobile ran into car-production problems, and output fell in 1951. Initially the moadel lineup for 1951 included updated versions of the 88 (redesignated 88A) and 98. The gap between them was filled in March 1951 by a new series called the Super 88. It was built on a 120-inch wheelbase, with a shortened B-body, and used the leaf-spring rear suspension from the 98. The 88A continued with the coil-spring rear suspension. One feature of the Super 88 that attracted much attention was the wraparound rear window, giving fifty percent more view.

Fastback body styles were taken out of production altogether. That was a corporate decision, affecting all divisions. According to GM insiders, the hardtops had made the fastback redundant, and demand for it dried up. Prices were stable, and the lineup simplified:

Model	88A	Super 88	98
Two-door sedan	$1,815.43		
Deluxe two-door sedan	1,892.43	$1,969.42	
Four-door sedan	1,871.89		
Deluxe four-door sedan	1,948.89	2,025.88	$2,277.40
Deluxe club coupe		1,928.36	
Holiday coupe			2,267.14
Deluxe Holiday coupe		2,231.20	2,518.65
Deluxe convertible coupe	2,333.86	2,644.23	

The 1951 models were Skinner's parting shot as boss of Oldsmobile. In 1951 he was promoted to group vice president for the accessory divisions, where he was to prepare a wide-ranging rationalization program.

Any assessment of Skinner's performance during his years at Oldsmobile must start with a look back at what his predecessor left for him to take over.

From 1933 to 1940, Oldsmobile had fared well financially under the general managership of Charles L. McCuen. An engineer with solid experience in product design, McCuen became extremely cost-conscious when saddled with the responsibility of turning the division around from a money-loser to a profit-making organization. He authorized no spending above a bare minimum on product development, and Oldsmobile, apart from its lead in automatic transmission studies, was reduced to keeping pace with the other GM divisions in terms of technical progress.

went from standstill to 60 mph in 12.2 seconds. It was the fastest car the magazine had ever tested. The report indicated an average gasoline mileage of 16 to 18 mpg, but it was possible to do even better. An Oldsmobile 88 took part in the 1950 Mobilgas Economy Run and averaged 20.19 mpg from Los Angeles to the Grand Canyon.

Big revisions in model policy followed for 1951. Oldsmobile discontinued station wagon production, for one thing. Why? Some dealers complained they were too high-priced. Others said that those dowdy wagons clashed with the hot-shot hellfire image of the 88 and did not belong in the same showroom. The factory sales department was short of fresh ideas for promoting wagons, and Skinner told them in plain words that if they couldn't get trade volume up, the division couldn't afford to build any more wagons. Unit cost went skyrocketing when sales went down. Midway in the 1950 model year, he determined to suspend station wagon output. Many years were to go by before Oldsmobile got back into the wagon market.

Skinner also shut down six-cylinder engine production, and killed the 76-series. These moves had been planned well ahead of time, and saved a lot of money for the division.

1951 Oldsmobile 98 Holiday coupe. New wraparound treatment for the backlight and heavier chrome moldings along the body sides distinguished this model from the previous year's.

Much of Oldsmobile's success in this pre-Skinner period can be attributed to good management in the sense of not doing anything wrong. If no big steps ahead were taken, neither did the division make any big mistakes or commit sins which set the product behind that of its competitors. In 1940 McCuen left Lansing to become vice president in charge of the GM Research Laboratories, and Skinner acceded to the post.

Oldsmobile's product and industrial programs for 1941-42 were fixed prior to his arrival. We see his influence first as the leader of Oldsmobile's fantastic war-materiel production record. How did he cope with the tremendous challenges of the postwar situation? He showed bravery in his decisions of product policy, but always stopped short of recklessness. He was not just achievement-oriented—he had a total commitment to standing out as an achiever.

Skinner looked muscular and athletic. He was built like a middleweight boxer, but his immaculate physique showed that he had enough sense not to risk his nose, teeth and ears in the pugilistic ring. He was not a sharp dresser, for he wore an ordinary business suit whatever the circumstances, but he was invariably well groomed and a picture of health and acumen. By the time he left Oldsmobile, he was balding, graying at the temples, but with steady eyes, a strong jaw and a wry smile.

1951 Oldsmobile Super 88 convertible coupe. Styling differences from the 88 were concentrated in the rear fender area (chrome sash and gravel shield).

1951 Oldsmobile 88 two-door sedan. The fastback was a thing of the past, and all 88 sedans had notchback rooflines that year. At the same time, one-piece curved windshields were standardized.

Opinions of Skinner among the people who worked under him are not unanimously favorable, however. "Skinner wasn't a car man," said a now-retired Oldsmobile engineer. "I think he really didn't care strongly about the product as long as it would sell."

An engineer who left Oldsmobile to go to work for another division told us: "Half the time I'm not sure Skinner knew what was involved whenever he made a decision. He was very quick to make up his mind, sometimes too quick."

We know that Skinner got along well with his superiors, and it turns out that he was held in respect and generally well liked by the personnel at Oldsmobile. "Skinner was the all-American businessman, extremely clear-headed, and he would have been successful in running just about anything. I don't know what not, a steel

company or an airline. He was quick to make decisions, and knew why he was making them," a former sales staff member told us.

"On the whole, Skinner was a good leader. He cared about Oldsmobile and its reputation for quality. He was deeply involved with the plant, and was always ready to order new tooling when it could give us higher productivity with closer quality control. Also, he was concerned about having safe conditions for the workers, and took the initiative in accident-prevention measures," we learned from a manufacturing staff member.

The man who followed Skinner as general manager of Oldsmobile turned out to be a much more controversial character. His name was Jack Wolfram, and he had been the division's chief engineer since 1944. Jack Wolfram was born in Pittsburgh, Pennsylvania, on December 18, 1899. His name was not John, it was really just Jack, with a middle initial F whose meaning he never revealed.

After high school graduation, Wolfram took correspondence courses in drafting, machine design and business administration. In 1918 he was working as a reporter for the F. W. Dodge Corporation for a while, and then joined the civil engineering staff of the Baltimore & Ohio Railroad in its Pittsburgh office. He left Pittsburgh in 1920 to go to Cleveland, where he had found a job as a design engineer with the American Heating and Ventilating Company. He did not stay there long, signing up with the Enterprise Tool Company later that year as a tool designer.

On the strength of this experience and background, he was able to land a job as a draftsman with Chandler Motor Car Company in Cleveland in 1921, a company that was then doing well in the market and expanding rapidly. Chandlers were good cars of conventional design and construction, competing in the middle price class, a rival to makes such as Nash, Buick, Oldsmobile, Studebaker and Graham-Paige.

Wolfram got to really know cars at Chandler, working in one department after another, and gradually learning the car's progress from the drawing board to the production line.

He was ambitious, a fast learner and a tireless worker. Within two years, Wolfram found himself promoted to designer. Later, he was able to move laterally and work as an experimental engineer. Eventually, however, he found his career prospects limited at Chandler, and began to look for a more promising position somewhere else. He ended up at Oldsmobile in 1928, and began his long march upward through the ranks of the engineering staff.

His tenure as general manager was to be a long one, and the reader is about to become familiar with the man and his methods.

CHAPTER
6
Springboard to Decadence

THE COURSE OF EVENTS at Oldsmobile during the early 1950's was in many ways determined by corporate moves in personnel and planning. In 1948 C. E. Wilson had promoted a number of younger men to high positions. Buick's flamboyant boss, Harlow H. Curtice, was made executive vice president of General Motors, and Ivan L. Wiles took over as general manager of Buick. Louis C. Goad, who was then forty-seven, became general manager of the Body and Assembly Division.

Jack Wolfram, aged fifty-two when he took over the reins at Oldsmobile, therefore had a different team of corporate officials to deal with than the individuals with whom Skinner enjoyed such friendly relations.

No charge can be laid against 'Red' Curtice, however, that he disfavored any other division to give Buick an extra advantage. He ran the corporation as an extension of Buick, imposing his will and management style even on Chevrolet, where Tim Keating had succeeded W. F. Armstrong in 1949.

Under Curtice, the corporation's plans for the future role of each division took account of their traditional image and clientele, price range and profitability record, while allowing each division greater freedom to develop new images and cultivate different market segments.

Curtice's staff prepared short-term and mid-range market projections, and its conclusion was that domestic passenger car sales could be expected to double in the coming decade. At Curtice's initiative, a corporate expansion plan was formulated in February/March 1951, to raise GM's overall capacity of 4.5 million cars and trucks a year in the United States and Canada. In the first phase, it was intended to boost Cadillac's capacity by thirty-five percent and Oldsmobile's by twenty-five

percent. Buick was allotted only fifteen percent growth, compared with twenty-one percent for Chevrolet and thirty-one percent for Pontiac.

As time passed, plans were to be revised, with an upward adjustment for Oldsmobile and a less ambitious growth rate for Cadillac. Estimates for the cost of implementing this plan centered around a figure of $750 million, of which $300 million would be needed for sites and buildings, and $450 million for machinery and equipment.

The percential growth targets must be regarded in relation to the actual sales of each division during the preceding years and present levels of business.

	1949	1950	1951
Cadillac	80,800	101,825	97,098
Buick	372,425	535,807	392,285
Oldsmobile	269,351	372,519	273,472
Pontiac	321,033	440,528	337,821
Chevrolet	1,031,466	1,420,399	1,067,042
Total GM	2,075,075	2,871,078	2,167,718

And the following figures will put Oldsmobile's situation in proper perspective:

	1949	1950	1951
Rank in sales	7th	6th	7th
Olds market share	5.57%	5.89%	5.40%
GM market share	42.9%	45.4%	42.8%

With a four-barrel carburetor and higher compression, the Rocket V-8 was made to put out 160 hp with no increase in displacement. This version was used in the Super 88 and 98. The four-barrel carburetor was made by Rochester Products Division and known as the Quadri-Jet. The automatic choke had a heat-sensitive coil for its release mechanism.

Oldsmobile got ahead of Dodge in 1950, but lost again the following year.

During the Korean War, Oldsmobile converted about thirty percent of its capacity to war-materiel production. In 1952 Oldsmobile completed a new plant for producing turbines and compressors to be used in the J-65 turbojet engine.

The war was to affect General Motors in other ways, too, notably in terms of personnel changes. Harlow Curtice took over as acting president of GM on December 1, 1952, as Wilson was picked to serve as secretary of defense in the Eisenhower administration (taking a cut in salary from $550,000 to $25,000 a year). Wilson had been an excellent chief executive officer in private enterprise, and he brought to his government post a degree of honesty, candor and lack of self-interest that were suspect in the eyes of seasoned Washington politicians.

Wilson made many enemies in Washington and elsewhere because of his blunt manner, simple language and horror of hypocrisy. His definitions of fashionable topics were clever, merciless and killing. He deflated technical experts by saying "An expert is a mechanic away from home." He undermined publicity men by remarking "A brochure is just folded baloney."

The American public never learned to appreciate Wilson. Most people thought of him as the blunderer who uttered the famous misquote: "What's good for General Motors is good for the U.S.A." That earned him the dubious honor of standing model for Al Capp's General Bullmoose in the Broadway production of *Li'l Abner*. But what Wilson had said in fact was quiet different. He was asked during a Senate hearing whether he would be able to make a decision—as U.S. Secretary of Defense—that was in the interests of the United States government but unfavorable to General Motors. Wilson's exact words of reply were: "Yes, sir, I could. I cannot

1952 Super 88 two-door sedan. This model had a curb weight of 3,783 pounds, which gave an excellent power/weight ratio with the 160-hp Rocket V-8 engine. With the standard 3.64:1 axle ratio, it was geared for sparkling acceleration rather than maximum speed.

1952 Oldsmobile Super 88 chassis had leaf-spring rear axle suspension. Olds engineers still hesitated to move the engine forward, seeking to maintain even weight distribution. Air cleaners were continually redesigned to allow lower and lower hood lines.

conceive of one [such situation] because of years I thought what was good for our country was good for General Motors, and vice versa.''

On February 2, 1953, Alfred P. Sloan, Jr., formally announced the appointment of Harlow H. Curtice as president of General Motors.

Having a man of Curtice's caliber at the head of the corporation was bound to steer product planning and evolution in the direction of his personal taste in cars. He was not an engineer, but an accountant who had come up through AC Spark Plug at Flint, and mounted a spectacular rescue operation at Buick in 1934. He had many talents; his persuasive salesmanship perhaps overshadowing his managerial skills. He understood styling better than engineering, and with predictable regularity he fell in love with the wildest designs Harley Earl's advanced-studio artists felt free to prepare.

Curtice liked big cars, flashy cars, and detested bland-looking cars. Along with the other GM divisions, Oldsmobile was to enter an era of styling excesses and poor taste that rankled many of the best designers on the Styling Staff.

With the 1951 models, Art Ross permitted himself to make the first fateful concession to ugliness by permitting a chrome-plated sash to mark the Super 88's rear fender line, in complete violation of the main body lines and in conflict with all other accent lines. The sash extended from the shoulder of the rear fender, running diagonally down and back to the massive chrome-plated gravel shield, where a horizontal molding pierced the brightwork assembly. The grille design became heavier, and the lower of the two horizontal bars was carried by the bumper guards—its ends separated from the upper, or frame, bar. Chrome was loaded on in thicker slices in various places, apparently in the belief that it would cover up a design goof when in fact it only called attention to it.

On the engineering side, the quietly competent Harold N. Metzel was appointed chief engineer. Gil Burrell was motor engineer and George T. Jones was named chassis engineer. Andy Watt became transmission engineer; and Jim Lewis, body engineer. This was a team of confirmed Oldsmobile veterans; who, in the words of a junior member of the engineering staff at the time, ''could do no wrong.''

Harold N. Metzel was born in Peoria, Illinois, on May 1, 1904. He attended local schools and entered Bradley University, from which he graduated in 1926 with a bachelor's degree in science. He wanted time to think about a career, and found a way to avoid leaving school by teaching mathematics at the Community High School in Armstrong, Illinois. The following year he got a chance at an engineering position with Western Electric in Chicago—and took it. That was fine for making a living, but the work did not give him great satisfaction. He wanted to work on cars, and in 1928 went to Oldsmobile as a test driver. ''At this period in my life, I drove more than 100,000 miles a year,'' he recalled later.

Metzel became assistant foreman of dynamometer tests in 1929, and the following year was placed in charge of the engine laboratories. By 1935 he held the title of development engineer and divided his time between the desk at Lansing and the Proving Grounds at Milford.

This was the time when Oldsmobile was taking the lead in experimental work on automatic and semi-automatic transmissions, and Metzel got involved with testing and evaluating the forerunners of the Hydra-matic. He did so much work on these experimental units and other drive line problems that he was appointed transmission engineer in 1937. Two years later, he and his staff carried out the testing and inspection of the first five thousand Oldsmobiles equipped with Hydra-matic.

During World War II, Metzel headed Oldsmobile's gun and cannon engineering development. When the war ended, he was named assistant chief engineer to Jack Wolfram, and while Gil Burrell was busy on the Rocket V-8, Metzel served as supervisor and development engineer for that project.

Development work on the Rocket V-8 engine was, of course, something that never stopped. After continuing unchanged for 1950, the 1951 version had its compression ratio raised to 7.5:1, with no increase in power output or bulging in the torque curve. At the same time, the engine received high-resistant Auto-Thermic aluminum pistons, reinforced with double steel struts with a chrome-plated top compression ring. Since these pistons were heavier, it became necessary to increase the size of the crankshaft counterweights.

For 1952, the output of the baseline engine was raised to 145 hp, mainly by new came profiles giving higher valve lift, plus minor alterations in the rocker arm mechanism.

This engine had a downdraft two-barrel carburetor by Rochester or Carter, but Oldsmobile also had a more powerful version with a four-barrel Rochester Quadri-Jet, delivering 160 hp at 3600 rpm.

The 145-hp unit was standard in the Deluxe 88 (which replaced the 88A), and the 160-hp unit was standard in the Super 88 and Classic 98. All cars equipped with synchromesh transmission received a new 10.5-inch semi-centrifugal single-plate clutch.

More important alterations were made in the automatic transmission. A cone-type friction reverse clutch had been adopted for the 1951 Hydra-matic, improving the transmission's ability to permit 'rocking' between drive and reverse. The revised Hydra-matic, used for the 1952 Classic 98 and Super 88, introduced the super range, with a separate position of the selector lever. This prevented upshifting to fourth, holding third until the car reached a speed of 70 mph or the driver manually shifted to drive.

The super range had its own position on the shift quadrant, marked S, placed immediately to the right of the drive position. Thus the shift pattern became N-D-S-L-R. There was not, as yet, a P for park. Shifting into S gave extra torque for acceleration, improved engine-braking on steep downgrades, and a feeling of better control when driving on twisting mountain roads. With the lever in super position, the car started off in first gear and shifted through second to third in normal order. By

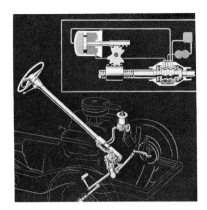 

Power steering became optional on Oldsmobile for the first time in 1952, with an engine-driven hydraulic pump and a power cylinder working directly on the steering gear. The system was developed by the Saginaw Steering Gear Division of GM. Auxiliary wheel clamped to steering wheel measures the effort put into the system by the driver. It was an indispensable instrument in the development of power steering. The 1952 Olds had a half-circle speedometer.

holding third, engine rpm were kept higher on the power curve, giving markedly higher performance.

Super-Drive Hydra-matic also introduced the variable-capacity pump, which permitted large capacity at low rpm (where it was most needed) but allowed the capacity to drop off toward zero at high speed (and thereby assuring a dramatic reduction in pumping losses).

Because of the engine and transmission changes, it became possible to bring down the axle ratio from 3.42:1 to 3.23:1 in the Super 88, and from 3.64:1 to 3.42:1 in the Classic 98. The use of 'longer' gearing increased highway fuel mileage and reduced engine noise.

Chassis changes were few. The wheelbase of the Classic 98 was stretched two inches to 124. But the important thing was that a big standardization move took place with the disappearance of the 88A, with its A-body and coil-spring rear suspension. Its replacement, the Deluxe 88, shared the body and 120-inch wheelbase chassis of the Super 88. Thus Oldsmobile had only one rear suspension system for the whole model range, and one basic body, the Fisher B-body, with two wheelbases.

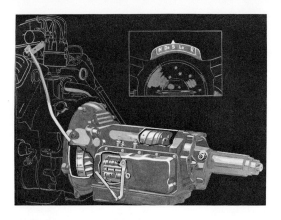

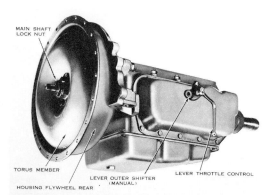

MAIN SHAFT
LOCK NUT

TORUS MEMBER

HOUSING FLYWHEEL REAR

LEVER OUTER SHIFTER
(MANUAL)

LEVER THROTTLE CONTROL

Hydra-matic transmission was labeled 'Super Drive' in 1952, to stress the addition of an intermediate (super) range, locking in third gear up to 75 mph. Reverse was still on the other side of lo rather than left of neutral. Outwardly (middle) the Hydra-matic was the same as in 1940, with a single shift-control lever on the side, and a very compact housing. A look inside (right) the Hydra-matic. The fluid coupling is shown on the right, with two members only: one impeller and one follower. The gear at lower left is for the speedometer drive.

Jack Wolfram (right) holds the banner for the four-millionth Oldsmobile with his production manager at the opposite end. The date was May 12, 1953.

Two important new options were added: power steering and power brakes. The servo-assisted steering had been developed under Philip B. Zeigler at Saginaw Steering Gear Division. It used a hydraulic pump, belt-driven from the engine, to add extra force behind the driver's movements of the steering wheel.

The power brake system was based on the Bendix Hydrovac (which was common on trucks) and purchased from Bendix. The system consisted of a vacuum chamber connected to the intake manifold, with a diaphragm linked to the master cylinder. Movement of the master cylinder piston (in response to pressure on the brake pedal) was instantly supported, and the pressure magnified, by the vacuum booster.

Oldsmobile also made factory-installed air conditioning optional for the 1952 models.

A minor convenience option known as the Autronic-Eye, an automatic headlight dimmer that responded to extraneous light hitting a photoelectric cell from the direction of oncoming traffic, was also introduced in 1952.

Despite a lot of new sheet metal, styling changes for 1952 appeared relatively minor. The 98 had a sculptured rear fender in 1951, with a horizontal spear in the

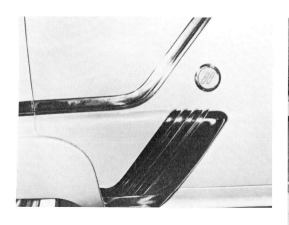

1953 Oldsmobile Super 88 convertible coupe. A lighter touch in the use of chrome accompanied the trend toward boxier shapes. This year the width of the body increased from 75.7 to 77 inches. The convertible weighed 3,904 pounds. Side decor on the 1953-model 88 featured this simulated gravel shield to create the impression of a rear fender line, along with the bent molding coming down from the belt line.

New instrument panel in the 1953 models returned to use of the circular speedometer. Brake pedal in Hydra-matic equipped cars was still narrow. Glovebox is in the middle.

form of a long-tailed flounder. There was also a chrome molding running straight from the front fender through the door panels, then kicked up to avoid collision with the fender sculpturing. On the 1952 model, this was replaced by a new fender carrying the diagonal sash of the Super 88, with a horizontal molding to separate it from the vertical-striped gravel shield on the lower part.

Oldsmobile bodies were becoming boxier, and Pete Coltrin, who was then working for an Oldsmobile dealer in Pasadena, was aware of the deterioration in streamlining: "From being fairly well off in the aerodynamics department with the '49's, the 88's of 1951-52 were pushing a lot of air, so to speak."

The 1953 models presented the final facelift of the basic body generation that began with the Futuramic in 1948. The same model lineup was carried over, and no changes were made in wheelbases or overall length. Styling features centered on the grille and side decor. The bumper was integrated with the grille, the bumper guards bent inward to follow the contour of the grille frame, and carrying pods resembling turbojet-engine cowlings on top, linked by a horizontal bar.

Interior of the Fiesta prototype shows normal bench seats with special upholstery, standard instrument panel. Top was power operated.

1953 Oldsmobile 98 Fiesta convertible coupe. The Fiesta was an attempt to make the 98 sportier without losing its luxury. It was the first Olds design with wraparound windshield, due for production in 1954.

Rear fender sculpturing was toned down, and the diagonal sash was slimmed down on both Super 88 and 98 (no longer Classic, after just one year). The rear fender crown was raised, and the trunk enlarged with a higher deck contour, which in combination gave the car a new silhouette and the illusion of additional length.

As Harley Earl was to confess a year later, "My primary purpose for twenty-eight years has been to lengthen and lower the American automobile, at times in reality, and always at least in appearance. Why? Becasue my sense of proportion tells me that oblongs are more attractive than squares...."

An all-new instrument panel was put into the 1953 cars, reverting to a full-circle speedometer, with N-D-S-L-R in a large window below the odometer. It was placed immediately in front of the driver, and to match it, facing the front seat passenger, was a circle of equal size filled by a grooved dish containing a tiny dash clock in the center. On top of the instrument panel of the 98 was a cushion of soft foam rubber under a plastic cover, intended as safety-padding but subsequently proved to be ineffective due to excessive softness in the foam. The glovebox was moved to the center, below the radio. The steering wheel was redesigned with two spokes only, and the full-circle horn ring returned. On cars with Hydra-matic drive, the brake pedal was widened to make left-foot braking easier.

On the engineering side, the Rocket V-8's compression ratio was increased to an even 8.0:1, and both engines (two-barrel and four-barrel carb types) found five extra horsepower. The rating for the Deluxe 88 was 150 hp, and for the 98 and Super 88 it went up to 165 hp. That was barely enough to maintain performance levels, for the cars were gaining weight fast, at the rate of fifty to one hundred pounds a year. The 1953 models had curb weights of 3,827 pounds for the Deluxe 88, 3,864 pounds for the Super 88, and 3,975 pounds for the 98, for four-door sedans with synchromesh transmissions.

The price for Hydra-matic had increased to $178.35. Power steering cost $177.40, and power brakes were a bargain at $35.50.

During the 1953 model year, Oldsmobile made its first experiment with a limited-production model. The Fiesta was a custom sports convertible based on the

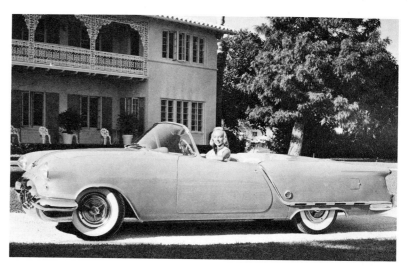

A special 200-hp Rocket V-8 with 9:1 compression ratio was jammed in under the Starfire's hood. Air cleaner looks big enough for a Mack truck.

The Starfire prototype was a driveable car, fully equipped for road use. But Oldsmobile's market research revealed that there were few buyers for a car of that type in its price class—above the 98.

98, outfitted with just about every option in the book. It was the first GM car offered for sale that had a panoramic windshield (a feature that Harley Earl had originally used on Buick's Le Sabre and XP-300 experimental cars of 1951).

If Oldsmobile was sincere in offering it as a limited-production model, they were right on target. On the other hand, if that was just a coy trick aimed at snob appeal, and the factory really intended to sell thousands of them, then Olds must have learned a very severe marketing lesson, for only 458 Fiesta cars were made.

Much greater interest was attached to a pure show car that was not for sale—the Starfire. It made its first appearance at the GM Motorama in New York City, alongside the Buick Wildcat, Cadillac Le Mans, Cadillac Orleans and Pontiac Parisienne. It was a futuristic sports convertible of very low build and presented several new styling ideas. Art Ross had finally got it all together after straying all over the map in bumper-and-grille designs. Here, at last, was an elegant combination, with an oval grille enclosed in the bumper structure, and a sloping hood line with a prominent 'ring-around-the-world' emblem centered between the headlights. The

diagonal sash line for the rear fenders was still there, but only as an upward extension of a horizontal molding, curving around a circular Oldsmobile badge.

The interior featured front bucket seats and a split rear bench for two. The Starfire was to have great influence on the styling of the 1956 models—and subsequent Oldsmobiles. The public reaction was overwhelming and favorable, and it encouraged Oldsmobile to prepare more 'dream cars' for public showing, as barometers of trends in consumer preferences.

To add to the glamor of the Starfire, Oldsmobile endowed it with an experimental Rocket V-8, running on a 9.0:1 compression ratio and putting out 200 hp. The way car size and weights were going, such power outputs were beginning to seem quite realistic, and forward-looking planners were speaking openly of 500-hp cars for the long-term future.

Oldsmobile was prospering under Wolfram's management. The division had built its three-millionth car on February 15, 1950. Despite the production cuts due to the Korean War, the four-millionth car followed on May 12, 1953; and the five-millionth car, on July 27, 1955.

Oldsmobile had planned for automatic-transmission installations in ninety to ninety-three percent of 1954-model production. The news of the catastrophic fire

Styling mockup for the 1954 Oldsmobile shows the panorama windshield on a four-door sedan. Front end indicates retention of the former grille design, and side decor is still tentative.

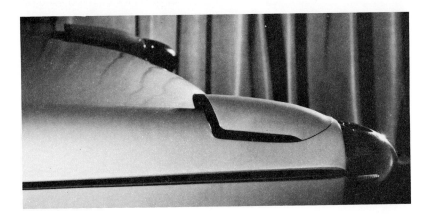

Simulated air scoops for the taillights? A styling idea that was nixed, but not until it had got to the finished prototype stage.

1954 Oldsmobile 88 two-door sedan. Production model has cleaner side treatment and smooth rear fender tops. Wheelbase was increased to 122 inches; overall length, to 205.3 inches; and the weight, to 3,838 pounds.

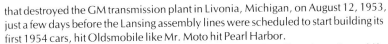

that destroyed the GM transmission plant in Livonia, Michigan, on August 12, 1953, just a few days before the Lansing assembly lines were scheduled to start building its first 1954 cars, hit Oldsmobile like Mr. Moto hit Pearl Harbor.

Stocks of Hydra-matics were quickly used up, and Wolfram knew it would be a bad time to tell Oldsmobile buyers they could only get synchromesh transmissions. Fortunately, Buick had excess capacity for the Dynaflow, and supplied many thousands to Oldsmobile (and Cadillac, which was in the same boat).

Oldsmobile engineers did not hold the Dynaflow in very high regard, however, and Wolfram was most insistent, vis-a-vis the corporation, that makeshift production of Hydra-matics must be set up until the plant could be rebuilt. No time was lost in finding a plant, but tooling problems were not immediately solved, even when machines were salvaged from the burned-out factory. As it turned out, the Livonia plant was never rebuilt, but Hydra-matic found a new home when GM purchased the giant Willow Run assembly plant from Kaiser Motors Corporation, and then retooled for making automatic transmissions.

Oldsmobile made a big leap forward with its 1954 models, which were truly new cars, fully restyled, with more powerful engines. That year Oldsmobile moved up to fourth place in the industry by overtaking both Pontiac and Plymouth. That

would have put Oldsmobile third, right behind Chevrolet and Ford; but for Buick, which made over half a million cars that year.

Here is the statistical picture in a nutshell:

	1952	1953	1954
Total market (millions)	4.158	5.739	5.535
Olds sales	281,189	305,593	407,150
Olds rank	7th	6th	4th
Olds market share	5.25%	5.32%	7.35%
GM market share	41.7%	45.1%	50.7%

1954 Oldsmobile experimental Cutlass coupe. A wild, space-age styling project, not without its merits. Cadillac later used the rear fender design. Swivel seats were features in the experimental Cutlass intended to make entry and exit easier. The idea had to wait till 1973 for optional use on production cars, and was soon given up for lack of demand.

The 1954-model Oldsmobiles went on display on Wednesday, January 20, in dealer showrooms all over the country. This was the biggest change the buying public had seen in Oldsmobiles since the first showing of the Futuramic in 1948.

"The new 1954 Oldsmobile models were originally planned for release in 1955," J. F. Wolfram revealed at a press conference on January 18. "But original plans were scrapped early in 1953 when it was found possible to move the 1955 models up to 1954."

He wasn't bluffing. It was really true that Oldsmobile was putting out its planned 1955 models one full year ahead of schedule. But it wasn't Oldsmobile's or Wolfram's doing.

As the story goes, pieced together from bits of conversation with colleagues in the press, GM insiders and other sources close to Detroit, the cars that were first designed for 1954 were shown to the top management of GM in Movember 1952. Red Curtice blew his stack. The cars were lumpy, warmed-over, unimaginative—worse than the '53 models, he is supposed to have said. No doubt he added other, less printable adjectives to color his description.

Harley Earl was stunned. The general managers of the car divisions were embarrassed. Styling Staff and Fisher Body executives rushed into explanations of how this was the most that could be done within the tooling budget, proposed by the manufacturing staff and approved by Curtice. When tempers settled, meetings were held where incriminations were forgotten and excuses waved aside in favor of a concerted effort to reach a solution.

Curtice would not soften his stand, however. "General Motors can't come out with those . . . things . . . in a year when we'll be facing drastically redesigned cars from both Ford and Chrysler," is how he is reported to have summed up the marketing problem.

"It was difficult to disagree with him," admitted a Styling Staff member, many years later. "I never knew who first had the idea of going into a crash program to skip a year and get the '55 bodies into production for '54. Perhaps it was Ragsdale. Perhaps it was Goodman."

Both are plausible. Edward T. Ragsdale was then general manager of Buick, having previously served as Buick's body engineer since back in the six-cylinder days. James E. Goodman was general manager of Fisher Body, and a man who had worked his way up from a Fisher-plant production-line worker to general manufacturing manager of the division in twenty-one years. Another source claims Kenneth E. Coppock was the brain behind the plan—he was a top body engineer with Fisher Body at the time.

1954 Oldsmobile Super 88 Holiday coupe. New grille design within old framework features two bomb-like pods. Engine size had been increased to 324 cubic inches and output to 185 hp.

1954 Oldsmobile 98 Starfire convertible coupe. Though it got the Starfire name, it's basically the Fiesta in production form, with the side decor from the new 98 sedan.

One story has it that Louis C. Goad, then executive vice president with overall responsibility for the Car and Truck Group, simply asked the question in a meeting: "The designs for the 1955 cars are pretty well finished. Would it be possible to get them into production sooner?" No matter how it came about, it *was* possible. And it was done.

The cars were about three inches lower than the previous models. Hood lines were lowered almost down to fender height, and the rear fenders maintained what was nearly full height, right back to the taillights. The sweep-cut wheel openings gave an impression of speed, and the new grille continued the previous theme, with increasing horizontal emphasis, and continued use of bumper elements to fill the grille pattern. The new panoramic windshield and wraparound rear-window design gave a greenhouse effect to the whole passenger compartment. Interiors were bright and spacious, for the space lost in height had been gained in length. Wheelbases

were up for all models: 122 inches for the 88 and Super 88, 126 inches for the new 98.

The model lineup was simple, and prices remained competitive:

	88	Super 88	98
Two-door sedan	$2,271.62	$2,410.25	
Four-door sedan	2,337.09	2,476.71	$2,805.82
Holiday coupe	2,449.00	2,688.39	2,826.00
Deluxe Holiday coupe			3,041.75
Convertible Coupe		2,867.59	
Starfire coupe			3,248.84

The Starfire coupe was a convertible with hydraulic power top, power windows and power seat-adjusting mechanism for the four-way front bench seat. It was available in sixteen single body colors and seven two-tone combinations in which the rear fenders, lower body and rear deck were painted one color; and the front fenders, hood and roof, a second color.

The engineering story for 1954 was quite impressive, and it must have been a considerable strain on the organization to rush all the changes into production to match the schedule for the new bodies.

Wolfram had insisted on plenty of room to expand engine displacement without going into a redesign. That's why Gil Burrell spaced the cylinder centers so far apart, why he did not use a shorter stroke still, and why the engine was relatively heavy in its original form. When the 1954 program started, Wolfram told Burrell this was one time he didn't want any lack of power in any car in the Oldsmobile stable; and Burrell simply bored it out to 3.875 inches, which raised displacements to 324 cubic inches.

At the same time, compression ratio was raised from 8.0 to 8.25:1. The baseline engine, equipped with a two-barrel carburetor, used in the 88-series, put out 170 hp at 4000 rpm. The four-barrel version used in the Super 88 and 98 delivered 185 hp at 4000 rpm. Torque readings went up to 300 pounds-feet at an even 2000 rpm, and it was deemed prudent to go to a bigger clutch for cars with synchromesh transmission—the new one was a full eleven inches in diameter.

Brake drums of eleven-inch diameter were put in all wheels for adequate stopping power, since the new cars were forty-four to ninety-six pounds heavier than their predecessors. Despite increased car weights, it became possible to alter the overall gearing so as to let the engine run at reduced rpm for any given road speed. The axle ratio for the Hydra-matic 98 went down to 3.23:1, remaining at 3.42:1 for the synchromesh version of the 98. The same ratios were used in the Super 88. The manual three-speed 88 also had a 3.42:1 axle ratio, but with Hydra-matic this car was able to pull a 3.07:1 ratio, making it relatively economical on fuel.

The new low-profile bodies demanded a redesigned frame. The basic shape was retained, with nearly straight side-members and a hefty X-bracing plus five lateral cross-members. The mounting for the Hydra-matic transmission was altered to obtain the necessary clearance, by tilting the unit twenty-two degrees counterclockwise. And finally, the rear suspension was reworked. The leaf springs, which had a slight toe-in in the earlier design, were now laid parallel with the wheels, and were moved even closer to the wheels for improved stability.

The ride became softer, and shock damping remained inadequate, both front and rear. The lower center of gravity would theoretically help reduce sway on curves, but in practice, the effect was minimal. Fortunately, G. T. Jones, the chassis engineer, had enough sense to keep the anti-sway bars at both ends. The cars had lost something in maneuverability and steering reponse, but that was a general, industry-wide pattern, and did not cause Oldsmobile any sales resistance. People were, more than ever before, buying cars on the basis of appearance. It was to get worse before the decade was out, since the public's approval of some of the most senseless and outrageous attempts to make cars look new and different had the effect of egging the industry on toward less and less rational designs.

1954 Oldsmobile experimental F-88 sports prototype. It was an Oldsmobile version of Chevrolet's Corvette, built on the same 100-inch wheelbase. It turned out to be a useful styling exercise.

CHAPTER
7

The Price of Fashion

DESIGN TRENDS HAD BEEN altering the shape of Oldsmobile since about 1930, so what was happening in the mid-fifties was nothing new. Oldsmobile had in fact been a trend-setter rather than a follower all along, which increased the burden on its designers and management to keep the appearance of the product more future-oriented than its rivals. What did the future look like to Oldsmobile designers? "Harley Earl had been impressed with the P-39 Lockheed Lightning during the war," we learned from a GM Styling Staff member, "and every jet-fighter that came out after the war gave him inspiration for new car-styling themes. Then Oldsmobile had the Rocket name, and ballistic missiles lent their profiles to body ornamentation of all kinds."

Regardless of the contrasts in operating conditions, Earl continued to push aerospace influences on all GM cars. As a matter of fact, architecture and styling went hand in hand. Paramount in importance to Harley Earl was a low, long look. Of course, he was well aware of the fact that consumers expected next year's model to get roomier, and not less roomy, as it grew lower and longer. Essentially, he was trading off height for length. If headroom was cut down, more legroom was needed. Seats were lowered, but spaced farther apart.

In this, Earl was helped by the shortness of the new V-8 engines which all divisions had either in production or in preparation. The engines could also be pushed forward, freeing more space inside the wheelbase for the passengers. The V-8 engines had lower profiles than their in-line, vertical predecessors, too, which made lower hood lines possible. Increasing front overhang was balanced by increasing deck length.

Oldsmobile had to conform to the overall evolution of General Motors, for although the division still designed its own frames, suspension and steering systems, engine and drive train, the total concept was dictated by the corporation. Such a plan left no room for Oldsmobile to deviate from the other GM car divisions in basic body types or proportions, chassis layout, weight distribution or structural principles.

The 1954-model B-body was reserved for Buick and Oldsmobile only, since Cadillac based all models on the C-body, and Pontiac had to share the A-body with Chevrolet. The Oldsmobile 88 and Super 88 were built on the same 122-inch wheelbase as the Buick Special and Century, so that body-and-frame parts for these four high-volume series were extensively interchangeable. For the Ninety-Eight, Oldsmobile had a stretched B-body and a 126-inch wheelbase, which made it a lighter car than if it had shared the C-body with Buick's Roadmaster.

The whole body-sharing plan was flexible, so that Pontiac, for instance, could be 'given' a B-body car at any time if market demand warranted it and Fisher Body had the capacity; just as Oldsmobile could propose sharing the C-body any time it wanted to. The outcome depended on the concensus of high-level opinion in the corporate management.

Because of this flexibility, all divisions did enjoy some freedom to explore design concepts that lay outside the current range of Fisher production bodies, for if

Jack Wolfram at the wheel of the five-millionth Oldsmobile, produced on July 27, 1955. Standing is R. T. Rollis, general manufacturing manager.

and when a given project got as far as being considered for production, interdivisional coordination would become necessary. Only Chevrolet was big enough to be placed above such restraints, with the Corvette providing proof of its own unique status within the corporation.

Because of the Corvette, indeed, the other divisions felt encouraged to play with sports car designs. During 1954 the Oldsmobile studio, under the direction of Art Ross, prepared two cars that were to become influential on future Oldsmobile styling. One was the F-88 roadster, built on a 102-inch wheelbase. The second was a coupe on a 110-inch wheelbase, called Cutlass, which had a spectacular fastback

roof with a rear window styled with slats, like Venetian blinds. Both had bodies made of fiberglass-reinforced plastic.

These two cars introduced the oval air intake as an Oldsmobile identification mark, fitting below the bumper on the F-88, and as part of the bumper design on the Cutlass.

Both were powered by a 250-hp experimental version of the stock V-8, featuring 9:1 compression and improved carburetion. Chassis features remained

Improved crankcase ventilation was claimed to have been used for the 1955 model Rocket V-8. But it vented into the atmosphere. It was not until 1963 that Oldsmobile adopted positive crankcase ventilation.

1955 Oldsmobile Super 88 two-door sedan. The grille was made oval by scooping out the bumper face. Wraparound rear window became standard for two-door models.

very close to production-type design. On both cars, fender lines included new themes. The trailing edge of the wheel openings was opened up in a severe sweep-cut, changing the cutout line from semicircular toward wing-profile.

In keeping with the trend of the time, the upper fender lines merged in and out of the belt lines. On the F-88, the front fender tapered off in the door panel, but was picked up into an arch to form a rear fender, which ended in a rocket-line cylinder with the taillight at the end. The lower fender continued as a louvered skirt to form part of the rear bumper. Chromed bumper horns in the fender tips contained exhaust outlets (jet syndrome, again), while the main bumper bar was painted body color, and inset with seven tooth-like chrome guards spaced across its surface.

On the Cutlass, the front fender held to belt line height into the door panel, and then veered gently lower; while the belt line developed into a tailfin running horizontally back to an acute angular cutoff. The fastback roofline also tapered in width, coming to a point in the middle of the rear deck, an idea that was to be used again for Oldsmobile show cars (but discarded by Olds officials for use on production cars and left for others to pick up: Chevrolet for the Corvette Sting Ray coupe of 1963 and Buick for the 1971-model Riviera).

Both the F-88 and the Cutlass had spinner-type wheel covers with turbine-pattern rims, and big-world-in-a-ring emblems on hood and deck. Interestingly,

rocket-type hood emblems were not used, and chrome moldings were sparsely used on the sides. The F-88 merely carried a reverse-slant accent line for the rear-fender kickup. On the Cutlass, a simple horizontal spear ran along the widest point of the fender curve, starting in the door panel and widening horizontally toward the tail end. Both cars had bucket seats, sports-car instrumentation and spaceship interiors.

Before any of their styling ideas could come into use for a production-model Oldsmobile, however, the division's studio had turned out another show car, the Delta, in 1955. It was a four-seater hardtop built on a 120-inch wheelbase using a modified standard frame, with a 253-hp V-8 engine, having a 10:1 compression ratio.

This hardtop coupe was very low and sporty, no more than fifty-three inches high overall, with panoramic windshield and wraparound rear window. A split-oval grille was inset in the bumper, whose ends rose to twice its height to provide a framework for the recessed headlamps, thus reaching up right to the fender crown and covering the entire fender tip. Cast-aluminum disc wheels were used.

Wheel arches had a new sweep-cut treatment, featuring extended chrome-plated cavities aft of each tire—the outline growing more bulbous and less winglike than on the previous year's designs.

Side decor was a two-level affair, starting with a wide spear at headlamp height, curving down to top-of-bumper height in the door panel and then leading horizontally back to the rear bumper.

A steel roof with brushed-aluminum finish was used, but the rest of the body was made of fiberglass-reinforced plastic. Among its innovations were front seats that swiveled for easier entry or exit, and dual fuel tanks positioned in the rear fenders (as Jaguar had done on its Mark VII Saloon in 1950).

What is most interesting about Oldsmobile's styling prototypes in these years is that they tended farther and farther away from what the division was actually putting into production. As the show cars got cleaner, shedding chrome and heavy rocket emphasis, the production models went in the opposite direction: overdecorated with a heavy hand, as if their basic shape and proportions were someting to be ashamed of.

The climax for show-car design by Oldsmobile was reached in 1956 with the Golden Rocket. It was a fastback coupe inspired by the Cutlass profile, but with different emphasis. The Venetian blinds were reduced to four symbolic gills below the backlight base, and a two-piece rear window was split down the center, as if to make a backbone, with compound curved glass on both sides. The whole cockpit cover was formed of lift-up glass panels in chrome frames, made to remind the viewer of the fighter-plane canopy. Tailfins—in which running-lights were mounted—were miniaturized and restricted to an area immediately above the rear wheels.

The fenders introduced a new pontoon look that the 1961 Thunderbird later became famous for. There was no break at all between front and rear fenders, just a steady taper from front to rear. There was no chrome at all on the body sides, just a plain curvaceous panel from chrome-plated headlight bezels to chromed bomb-nose rear fender tips. Taillights were recessed below these tips.

The weirdest part of the car, however, was the front. There was no grille as such. The hood came to a point, forward of the fenders, with aircraft-style blending of the sheet metal between these elements. The front could also be called bow-shaped, for the foremost part was a narrow chrome shield with shark-like teeth on both sides, covering a forward-sloping slot that served as an air intake. In case it could not provide sufficient cooling for the 275-hp V-8 engine, the surrounding panels were fitted with flaps that opened to admit air to the radiator.

As on previous show cars, the Golden Rocket body was made of fiberglass-reinforced plastic. In addition to swivel seats, it also embodied a new development from Saginaw—the tilt-wheel.

After this experiment, Oldsmobile stopped showing its advanced styling prototypes to the public. What was to follow were merely pale elaborations on current production models or offbeat studies already rejected as a base for future production-car design.

On the theory that women influence many car purchases, Oldsmobile assigned Miss Peggy Sauer of the GM Styling Staff to concoct some special interiors with a heavy accent on appeal to the female. The first result was a 1957 show car called Mona Lisa, using the standard 98 Holiday coupe body with a special paint job and an interior, finished in pearlescent tangerine to match the exterior paint, in a striped pattern with a Caribbean motif.

The Chanteuse was another creation by Miss Peggy Sauer, using the Starfire convertible as a base. There was no material restyling, as it was all done with colors,

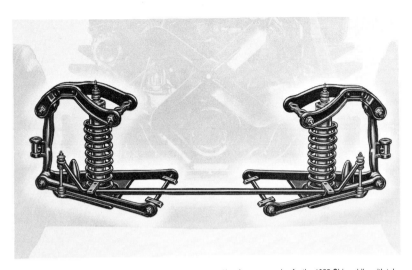

New front suspension for the 1955 Oldsmobile, with telescopic shock absorbers mounted concentrically within the coil springs, was designed by Jim Lewis.

the exterior being painted a sparkling violet which was repeated inside, with chartreuse accents.

Finally in 1958, there was the Carousel, a station wagon (which had recently been reintroduced in the Oldsmobile production program) specially tailored for family life with children—how to keep them safe, comfortable and entertained, and how to store their outdoor apparel for instant readiness.

Two roadsters presented in 1958 and 1959, the F-88 Mark II and F-88 Mark III, evidently came from the Advanced Styling Studio and had bodies that deviated to an extreme degree from the styling of contemporary Oldsmobiles.

The F-88 Mark II was not unlike the 1958 Corvette in overall shape. The Oldsmobile oval was retained for the grille, though the lower part was flattened, which gave the frontal aspect the down-at-the-mouth look of Emmett Kelley the clown. Delicate bumper strips ran around the fender tips on each side, blending discreetly into the protruding body nose. Side-by-side dual headlights were housed in oval bezels, and below the bumper strips were parking lights/turn signals shaped like jet-engine pods emerging from the lower fender panel. Along the side was a sculptured spear, mainly horizontal but having a slight rise in the middle so as to underline the belt line. The F-88 Mark II had the small tailfins from the Golden Rocket, and the same absence of chrome moldings. Of all its styling features, only

Oldsmobile experimental Delta coupe was built in 1955 with a body made of fiberglass-reinforced plastic having a brushed-aluminum roof. The four-passenger coupe was only 53 inches high overall.

Oldsmobile 96 chassis for 1955. The rear leaf springs were 58 inches long and nearly flat with the car in static condition, to improve ride comfort. The frame had many reinforcements.

the bulging spear protruding from the body sides was to be used on an Oldsmobile production car.

The F-88 Mark III was basically similar, with certain refinements. The front air intake became truly oval, and the grille mesh was recessed in the frame. A hood scoop à la Ferrari appeared prominently, and the bumper strips were lowered closer to the wheel-hub level. The side spears were played down and survived only as an accent line, while the front fenders were decorated with dummy National Advisory Committee for Aeronautics (NACA) ducts, a styling trick that Chrysler was to pick up and use on the 1968 Dodge Charger.

Both the Mark II and Mark III versions had fiberglass-reinforced plastic bodies, but while the former was an open car with a canvas top concealed under a panel on the rear deck, the latter had a retractable hardtop recalling the styling of the

1955 Studebaker Starliner coupe. On both cars, the wheels were heavily styled with spinner-type covers and radial vanes to carry the turbine theme. Nothing from this design was to appear on subsequent Oldsmobile production cars, which leaves a lot of question marks about the value of styling exercises not tied to the type of car being produced and marketed by a division such as Oldsmobile.

The styling of production-model Oldsmobiles went its own way, independently of the show cars, but increasingly dependent on the commonality with other divisions using the same Fisher bodies. The Oldsmobile studio found its main task reduced to finding ways to play with front ends, side decor and various body ornamentation, so as to make the Olds product look different from those of Buick and Pontiac. The other divisional studios were forced into the same preoccupations, while the all-important questions of size, proportions, seating space and overall form and structure had been settled at the corporate level.

Of course, there was input from the divisional studios, just as Fisher Body had to be involved at an early stage for all restyling programs, but it was the central command of the GM Styling Staff under Harley J. Earl that made up the final package, which was then submitted to the vice president in charge of the Car and Truck Group, the divisional general managers and the top corporate management. Then followed discussion of the variety of different bodies Fisher would build (A, B and C, at this time) and which car lines would use which body—production schedules were worked out on that basis.

For 1955, Oldsmobile made few alterations in the model lineup. The 88-series continued with a Holiday coupe (HC), two-door sedan (K) and four-door sedan (S). The same three bodies also existed for the Super 88's, their code symbols being given a D prefix (DHC, DK and DS). In addition, the Super 88 range included a convertible coupe (DCR). In the 98-series, we find a four-door sedan (DS), Deluxe Holiday coupe (DHC) and Starfire convertible coupe (DCR).

The price structure reflected the increased weight and more luxurious equipment, but it should be kept in mind that automatic transmission, power steering and power brakes were extra-cost options.

Body Style	88	Super 88	98
Two-door sedan	$2,091	$2,215	
Four-door sedan	2,151	2,278	$2,869
Holiday coupe	2,255	2,474	3,088
Convertible coupe		2,641	
Starfire convertible coupe			3,280

Wheelbases were continued unchanged for 1955, and while the cars were shortened overall, all models gained weight, mainly in the form of noise-insulation and sound-deadening materials. Some structural reinforcements also played their part.

Restyling centered on the full-oval grille, the bumper face being dished out to provide the balanced symmetry that had been lacking in 1954. Side decor was modified, the main idea being to play down the reverse-slant remnants of the old rear-fender sash. The new accent line was swept back from near mid-point in the old sash line to meet the horizontal molding which ran from the top of the front wheel opening to a point deep into the rear fender panel.

"If you look at all the GM cars of the period," a high ranking GM Design Staff official told us, "the script was on the wave length of getting the chrome down low, hopefully to make the car appear closer to the ground. It was management's philosophy."

The different makes tried to do this in different ways. "Cadillac was rather stiff," the stylist nodded agreeably, "and Buick had a round header that poured out to the sides. Olds used the oval. Art Ross created that face and developed it into something of a trademark for Oldsmobile."

The 1955-model Rocket V-8 had a revised combustion chamber design, permitting the compression ratio to rise to 8.5:1. This in combination with a new camshaft having higher-lift cam lobes, produced an increase in output to 202 hp.

As tested by *Motor Life* (April 1955), the Super 88 had a top speed of 106 mph and covered the standing-start quarter-mile in 18.1 seconds! Wide-open throttle acceleration from standstill gave the following times: 3.5 seconds to 30 mph; 6.1 seconds to 45 mph; and 11.8 seconds to 60 mph.

Fuel consumption at steady speeds on level roads proved quite reasonable: 21.2 mpg at 45 mph, and 19 mpg at 60 mph. The power brakes were said to be

Factory keeps expanding northward. This is what Oldsmobile's home plant in Lansing looked like in 1955.

excellent, with enough boost left to make several stops after switching off the engine. Also noted was the lowering of the brake pedal to near accelerator level for easier changes from go to stop.

The 1955 models had a new front suspension system, using the new principle of mounting the shock absorbers vertically on the centerline inside the coil springs.

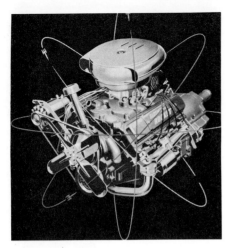

Rockets in orbit around the engine. An advertising ploy, pure and simple, and not a clever graphic way to show rocking couples, secondary unbalance or the basic theory of engine mounts.

The change involved new upper and lower control arms, plus frame reinforcements to provide top-end anchorage points for the shock absorbers.

The first four-door hardtop in the industry, the Holiday sedan, was introduced in March 1955, and listed at $3,154 in the 98-series; $2,541 as a Super 88; and $2,322 as a basic 88. It was an immediate hit, and before long, nearly two-thirds of Oldsmobile production was coming off the line with Holiday bodies. Production of this body was a major technical feat for which most of the credit must go to the Fisher Body engineers.

Production bottlenecks still existed in the Oldsmobile plant, however, mainly in connection with engine machining and body assembly processes. Something had to be done.

In January 1955, Harlow 'Red' Curtice increased the total GM plant-investment program from $1 billion to $1.5 billion. Within a year he had raised the plant-expansion budget to a full $2 billion. Oldsmobile's need for new and improved facilities was not neglected, and Wolfram found himself with a generous budget.

He took a few months to make up his mind, in close consultation with Oldsmobile's top manufacturing expert, R. T. Rollis, on the priorities for new plant investment. Robert T. Rollis was born in Stoughton, Wisconsin, in 1911, and had graduated from the University of Wisconsin. He had joined General Motors in 1935 as a plant engineer with Chevrolet. In 1942 he left Chevrolet and joined Oldsmobile, and in 1945-46 he was Skinner's key lieutenant on the production front. Wolfram named him general manufacturing manager of Oldsmobile in 1955.

It was June 1955 before Jack Wolfram announced Oldsmobile's gigantic new expansion program, which would raise production capacity by fifty percent.

The Rocket V-8 engine plant was equipped with new machinery, and new facilities and equipment were added to the sheet-metal stamping plant, the axle plant and the forge in Lansing. In 1956 more automatic machinery was installed in the Rocket engine plant, including a unique cylinder-head assembly line.

Manufacturing of crankshafts was moved out and installed on Saginaw Street, where J-65 turbojet parts had been made up to 1955. Axle shafts were also machined there.

In 1957, Oldsmobile added 460 feet to the V-8 assembly line which made room for more automated machinery to speed production and tighten quality control. At the same time, new presses were put into operation in the stamping plant, providing greater press capacity for hoods, fenders and other sheet metal parts.

Oldsmobile had gone into the 1955 model year without a major styling change, while all others (except Buick and Cadillac) had prepared new styles. It was a 7.2-million-car year, and Oldsmobile made the best use of its existing facilities to draw maximum benefit from the public's buying spree.

Oldsmobile increased its sales by thirty-one percent (to 589,515 cars) and boosted its market share from 7.35 to 8.22 percent; but still the division lost its fourth-place rank to Plymouth, which had more unused factory capacity, attractive new models and lower prices.

The market was taking a turn toward concentration that promised to benefit the biggest and healthiest of survivors. Places to be filled were those of Kaiser and Willys, who produced their last passenger cars in 1955. One of them—Kaiser—had been competing in Oldsmobile's price class. Nash and Hudson had merged on May 1, 1954, to form American Motors Corporation, closing the Hudson plant and putting the Hudson label on some Nash models until June 1957, when all AMC cars were renamed Rambler. That also removed makes selling opposite Oldsmobile, while substituting a lower-priced brand. Wolfram rubbed his hands.

Studebaker and Packard had united on October 1, 1954, and by the end of 1956, the Packard nameplate was dead. Studebaker decided to concentrate on the lower-priced market and Harold Churchill rushed the Lark into production. As Wolfram and his sales executives saw the situation, this left Buick and Pontiac as

Oldsmobile's direct competitors, while Mercury, Dodge and DeSoto made up the supporting cast on the adversary side.

Jack Wolfram looked forward to further growth in the 1956-59 period, confidently facing the challenges in the marketplace, secure in the knowledge that much needed capacity would be on hand as soon as the plant expansion programs were completed. Apparently he was totally unprepared for what actually happened, for no fear of excess capacity was ever expressed in his memos or in the minutes of meetings Wolfram had with the corporate leaders.

Instead of continued growth, Oldsmobile was to suffer a severe setback, its sales running at a depressed level from 1956 through 1961, its market share dropping back to 5.4 percent in the deepest of this period of gloom (1960).

The market as a whole had not collapsed, and the total market in 1956 and 1957 was well above the figure for 1953, the previous record year. The national economy fell into a slump of short duration during 1958, when only 4,651,000 cars were sold in the U.S., and GM's market share fell to a crippling 42.1 percent in 1959.

Not all the corporation's losses could be blamed on Oldsmobile. In fact, Buick was in even worse trouble, and things were difficult for Pontiac. Cadillac was relatively unaffected, while Chevrolet went ahead. What could be the reason for Oldsmobile's problems? Were they the same as Pontiac's and Buick's? Was it the similarity in their cars, or something in the B-body cars that the consumers disliked? Or was it more a matter of money, a reluctance to spend extra for a higher-class name, more style and luxury, when a cheaper car could do the same job?

Jack Wolfram never shared his private thoughts on the matter with anyone, and from what we do know of his actions and utterances, it is clear that he always considered himself blameless, just as he never sought a scapegoat inside the Oldsmobile organization or in the corporation as a whole.

CHAPTER 8

A View of the Abyss

WHEN OLDSMOBILE BROUGHT OUT its 1956 models, Olds dealers across the country were happy. "It's got more power, which gets everybody interested," said an Oldsmobile salesman from southern California.

"It looks more refined now, and the interiors are even better than I expected," was the opinion of an Oldsmobile dealer from Atlanta, Georgia. And from right in the center of Michigan to the far corners of the nation, there were customers who expressed their faith in Oldsmobile's quality, and would buy a new Oldsmobile when their present one gave out.

"Fresh new styling, important engineering improvements and outstanding comfort and safety characteristics make our 1956 car the best value we ever have offered the motoring public," said Jack Wolfram at the press preview on October 26, 1955.

Body changes for what Oldsmobile's ads loudly proclaimed as "Starfire Styling" did not involve any new sheet metal, but the bumper/grille assembly was a new design, with a central vertical split in the oval. From the side, the rear-fender sash line was combined with a downward sweep from the belt line to the horizontal accent line at the widest point of the body. Rooflines and window arrangements were unchanged, and the world-in-a-ring remained the predominant identification motif.

At the wheel, the driver faced an oval-frame speedometer, padded instrument panel, dash clock with a sweeping second hand and pivot-type ashtrays.

The space for the glovebox was increased, still located centrally, below the radio, and the size of the mirror was increased. Wipers covered an enlarged area, and the pistol-grip handbrake was replaced by a pedal-operated parking brake, with release knob under the dash.

Technical innovations were concentrated in the engine and transmission. The Rocket V-8 again received a new camshaft, with valve lift increased from .403 to .418 inch. At the same time, camshaft bearing journals had their diameter increased by $1/8$ inch, and a new cam contour was developed to reduce valve noise.

Exhaust valve head diameter was increased from 1.435 to 1.56 inches to improve breathing capacity, while the intake manifold was redesigned with a T-branch contour permitting freer gas flow to all ports.

Compression ratio was raised from 8.5 to 9.25:1, which resulted in a sizeable gain in power output and torque. The T-350 engine, used in the 98 and Super 88, put out 240 hp at 4400 rpm and generated a peak torque of 350 pounds-feet at 2800 rpm. The engine for the 88-series was called T-340 and delivered 230 hp at 4400 rpm. Peak torque was reached at 2400 rpm.

Both engines had modifications of the carburetion system. On the T-350 with its Rochester Quadri-Jet, a new linkage connected the throttle control to the automatic transmission. As a second change, vacuum control was utilized to automatically open the secondary throats, which had been enlarged for greater air

1956 Oldsmobile 98 Starfire convertible coupe. The new grille borrows something from the Cutlass, which also had fender skirts open to the rear. Rear fender treatment still lacks firmness.

The diagram labels (right cutaway image):

FLYWHEEL · DRIVEN TORUS · DRIVE TORUS · TORUS COVER · FLYWHEEL HOUSING · MAINSHAFT · F.U. DRIVE TORUS · F.U. DRIVEN TORUS · FRONT UNIT TORUS COVER · FRONT PUMP ASS'Y · CASE · FRONT UNIT DRIVE GEAR · FRONT PLANET CARRIER · FRONT SUN GEAR · INTERMEDIATE SHAFT · OVERRUN CLUTCH PISTON · FRONT SPRAG CLUTCH · OVERRUN CLUTCH · CASE SUPPORT · NEUTRAL CLUTCH PISTON · NEUTRAL CLUTCH · REAR SPRAG CLUTCH · REAR CLUTCH · LOW BAND · REAR INTERNAL GEAR · REAR SUN GEAR · REAR PLANET CARRIER & OUTPUT SHAFT · PARKING BRAKE GEAR · REVERSE STATIONARY CONE · REVERSE INTERNAL GEAR · REVERSE CONE PISTON · REVERSE PLANET CARRIER · REVERSE SUN GEAR · REAR PUMP ASS'Y · GOVERNOR ASS'Y · REAR EXTENSION HOUSING

Jetaway was the new label for the 1956 Hydra-matic with its dual-range feature and twin fluid couplings. It had higher torque capacity, and became heavier and bulkier. The size of the complete assembly is impressive—far bigger and heavier than a synchromesh transmission.

The new elements in the dual-range Hydra-matic center around the second fluid coupling, labeled F.U. (front unit) drive torus and driven torus. The second coupling worked to blend the power flow for smoother shifts.

flow capacity. The T-340 engine had an entirely new Rochester two-barrel carburetor.

The newest version of the Hydra-matic transmission was called Jetaway in advertising lingo. Behind that meaningless term, however, were technical intricacies of great ingenuity.

The 1956 Hydra-matic was developed to remedy shortcomings which had hitherto been acceptable, such as frequent and jerky shifts, while retaining the outstanding efficiency of the old Hydra-matic (which meant continued use of the fluid coupling as opposed to the torque converter), the passing ability, dual-range feature and engine-braking ability.

Starting in 1952, Hydra-matic engineers hit on a new principle for shifting gears, and it was perfected and made part of the 1956-model Hydra-matic.

The 1952-55 Hydra-matic did not have enough input-torque capacity for the engines that the car divisions then had under development. That alone necessitated going to stronger transmissions. In addition, the package was not properly arranged for installation in the body designs then in preparation. Finally, the Hydra-matic engineers admitted that the existing version was not as smooth as the torque-converter type of transmissions used by Buick and Chevrolet (Dynaflow and Powerglide).

The 1952-55 Hydra-matic had a multi-plate clutch between the fluid coupling and the planetary gearing, whose function was to lock the front gear set in direct drive. On the 1956 models this clutch was replaced by a second, small-diameter hydraulic coupling, giving a much smoother action. This second fluid coupling reduced the torque-capacity demand on the main fluid coupling, and permitted the engineers to reduce its diamter to the dimensions desired for installation in the future low-profile cars.

Advantage was taken of the second hydraulic coupling to rearrange the whole method of torque transmission, with the principle of torque-division being utilized to obtain smoother shifts in a new shift pattern. The power flow from the engine went straight to a planetary gear set instead of directly to the main hydraulic coupling.

The planetary gear set acted as a differential torque divider with sun- and ring-gear torque split in proportion to the number of teeth contained in these gears. In second and fourth speeds, the front gear set alone divided the torque. The sun gear took 35.6 percent of the input, passing it through the smaller fluid coupling and then through the gear set to the main fluid coupling. The ring gear, therefore, carried 64.4 percent of the input torque directly through the gear set to the main fluid coupling.

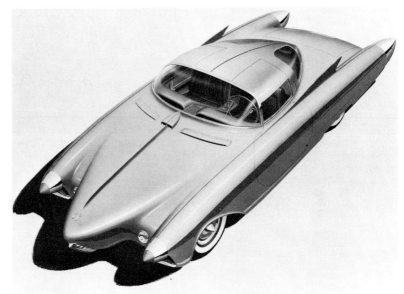

Proposal for the 1957 Oldsmobile 98, made in July 1955. Dual hood ornaments, and twin-oval grille dominated the front, and the rear fender lines marred the whole side. It was killed.

Styling mockup for the 1957 Oldsmobile 98, also completed in July 1955. This one was selected for further refinement.

1956 Oldsmobile experimental Golden Rocket sport coupe. The shark-like nose proved to be a dead-end idea, but the fender treatment was picked up by Ford for the Thunderbird, and both Chevrolet and Buick have used the roof design (for the 1963 Corvette and 1971 Riviera).

For engagement of first and third gear, the front planetary gears were in reduction and the secondary fluid coupling was empty.

Then the torque coming out of the front gear set planet carrier was divided by the middle gear set, so that 60.8 percent of the torque was tapped off before getting to the main fluid coupling. The remaining 39.2 percent passed through the main fluid coupling before reaching the sun gear of the middle gear set. The filling or draining of the secondary fluid coupling assured smooth transitions through all ratio changes, blending the two power-flow paths into a single continuous flow of power.

The small fluid coupling was never subjected to multiplied torque, and the thirty-five percent of torque it was called upon to transmit in second and fourth speeds always corresponded to thirty-five percent of engine torque.

The driver, of course, never got the slightest indication of how the power flow was routed and, except for full-throttle acceleration, hardly noticed the shifts. A couple of minor technical changes must be mentioned to complete the picture.

In the 1955 Hydra-matic, a cross-drive rear pump and governor assembly was used, while the 1956 model had its rear oil pump drive gear coaxial with the output shaft. Both brake bands in the 1955 Hydra-matic had to be applied to get first gear. This was changed for the 1956 model, since the neutral clutch could be arranged to provide this action without application of either brake band.

In addition to the 1952-55 shift sequence of neutral, drive, super lo and reverse, the 1956 Jetaway Hydra-matic had a new park position added to the left of neutral. This gave a positive guard against the car moving unintentionally with the engine running.

1957 Oldsmobile Super 88 Holiday coupe. The Rocket V-8 had grown to 371 cubic inches, and the weight to 4,327 pounds.

1957 Oldsmobile Golden Rocket 88 Holiday sedan. On this four-door hardtop, the rear door undercut the C-post, which, along with the swept-back A-post, reduced the roof's impact resistance to critically low values.

The Jetaway Hydra-matic was standard on the 98 and Super 88, with axle ratios of 3.42:1 and 3.23:1, respectively. Super 88 models were equipped with air conditioning, and the Super 88 convertible also had the 3.42:1 axle; while the 98 Starfire had a final drive ratio of 3.64:1. The same 3.64:1 ratio was standard for the 88-series equipped with synchromesh transmission, while those fitted with Jetaway Hydra-matic got the 3.23:1 rear axle.

Curb weight for the 88 four-door sedan had increased to 4,028 pounds, and that for the Super 88, to 4,061 pounds. The 98 four-door sedan had a curb weight of 4,211 pounds.

All 1956-model prices had been raised, from $45 to $100 over the previous year:

Body Type	88	Super 88	98
Two-door sedan	$2,166	$2,301	
Four-door sedan	2,226	2,363	$2,969
Holiday coupe	2,330	2,520	3,138
Holiday sedan	2,397	2,586	3,204
Convertible coupe		2,726	
Starfire convertible coupe			3,380

Power steering was included in the 98 prices; and automatic transmission, for the Super 88 and 98. Simultaneously, Oldsmobile lowered the price of air conditioning from $550 to $400. Despite the best-laid plans, the 1956-models failed to carry on the selling pace of the hot '55's. Jack Wolfram calmly put his trust in the 1957 models, which were extensively redesigned.

The 1957-model programs had started about the time the 1954 models went into production, and there were wide-sweeping changes under the skin as well as in appearance.

The 1957 chassis was new, with a wider stance and fourteen-inch wheels. A new front suspension system (again) featured ball joints (eliminating the king-pin). The upper control arms were angled up at the front, so as to reduce nosedive during braking. The coil springs were positioned closer to the wheel hubs, and the stabilizer bar was reinforced to minimize body roll on curves.

The new perimeter frame was eight inches wider, with a heavier structure, having rugged X-bracing along the full length of the widest section, and rigid cross-members at the front and rear suspension anchorages. Hotchkiss drive was retained, with fifty-eight-inch-long leaf springs, as before. What was new was a vertical-mounted shock absorber outboard of the spring clamps.

Engine size was increased to 370.7 cubic inches, with a new crankshaft giving a 3.69-inch stroke, and the cylinders bored out to an even four inches.

The new version of the Rocket V-8 was designated T-400 (referring to its 400 pounds-feet of torque at 2800 rpm), and it delivered 277 hp at 4400 rpm.

1957 Oldsmobile Golden Rocket 88 convertible coupe. With a four-barrel carburetor, the 371-cubic-inch V-8 delivered a total of 277 hp, and the car could do 110-115 mph in standard trim.

1957 Oldsmobile Starfire 98 Holiday sedan. Wheelbase was 126 inches and overall length, 216.7 inches. Weight had increased to 4,544 pounds, and tire size to 8.50-14 (1956 was the last year for 15-inch wheels).

All models had the same engine, with 9.5:1 compression, and Rochester Quadri-Jet carburetors. Engines were installed farther toward the front end of the frame, increasing the forward weight bias in the vehicle.

Bodies were also all-new for 1957, continuing the styling trends of the past three years, but their silhouette was two inches lower! Art Ross reached the ultimate oval for the front-end theme with an open bumper-grille design featuring an oval recess running the full width of the bumper. The name Oldsmobile was spelled out in big capital letters on the grillework in the recess, and above was an ovalized world-in-a-ring emblem, increasingly stylized and symbolic. The triple-fuselage hood ornament of 1955-56 was reduced to a single spear, but three-pronged rocket-type ornaments were placed on the fender crowns, above the hooded headlamps.

Side decoration on the Golden Rocket 88, as the baseline series had been renamed in honor of the sixtieth anniversary of the first Oldsmobile, was more elaborate than on the Super 88. In addition to the sweeping sash line, marking the start of the rear fender, its sheet metal was sculptured to give a rocket profile to the crown area, blending into the circular taillights.

But the 98 was a different matter. "It had a lot of chrome on it," a former Oldsmobile stylist told us in shamefaced admission. A contrasting accent stripe ran for more than half the length of the side panels, and had been put there by a sheer misunderstanding.

"The rear quarter-panel came along and bounced up and went into a bullet taillight," one designer explained. "This went back to the rear wheel opening. There were two proposals on how to treat this panel. One proposal had chrome on the whole panel—this was all chrome— and the other proposal had a body molding that was supposed to come over and encompass this panel. They were two separate designs and never appeared together on the same clay model. They just happened to be on the same drawing together, in the form of double overlays, when the design staff management walked in and said 'Now, that's IT!' 'But Mr. Earl, these are two separate drawings . . .' we tried to point out but were silenced by a bark: 'That's *it*.'" Incredibly, the 'double-overlay' Oldsmobile went into production—a monument to poor taste and lack of concern for artistic values.

Olds added four new body styles for 1957. They included three station wagons and one convertible coupe. The station wagons were called Fiesta (after the styling prototype wagon). Wagons had been absent from the Olds model lineup since the end of the 1950 model run, so the Fiesta represented a serious attempt from Oldsmobile to recapture a share of the family market.

Oldsmobile's 1957 chassis featured a wider track. The frame was eight inches wider and 45 to 67 pounds heavier. An extension of the front cross-member permitted the engine to be moved forward, opening the way for the cowl to come forward also.

Because of the popularity of the hardtop sedan, Wolfram decided to adopt hardtop styling also for some wagons (one in the 88-series and one Super 88). A Fiesta wagon using the B-body sedan with the normal B-post as a basis was available only in the 88-series. The tailgate was a flat design with a slight wraparound of the window. The window frame was hinged on top, while the lower part folded down to form an extension of the cargo floor.

All models for 1957 had a new panoramic windshield with about eighteen percent more glass area. Inside the 1957 Oldsmobile was a unique strut-mounted instrument panel, adapted from the Delta show car of 1955, and three-dimensional upholstery was used in some models. A technical 'first' for Oldsmobile that year was the use of printed electric circuits for the instrument cluster.

Interior design was becoming gaudier, flashier, and less and less associated with the real needs of passengers. The late 1950's were a low point for the layout and interior equipment of Oldsmobiles. Irv Rybicki, who took over as vice president of the GM Design Staff in 1978, gave his frank opinion on the subject: "I couldn't tell you what the basic philosophy was in the '50's relative to interior design. I can't tell you what motivated them to do what they did because they used a lot of two-tone bands, and the welts were a different color than the trim. A lot of things have been done in the interiors of domestic automobiles that I have never agreed with, such as a lot of buttons and bows and wrinkled fabric that looked like modern Italian furniture. And I don't come down on that side at all."

Prices increased proportionally with the gain in weight, or perhaps even faster:

Body Style	88	Super 88	98
Two-door sedan	$2,439	$2,648	
Four-door sedan	2,499	2,706	$3,350
Holiday coupe	2,552	2,845	3,532
Holiday sedan	2,624	2,917	3,603
Convertible coupe	2,856	3,093	3,792
Fiesta sedan	2,875		
Fiesta hardtop	2,978	3,181	

The average 1957 Oldsmobile was a soft car to drive, with sloppy springs and body motions that caused seasickness in many passengers. The car was stable going straight down the highway, but on winding country roads, its weaknesses showed up: slow steering, lacking in precision, excessive bounce and roll.

Still, the Oldsmobile was known as a goer. It had that marvelous power. Drivers with a heavy right foot would catch themselves spinning the wheels unintentionally when trying to move off smartly. Then in January 1957, Oldsmobile began offering the J-2 Rocket engine, equipped with triple two-barrel carburetors, for sale to the public. It was priced at only $83, and boosted the engine output to 300 hp at 4400 rpm, the torque rising to 450 pounds-feet. It was claimed to offer normal fuel economy when running on part-throttle, breathing through only one carburetor, with hair-raising displays of smoke-trailing acceleration being staged whenever the driver floored it.

According to a test report by Joe Wherry, published in *Motor Trend* (February 1957), the J-2-equipped 98 could go from standstill to 60 mph in 9.4 seconds when new (before break-in). Factory tests gave figures down to 9.1 seconds for the 0-60 run, with well-used test cars. Installed in 88's, the J-2 could beat the eight-second mark!

Despite offering more and more horsepower, luxury and gadgets of all kinds, Oldsmobile fell far behind its sales targets in 1957. Why? The Oldsmobile car was in a decline, viewed as true automotive value. It was increasingly perceived by the public as the wrong kind of car at the wrong price, and it was to get worse before anything could be done about it. How the market went is best shown in tabulated form:

	1956	1957
Total market (millions)	5.96	5.98
Olds sales	437,896	371,596
Olds rank	5th	5th
Olds market share	7.35%	6.21%
GM market share	50.8%	44.9%

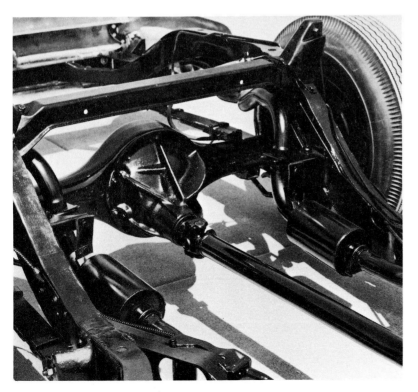

1957 Oldsmobile Golden Rocket 88 Fiesta station wagon. The Fiesta name was used for hardtop-style wagons, sharing the basic body structure with the Holiday sedan.

The J-2 Rocket engine was fitted with triple two-barrel carburetors and ran with a 10:1 compression ratio, delivering 300 hp under full load. Fuel economy was assured by doing all normal driving with one single carburetor at work.

Rear axle detail view of the 1957 Oldsmobile shows the low, low entry of the propeller shaft in the differential nosepiece. This was done to permit a lower floor with less of a tunnel.

Oldsmobile was subject to the same lead time constraints as the other GM divisions. In 1958, the total lead time was set at thirty months. A new-car project would start simultaneously in the car division's engineering staff and in the division's studio at GM Styling. The engineers would select preliminary specifications and type of body. The stylists would work on concepts, themes and accent lines in sketches and blackboard drawings at first, later adding preliminary clay models and the seating and trim buck. For the first twelve months, the project would be held in this definition phase, but then the hardware phase would begin.

The engineers would design and test experimental parts. Decisions would be made on existing production components that could be utilized in the new car. At

Proposed front end for the 1958 Oldsmobile, built as a full-scale clay model in February 1956. The design finally approved for production was even less coherent.

Miss Peggy Sauer included a vanity case in the Mona Lisa package she designed for the 1957 Holiday coupe.

Oldsmobile's general sales manager, V. H. Sutherlen, listens skeptically to Peggy Sauer's explanation of the umbrella that was part of the special fittings for the Chanteuse 98 Starfire convertible. Interior trim and upholstery were light green.

the same time, GM Styling would prepare final clay models, and when they were approved, go ahead and make drawings and templates. At this stage, Fisher Body would be brought in on the project to make body drawings. The car division's engineering staff would also be in contact with Fisher Body to supply chassis and interior requirements.

With fourteen months to go, the styling studio would build final appearance models in plastic; and with twelve months to go, Fisher Body Division would start making its clay die models. Fisher Body would then make body cost studies and submit tool data for the car division. Sample bodies would be built by Fisher Body with ten to six months to go, followed by structural tests and design releases. Body die designs would begin with ten months left, and orders would go out as soon as possible over the next four months. The procurement of manufacturing tools, dies and equipment would start with eight months to go and be completed two months prior to production startup. Chassis tool and equipment designs would begin with thirteen months to go, and stretch out over a six- to seven-month period.

With ten months remaining, the car division would build experimental cars and start testing. This initial test phase would have to be completed in four months. This period would overlap with durability tests and design releases, which would continue until only two months were left. Within the final four months, there would be an equipment, tool and die tryout. In the last thirty days, Fisher would start body production to avoid bottlenecks at the assembly plants.

General Motors spent $730 million on restyling all car lines for 1958. This work was directed by Harley J. Earl, and planned as a grand finale for his long career, before handing over the vice presidency of the GM Design Staff to William L. Mitchell.

With the switch to its new Mobile Look, Oldsmobile lost its oval-theme face for 1958. The grille became, instead, a low and wide design reminiscent of some recent Chrysler models. Nothing in the design identified the car as an Oldsmobile, so the name was written in very big letters across the panel on top of the grille. The world-in-a-ring emblem disappeared, and instead a shield derived from the older Oldsmobile trademark was mounted in the middle of the aluminum grille.

Side sculpturing became heavier, and purely horizontal, with a comet-tail stretching back from the headlights, a missile-silhouette bulge low down in the rear fender and a stack of chrome moldings higher up on the rear fender panel. Dual (four-beam) headlights were adopted, and the new wraparound rear window was a single piece of glass.

Gil Burrell and Gibson Butler had developed the Rocket V-8 to run reliably with a 10:1 compression ratio, and made a variety of minor improvements. A camshaft with new cam contours aimed at increasing low-end torque was adopted, along with wider cam lobes to improve wearing characteristics and durability. New valve springs of conical design were claimed to minimize noise in the valve gears, and the intake manifold had bigger ports and enlarged branches for freer gas flow. Finally, the breathing capacity of the four-barrel carburetor was increased.

A new two-barrel Econ-O-Way carburetor by Rochester was adopted for the 88 (now sporting the Dynamic name for the low-line series), which enabled Oldsmobile to claim fuel economy improvements up to twenty percent over the Golden Rocket 88 of 1957. The Dynamic 88 engine was rated at 265 hp, while the output for the Super 88 and 98 engine went to 305 hp. Torque was increased to 390 pounds-feet in the former and 410 in the latter.

Cars with standard suspension received a new rear end with coil springs and four locating links. This was done mainly to obtain conformity of the suspension members for the New-Matic Ride, and not because the leaf-spring suspension had been found wanting in some way.

1958 Oldsmobile Dynamic 88 Holiday sedan. Dynamic 88 was a new series in 1958, built on a 122.5-inch wheelbase. It was garishly overdecorated and had little Oldsmobile identification. Styling continuity was badly broken.

The axle was mounted on two parallel trailing arms located as close to the wheel hubs as possible, and anchored to the frame side-members just ahead of the rear-axle kickup. In addition, two widely splayed torque-reaction arms linked the top of the differential casing to the frame side-members.

For cars with New-Matic suspension, the coil springs were removed, and air-spring units installed in their place. The system had been developed by Cadillac, who was forced to share it with Oldsmobile, Buick and Pontiac in an effort to keep the cost down by raising production volume.

Each wheel had its own pneumatic chamber filled with compressed air, to maintain ride height and provide elastic absorption of roadway unevenness. High-pressure air was supplied by a two-cylinder compressor, engine-driven by dual

1958 Oldsmobile Fiesta Carousel station wagon. Tailgate and rear end design show how practical considerations were pushed aside in favor of styling gimmicks. The weight of the chrome must have caused a big loss in payload capacity.

1958 Oldsmobile 98 convertible coupe. It was the year of dual headlights and a new front end without the globe emblem. Wheelbase for the 98 was stretched to 126.5 inches.

belts. Oil and moisture were drawn from the air by an oil separator, from which the air was pumped into a high-pressure tank located behind the right rear wheel.

The amount of air in the spring units was regulated by three height-control valves: one at each rear wheel, and one in common for the two front wheels. The valves were intended to keep the car constantly at the same level, regardless of load; with spring rates (when fully loaded) *lower* than was possible with metal springs.

As more load was placed on the car, the height control valves directed air from the high-pressure tank to one or more spring units to compensate for the additional weight. When unloading took place, the spring units would exhaust air into a closed storage system with a low-pressure tank mounted behind the left rear wheel.

The theory behind the system was valid, and the engineering of it well executed. But when it came to production, too many shortcuts were taken, and

cheap parts substituted for expensive ones. The result was poor quality, which meant frequent failures in the field, to the long-lasting and quite undeserved detriment of the principles of air suspension. Oldsmobile gave up on the New-Matic ride after a year. The fascinating aspect of that decision is that Oldsmobile reverted to leaf springs and Hotchkiss drive for 1959.

Oldsmobile sales in 1958 dropped to 306,446 cars, but the division gained one place in the ranking, because of Buick's fall from favor. Thus Oldsmobile occupied fourth place, behind the low-priced three, and its penetration increased slightly to 6.6 percent of the market. The corporation's market share made a partial recovery to forty-six percent.

GM President Harlow H. 'Red' Curtice ended his career in the fall of 1958 by going into retirement, and his place was filled by the two-man team of Gordon and Donner.

Neither had got his hands dirty on Oldsmobile engines nor made his pants shiny on Oldsmobile office furniture. John F. Gordon was a former chief engineer and general manager of Cadillac, and Frederic G. Donner was an accountant who had been vice president in charge of the GM Financial Staff since 1941 and chairman of the Finance Committee since 1956. Jack Wolfram knew Gordon well, but had only a distant acquaintance with Donner.

Probably the change of leadership did not affect Oldsmobile's standing one iota, nor the division's ability to get approval (and corporate funds) for new projects. While Wolfram has been accused of having a very conservative attitude toward automobiles, and an outdated idea of where the Oldsmobile market was heading, he did push several important programs through to fruition. As chief engineer, Harold Metzel became responsible for two of the most important ones: The F-85 compact car and the front-wheel-drive experiments. Both of these were started in 1957-58. The former was part of a corporate thrust against imported cars, where Oldsmobile merely played a supporting role—but the corporate management viewed the matter as extremely urgent, and considerable pressure was brought to bear on the participating divisions to get the compacts to the market place. In contrast, the front-wheel-drive studies were pure research, with no timetable for completion, pursued independently by Oldsmobile Division, with an assist from the GM Engineering Staff.

CHAPTER 9

Compacting for Strength

FACED WITH THE GROWING sales of small European cars such as Volkswagen, Renault and Fiat, General Motors reacted in a predictable manner. There was no thought in the mid- and late-fifties of downsizing the standard cars, which were steadily gaining length and weight year by year. The success of the imports was seen as a temporary phenomenon, basically unconnected with the American market and its transportation needs. In line with the old pattern of annual model changes and continual upgrading, the GM planners determined that imported cars could best be fought with domestic products of a size and price closer to their own levels—but ready to be moved up to higher brackets when they had accomplished the primary task of "stopping the imports dead in their tracks," as one GM executive phrased it.

General Motors had considered smaller cars many times, long before the compacts were on the scene. Chevrolet was serious about making a small car called the Cadet in 1947, but the plan was called off when it was learned that the rumored low-priced small Ford was not forthcoming.

In studies for ways to retaliate against any domestic threat in any segment of the market, GM kept a close watch on all cars of sub-standard size, from the Henry J and the Hudson Jet to the Rambler. GM's conclusions were always the same: It was no cheaper to build a smaller car, as long as the same number of parts were used. The material saving of making a smaller door or a smaller wheel disappears in the overall cost-accounting, while the labor and handling costs are constant, regardless of the size of the individual part.

There, briefly, is the true reason why GM kept shying away from the idea of building smaller cars. In contrast, GM executives knew full well the financial rewards of dressing up a big car, by making a minor investment, and selling it for a lot more money. Model by model, series by series, that was the way GM had led the market since 1945.

This time, however, the imports had changed the situation, and GM began a rash of light-car programs. Chevrolet was first, when the fearless Ed Cole developed the Corvair along Porsche/Volkswagen lines, with an air-cooled engine mounted in the rear.

This was not at all what the corporation had in mind, nor did any of the other divisional heads share Cole's enthusiasm for the Corvair concept. But Chevrolet had forged ahead, and Cole really forced the corporation's hand into giving its reluctant approval. No alternative could be made ready for production in big numbers within reasonable time, and Chevrolet had made big investments in the Corvair that the financial brains were loth to write off. Thus, the Corvair was allowed to go ahead, appearing as a 1960 model in 1959.

Inevitably, Fisher Body was involved. And the Corvair body shell, the X-body, became the solution for the other divisions. If they could share it, the cost of one of the main items could be brought down to acceptable levels. Next, by sharing engines, the cost of a second major item might be reduced far enough to see the chance of a profit margin, even with the low target retail prices being discussed.

1962 Oldsmobile Cutlass sports convertible. With bucket seats in front and optional four-speed floorshift, the Cutlass had youth appeal and an attractive price. The grille was straightened but the unusual side sculpturing remained.

Jack Wolfram of Oldsmobile, Ed Rollert of Buick and Bunkie Knudsen of Pontiac agreed to use the X-body, which was a unit-construction shell, without a separate frame. They did not accept it without change, however; for the Corvair was built on a 108-inch wheelbase, and that was just too short for cars bearing Olds, Buick or Pontiac nameplates. They settled for a 112-inch wheelbase, and Fisher Body quickly engineered a bigger version of the X-body, essentially by inserting four inches ahead of the cowl structure.

The Corvair had only a small luggage bin in front, while the B-O-P compacts would have front-mounted engines, and that created a need for more space as well as beefing up of the body-members in that area.

Sharing the air-cooled Corvair engine was out of the question. Both Wolfram and Metzel were dead set against anything air-cooled (and noisy); nor would they

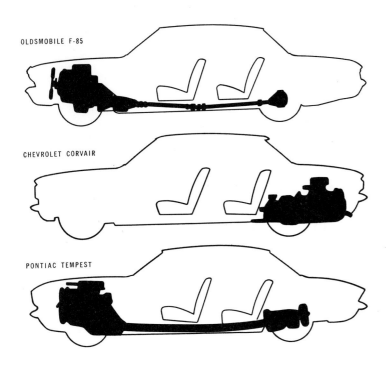

OLDSMOBILE F-85

CHEVROLET CORVAIR

PONTIAC TEMPEST

tolerate the rear engine position for which that engine was designed. Moving it to the front would have been possible, but not without serious installation difficulties, steering problems and prospects of higher cost.

Buick had been working for years on a small all-aluminum V-8 engine based on GM Engineering Staff designs, which all three divisions would use. Oldsmobile insisted on having its own combustion chamber in it, however, so it was arranged for Buick to make and machine the blocks for shipment to Oldsmobile, who made its own cylinder head, fixed, incidentally, with a stronger head-bolt pattern using a

greater number of bolts (six per cylinder). Buick also made the crankshafts and camshafts for both divisions.

Gil Burrell and Frank Ball undertook a thorough development program to make sure the engine would be good enough to power cars carrying the Oldsmobile name. The division not only carried out its own engine assembly, but also was responsible for its own pistons, rings, valve mechanism, intake manifolds, carburetion and air cleaner.

The block was a rigid deep-skirt design with iron liners, centrifugally cast in place in the cylinder block. Both the block and the aluminum cylinder heads were made by the semi-permanent-mold technique that had been developed by the Central Foundry Division of General Motors.

As an example of the advanced manufacturing methods employed, consider that the outside surface and pads on the head casting were finished by milling in a seven-station Snyder transfer machine, complemented by a two-section Foote-Burt transfer machine that completed all of the detail operations, including drilling and tapping the spark plug holes.

The combustion chambers were not machined but were very accurately cast because of the type of metal mold that was used. Chain drive was used for the camshaft, and hydraulic valve lifters were used, just as in the Rocket V-8. Rocker arms were cast-iron, and the rocker arm shaft was of tubular steel, held in aluminum brackets. The crankshaft was an Armasteel casting, supported in five steel-backed main bearings, while connecting rods were forged steel of I-beam cross section.

An unusual feature was the one-piece front cover, made of die-cast aluminum. It served as a mounting for the distributor and fuel pump; housing for the integral oil pump; retainer for the crankshaft front oil seal, water pump scroll and dual water outlets; timing chain cover and timing pointer; and integral connector for the thermostat by-pass water.

With a bore and stroke of 3.50x2.80 inches, it had a displacement of 215 cubic inches. With an 8.75:1 compression ratio and two-barrel carburetor, it delivered 155 hp at 4800 rpm, while generating a maximum torque of 210 pounds-feet at 3200 rpm.

Fitted with a four-barrel carburetor for automatic-transmission cars, the compression was raised to 10.75:1, which brought maximum output up to 185 hp at 4800 rpm and peak torque to 230 pounds-feet at 3200 rpm. For synchromesh-transmission cars, the four-barrel engine ran with 10.75:1 compression and put out 195 hp at 4800 (with 235 pounds-feet maximum torque at 3200 rpm).

The Corvair's front suspension, similar in principle to that of the Impala, was adapted to the B-O-P compacts (Bopettes, as they were often referred to collectively).

Pontiac wanted independent rear suspension for its Tempest, and that meant sharing the parts of the corporation's only car with that feature. Consequently, Pontiac adapted the rear end from the Corvair, with swing axles and coil springs. But Oldsmobile and Buick insisted on using rear axles, and subsequently designed their own four-link suspension systems with coil springs. The Oldsmobile version was closely akin to the coil-spring suspension used on the 1958 models.

Chevrolet made its own Powerglide automatic transmission for the Corvair—it was not, however, suitable for the rear-axle cars of Buick and Oldsmobile, though Pontiac adapted it to the Tempest. Instead, Oldsmobile and Buick prevailed upon Hydra-matic Division to produce a small, lightweight two-speed automatic to go with the aluminum V-8 engine.

Advertised as the Dual-Path Hydra-matic with Accel-A-Rotor action, the engineers knew it as the 61-05. It used a small torque converter with a very low stall ratio, and borrowed the torque-dividing principle from the latest four-speed Hydra-matic, thereby getting an extended range of torque multiplication from different but converging paths. This transmission also turned out to be extremely reliable in service.

Brakes, steering, electrical systems, and so on, were worked out in coordination with the supplier divisions and the other car divisions.

Irv Rybicki headed the team that was given the difficult task of styling the compact car for Oldsmobile. Difficult because it was a unit-construction body, giving less freedom to make alterations. The floor pan, cowl structure, windshield angle and backlight base were locked into fixed positions that neither Buick, Pontiac nor Olds could deviate from.

It is generally conceded that Oldsmobile did the best job of getting its own distinctive lines on the car. A raised knife-edge belt line ran horizontally for the full length of the body, blending in with the hood and the rear deck without the barest suggestion of a tailfin.

1962 Oldsmobile F-85 station wagon. The compact wagon on its 112-inch wheelbase was surprisingly roomy. Few styling frills were allowed, and the normal windshield design showed no loss of vision.

The side sheet metal followed a regular curve through doors and fenders alike, accented by a sweepspear curving to an end along the rear wheel opening. The grille carried the theme of the 88 and 98 models: the name Oldsmobile in big capital letters below a discreet grille swept back from its upper frame into the dark void of the main air intake. On either side of the grille were dual headlamps in hooded bezels.

Olds called its compact F-85, and the engine was known as the Rockette. At first, it was built only as a two-door sedan, four-door sedan and station wagon. The name F-85 was made up to create the impression of a relationship with the F-88 show cars, using a lower number to indicate reduced size.

Despite the fact that the F-85 was a compact, Wolfram felt that it must play its part in supporting the Oldsmobile image. He wanted it to bespeak power and

1962 Oldsmobile Jetfire two-door hardtop. Specific ornamentation was devised for the high-performance compact. Despite its brilliant engineering, the public preferred Pontiac's GTO.

but slow steering (power steering was optional). It was extremely stable, and despite soft springing, it did not have a lot of body roll except on very tight curves.

All in all, it was a most satisfactory car, built with Oldsmobile quality, and suited for a million typical duties. Oldsmobile claimed it had seating for six, and "yes, you could get six people in there, but it was a terrible mistake to stress that point, when we were building lots of bigger cars with a bigger profit margin, and they were running around with an average load of 1.7 people on board," said a former Oldsmobile executive. Yet it was amazing how many of the tasks the F-85 could handle, that most consumers thought only a big car could do, whether it was going from Miami to Chicago over a weekend, or hauling a trailer across the Rockies.

In view of the short time available to test the complete car before production was due to start, and the unusual combination of components and systems of so many different origins, it must be said that Oldsmobile did a great job of making the F-85 such a balanced car in every way, and so thoroughly reliable.

According to an article by Robert Sheehan in *Fortune* (June 1963): "In Wolfram's thinking, the big virtue of the F-85 was that it enabled Oldsmobile to get representation in the low-price market, something Oldsmobile couldn't do with a standard-size car without hurting its traditional image. It puts Oldsmobile in a position to jump in whatever direction the market takes. It is his hope that, in time, the new customers coming in by way of the F-85 will begin to grade-up: 'We'll get people into Oldsmobiles earlier in their careers.'"

In its first year on the market, the F-85 proved disappointing, with a sales volume not far above critical level, finishing ninth among compacts for the 1961 calendar year. Nationwide registration figures show a total of 70,813 F-85's (including 14,133 wagons), 20,000 behind the sister-model Buick Special and 39,000 behind the Pontiac Tempest.

Only two compacts were selling in numbers big enough to make their future seem assured: Ford's Falcon (355,000) and Chevrolet's Corvair (315,000). Third place was held by the Rambler Classic (212,000). The Falcon's sister, Mercury Comet, was fourth with 140,000 cars and the Plymouth Valiant, fifth, with 116,000 cars. The Tempest and Special were sixth and seventh, while the F-85 was outsold even by Studebaker's Lark (72,155).

An F-85 Cutlass coupe was introduced in May 1961, and was joined in September 1961 by a Cutlass convertible. Both were sport models, equipped with bucket seats, special trim, two-tone paint, and so on.

The Cutlass attracted a new type of customer to Oldsmobile showrooms, and without the Cutlass, the F-85's sales performance would have been pitiful indeed. Advertising and sales promotion were redirected to aim for a younger customer, stressing performance, styling and colors; while playing down the spaciousness, comfort and dependability of the car.

This opened the way for the production and merchandizing of an exciting engine the engineers had been toying with since October 1959. Jack Wolfram had asked Gil Burrell about making a very high-performance version of the F-85, and was told that the aluminum-block engine had strict limitations to the conventional ways

elegance—he was less concerned with price. The F-85 did indeed become quite expensive, with list prices from $2,403 to $2,971; but on a model-for-model basis, separated by a safe margin of approximately $400 from the Dynamic 88. Oldsmobile assembled the F-85 on its own brand-new assembly line at the main plant in Lansing.

"Designed for the buyer who wants the best in a smaller, lower-priced car with economy of operation," Wolfram said, "the F-85 offers outstanding economy—twenty-five percent more miles to the gallon than many full-size cars—but it never compromises on performance. It has safety power to spare—for passing and smooth merging with traffic on expressways. Its performance is outstanding."

He explained that the F-85's combination of lively performance and excellent fuel economy was due to two things: the car's curb weight of only 2,695 pounds, some 1,500 pounds less than its full-size brother, the Dynamic 88; and the efficiency of Oldsmobile's new aluminum Rockette V-8 engine.

Because it was so much lighter, the F-85 could outrun the Super 88 from traffic lights. Of course, it had typical Oldsmobile family-car roadholding, with light

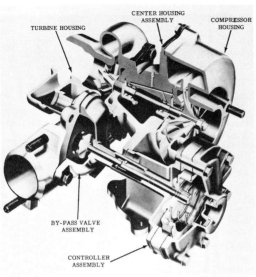

1962 Oldsmobile Jetfire engine. Intake manifold was fed with fresh mixture from the compressor (next to carburetor). Compressor shaft was driven by an exhaust-gas turbine, fed by curved pipe at upper left. Details of turbocharger unit (right). The working parts were extremely small, and the whole assembly was compact, lightweight and relatively easy to install.

of raising power output. Compression ratio could not be upped any more. Only about ten to fifteen percent more power could be obained by fitting larger carburetors, widening the ports and going to a hotter camshaft—and then only with the penalty of losing the smooth running and good low-range torque.

The safest way to increase the power was to enlarge the cylinders, but there was no room for that in the Buick block. It would be easy to revive a smaller-bore version of the Oldsmobile Rocket V-8, but that was a cast-iron engine, and perhaps unacceptably heavy for installation in the compact car.

Was there no way, then? Burrell shook his head at Wolfram's repeated prodding. Then he remembered a report on turbocharging from the GM Research Laboratories, which had done a lot of work in the 1953-56 period to establish whether the turbocharger could be utilized to raise power output in such a fashion as to permit the use of a basic production engine in a heavier vehicle.

1963 Oldsmobile Cutlass coupe. New body panels with slab-sides were more in line with 88 and 98 styling, and the longer tail made the compact look bigger.

The conclusions of the report had been pretty negative, Burrell remembered, but that did not deter him from digging out the report and looking at the evidence again. Yes, the Research Laboratories had built up an impressive bank of test results, mostly discouraging.

Burrell mentioned this to some of his closest collaborators, such as Jim Lewis and Gibson Butler. They decided to make their own tests. Various makes of commercial turbochargers were purchased and installed on the Rockette engine. Some were quickly discarded as having the wrong operating characteristics for an engine of this size and speed range. Others showed some promise, but there were times when no turbocharger looked like it could help the F-85.

As their test experience built up, experimental engineers Ed Rosetti and Ted Louckes began to find a pattern. Gibson Butler made up a new design for a turbocharger installation, assisted by the young Frank Ball.

"We did some things that were new and different," Frank Ball grinned at the memory. "Others who were working on turbocharging back then would lower the compression ratio—and when you do, you lose fuel economy in steady-speed down-the-road operation. We were not willing to do that."

The solution involved a special carburetor combined with an injection system for something Oldsmobile called Turbo Rocket Fluid. It was nothing more complicated than a fifty-fifty mixture of distilled water and methyl alcohol, but it enabled the engine to tolerate turbocharging with a compression ratio of 10.25:1.

The fluid was stored in a reservoir kept under pressure by manifold vacuum. Under part-load operation, when the turbocharger was hardly pumping at all, and there was high vacuum in the manifold, a check valve prevented fluid from being sucked into the engine. When the throttle was opened, gas flow increased, and the turbocharger began to stuff more and more tightly packed air into the cylinders, a diaphragm in the fluid metering valve opened a ball check, and the pressure on the reservoir forced the fluid through the discharge nozzle.

Injection started when boost pressure reached one pound per square inch. Not only was it effective in suppressing detonation, but the alcohol, which is a high-octane fuel, was found to contribute significantly to raising the power output. Of course, the idea was to restrict the use of Turbo Rocket Fluid to the times when it was needed for combustion control, and fluid consumption in ordinary driving was found to be between 5,000 and 8,000 miles to the gallon.

What was different in the new Rochester carburetor was not just that it was a side-draft design but rather that it lacked a throttle plate. Instead, there were two butterfly valves between the carburetor and the turbocharger inlet. One of them regulated the air admission in the manner of a throttle, while the other restricted the compressor inlet opening in case the engine ran out of Turbo Rocket Fluid.

The turbocharger unit was manufactured by the AiResearch Division of Garrett Corporation, and consisted of a radial-inflow turbine wheel and shaft made of Stellite steel with a centrifugal compressor wheel of aluminum on the opposite end of the shaft. The turbine and compressor wheels were tiny—not even 2½ inches in diameter. It had been tested at up to 150,000 rpm, but had a top speed of 90,000 rpm on the Rockette engine. At speeds under 30 mph with road-load conditions, the turbocharger idled at 6000 rpm; but stepping on the accelerator would send the shaft spinning to 38,000 rpm within a second. At a constant 70 mph, the turbocharger ran at 37,000 rpm, and flooring the pedal at that speed would immediately bring its speed to 83,000 rpm.

To prevent overcharging, the engine was equipped with a waste gate, a simple poppet valve on a side passage on the inlet side of the exhaust scroll. It was arranged to bleed off excess pressure into the tail pipe so as to keep the turbocharger boost from exceeding five pounds per square inch (for an overall maximum of 19.7 pounds per square inch, atmospheric pressure being equal to 14.7 pounds per square inch).

The turbocharged Rockette engine was found to run reliably with a maximum output of 215 hp at 4600 rpm, and a peak torque of 300 pounds-feet at 3200 rpm. It was cleared for production in December 1961, becoming America's first production engine with an output of 1 hp per cubic inch and 1 hp per 1.88 pounds of engine weight.

Compared with the four-barrel, high compression Rockette, the turbocharged version had sixteen percent more horsepower and thirty percent more torque. Relative to the basic Rockette, the gains obtained by turbocharging in addition to higher compression and the bigger carburetor amounted to thirty-eight percent for hp and forty-two percent for torque.

Wolfram wanted a special car for this engine, a new model with its own distinctive appearance. However, there was no money available for creating a new body, and because of the pressure to get the car out into the showrooms, there was no time to prepare any more than a few cosmetic touches for the basic Cutlass hardtop coupe body chosen for the limited-production model, available exclusively with the Turbo Rocket V-8. The car was called Jetfire and was introduced in April 1962 at the New York International Automobile Show.

Prior to that, the press had been invited to drive the car on the GM Proving Grounds at Milford, Michigan. We drove it there, and were impressed with the acceleration, smoothness and silence of the engine. It was something totally new and unique in compact cars.

It would go from standstill to 60 mph in 8.9 seconds, and within a relatively confined space we were able to see readings of 110 mph on the speedometer. We never learned its full speed capacity. Of course, it was geared for acceleration, with a 3.36:1 axle ratio, and not for setting speed records. The test cars were equipped with automatic transmission, having a new floor-mounted control lever, and a three-speed synchromesh transmission was listed as standard (with a column shift)— we never saw one. Later in the year, the Jetfire became available with a four-speed floorshift, which we drove extensively. What was most remarkable about it, however, was not the acceleration through the gears, but the incredible top-gear flexibility, the engine providing a strong pull from 1600 rpm upward, without knock or jerkiness.

Wolfram could not really have expected the Jetfire to build a new image for Oldsmobile, since it was a limited-production model, addressed strictly to the enthusiast market, whose flavor was never carried over into the Series 88 or 98. Though it was listed at a remarkably modest $3,048, there was no great rush to buy the Jetfire, and its effect on boosting the sales of the F-85 and Cutlass lines is open to question.

The Turbo Rocket engine was used in an experimental car Oldsmobile put on display to explore public interest in a glamorous sports car. It was called the X-215 and was a roadster built on a shortened Cutlass floor. Among its principal styling features was a plastic tonneau cover, incorporating an airfoil-section rollover bar,

Oldsmobile X-215 experimental sports car, 1963. It was built on a shortened F-85 floor and equipped with the Jetfire turbocharged V-8. Windshield and stylized rollover bar were racing-inspired.

completely covering the rear seat. The cockpit was surrounded by a low racing-type windshield which was carried over into the door glass. The hood was louvered down the middle, and front and rear fenders had functional air scoops for brake cooling. But the X-215 turned out to be a dead end for Oldsmobile's product planners, who had to concentrate on the bread-and-butter models.

Though compact Oldsmobile sales climbed to 94,893 cars (including 9,442 wagons) during the 1962 calendar year, the F-85 did not succeed in getting out of its ninth-rank slot among compacts. It built up a big lead on the Lark, but Chevrolet, having realized that the Corvair had lost the sales race to the Falcon, hurriedly brought out the Chevy II, which immediately took second place (340,000) behind

Oldsmobile experimental J-TR convertible was based on the 1963 Cutlass. Its particular styling features included rear-rectangular headlamps and louvered rocker-panel moldings which covered stainless steel exhaust outlets. It was also equipped with cast aluminum wheels, and the louvers on the hood matched those of the rocker panels.

"People who bought compacts wanted economy, not luxury or prestige. Most of them bought a Ford."

"The F-85 was too far ahead of its time. Wolfram should have let the compact market develop until it became clear where Oldsmobile might fit into it."

Many years later, Oldsmobile executives were able to explain the whole situation in much clearer terms. "We had not analyzed our problems properly, and the corporation misled us to some extent," we were told by a middle-management Oldsmobile man. "One of the basic misunderstandings was thinking that foreign cars cut into Oldsmobile sales. They did not. The market was changing, and it was hurting the low-priced domestics, not us. We had other problems, which is why our sales were in a decline. The way some of our cars looked it's a wonder that people would even think of buying them. The way the 98 was developing, it couldn't have looked pretty to anybody but a jukebox."

An Oldsmobile sales executive corroborated this analysis: "The F-85 didn't solve the problem it was supposed to, for it was aimed at the wrong problem. Instead of being a solution, it became part of the problem."

Jack Wolfram knew the F-85 was a good car, and expected his staff to find ways to sell it. Fortunately Pontiac came to their aid, with a restyling proposal that would add four inches to the length of the X-body. Both Buick and Oldsmobile were in favor of making the compacts longer, and Fisher Body made the necessary tooling changes in coordination with the divisions. The revised body was ready in time for the 1963 model year, and the F-85 looked like a totally new car.

The Oldsmobile studio had broken away from the original lines and developed a new theme, which made the F-85 show a stronger family likeness to the 88's and 98—a profile which could not so easily be confused with a Rambler when going by on the road.

The body was also 2½ inches wider, with fairly straight sides, free of chrome, discreetly accented horizontally at two levels—back from the headlamp bezel in front, and forward from the bumper at the back. The belt line was straight, from fender tip to fender tip. Dual headlights were adopted, fitted into a grille design that perhaps lacked distinction, failed to state an Oldsmobile identity and seemed bland and forgettable, but was also totally inoffensive. New rooflines were adopted, with a knife-edge treatment of the C-post.

The 1963-model F-85 also received a new standard engine of reduced displacement and power, giving improved fuel economy without losing acceptable performance levels. The aluminum V-8 was extremely expensive to manufacture, and not free of service problems. Buick had gone into a crash program to develop a low-cost cast-iron-block V-6 to be machined on the same line, and this engine was made available to Oldsmobile. The Rockette V-8 remained optional, but was phased out as soon as practical. The V-6 had a 198-cubic-inch displacement and was rated at 135 hp.

F-85/Cutlass sales spurted ahead to a record 121,483 cars (including nearly 10,000 wagons). The compact car market had swelled to 1.75 million cars, with the

the Falcon (482,000), and ahead of the Corvair (290,000). Interestingly, Buick's Special pushed ahead of the Pontiac Tempest, 152,000 to 138,000.

Many explanations of the F-85's poor showing were voiced, in Lansing, on many floors of the GM Building, and on the street: "Oldsmobile dealers just don't understand how to sell compact cars."

"The car was never promoted right. Oldsmobile did not know what they wanted it to be, and the public didn't care."

"Perhaps it was just too small, or it looked too small, for the kind of people who were buying Oldsmobiles in those days. They just didn't believe it was an Olds."

result that Oldsmobile was still near the bottom, in eighth position. Ford was still in front with the Falcon (325,000), with two Chevrolet lines on its tail: Chevy II (310,000) and Corvair (244,000). Plymouth Valiant (179,000) led the Buick Special (144,000) and Mercury Comet (141,000), followed by the Tempest (139,000).

As early as 1961, Wolfram had begun to entertain doubts that Oldsmobile really had any business competing in the compact market, and had argued the case against it strongly in meetings with Ed Cole, who had left Chevrolet to become vice president in charge of the Car and Truck Group.

Ed Rollert of Buick was also leaning away from the compacts. Ed Cole had been watching the market giving particular attention to the sales of Ford's Fairlane, all alone in a new class, sort of midway between the compacts and the big cars. Ford built the Fairlane on a 115.5-inch wheelbase, compared with 109.5 inches for the Falcon and 119 inches for the 500 and Galaxie.

Cole thought Ford should be stopped from running away with the intermediate market, and his successor at Chevrolet, Bunkie Knudsen, was preparing a rival for the Fairlane. It was to be the Chevelle, appearing as a 1964 model. Cole was convinced that Wolfram and Rollert were right. He made a plan to kill the Bopette compacts and replace them with B-O-P versions of the Chevelle. He called Gordon and briefed him. He said ok, as long as Donner would agree. Gordon prepared a full-dress meeting with the chairman, the divisional general managers and the various group vice presidents involved. It was a short meeting, and general agreement was in the air. Knudsen, who could have opposed it on the grounds that Chevrolet should have the intermediate-size car exclusively for one year before it was given to the other divisions, seemed happy to have the tooling costs shared with three partners, and heartily approved.

At the end of the 1963 model year, the F-85 was no longer a compact. But the division's involvement with compact cars was only temporarily at an end. A few years later, the compact would appear as unquestionably the right solution to the problem of a new market situation, and Oldsmobile called it . . . not Eureka, but Omega.

CHAPTER 10

Years of Reform

AS IF THE COMPACT CAR would liberate the big Oldsmobile from any obligation that might have been imposed earlier to exercise a certain moderation in vehicle size and weight, the 88's and 98 took another step toward dinosaurhood while the division was preparing the F-85.

The 1959 models were to set new records in more than one dimension, as the Dynamic 88 and Super 88 went to a 123-inch wheelbase and their overall lengths, to 218.4 inches. The curb weight for four-door sedans with Hydra-matic transmissions went up to 4,396 pounds for the Dynamic 88 and 4,441 pounds for the Super 88. The 98 had its wheelbase stretched to 126.3 inches and its overall length, to 223 inches. Curb weight for the four-door sedan increased to a total of 4,593 pounds.

These were the biggest and most powerful Oldsmobiles ever built, representing the start of a new styling cycle, as Jack Wolfram put it. It was another corporate program of making new bodies, starting in 1956 against the background of a decline in GM sales and the news of Chrysler's 1957 models with their gigantic tailfins, Ford's launching of the Edsel and the creation of the Interstate Highway System.

Then America was prosperous, the dollar was stable and no Sputnik had yet sent its beep-beeps from space to shatter the national complacency. Thus the 1959-model Oldsmobiles were created for a different era than the one they were plunged into; caught in the inertial web of the huge industrial apparatus that ceaselessly lowered the price of a new car relative to the public's purchasing power, year by year.

The styling change for 1959 was spectacular, more stunning than if the show cars of 1956-57 had suddenly gone on sale. Irv Rybicki talked about the creation: "I went into Olds as a designer in the early 1950's and then I got transferred to Pontiac as an assistant chief designer. I put a little bit of Pontiac into Olds when I went back as assistant chief designer of the Oldsmobile studio.

"Then there was a bit of a shakeup in the styling management and I became the chief designer of Oldsmobile. I took over about midway through the 1959 program, when everybody was doing fins and all of us had a couple of tubes that went along the top of the body and just below the belt line and developed into two oval-shaped lenses.

"The fact that I had complete control over the appearance of the product made me very proud. I felt the responsibility and I could control it all. I did not do it all. There was a team of designers and sculptors and engineers and these people were constantly coming up with ideas, but the fact that I made the last decision in the room was a hell of a big step forward."

Was there a 'rocket concept' in the 1959 styling?

1959 Oldsmobile Super 88 Holiday SceniCoupe. Its Vista-Panoramic windshield was the ultimate in wraparound design, and the rear window had compound curves, contoured deep into the roofline.

"I imagine the 1959 design was influenced by the rocket idea, for that form along the belt line did open up like a rocket, but the car was set—the basic design was set when I became the chief—and there was no turnaround time. Even if I didn't enjoy it—that particular approach—there would have been nothing I could have done. We were committed, and the release process had begun. After the 1959 models we never did play on the idea of integrating the rocket feel into the forms of the car."

Why?

"The automobile is a land vehicle and I prefer that automobiles look like land vehicles. Functional, people-carrying land vehicles. I don't think they should look like aircraft or boats or rockets. They ought to look like *cars*. To me, an automobile is an automobile, pure and simple," Rybicki stated his credo, adding insistently: "And every part of the car should reflect the fact that it runs on four wheels and carries people."

Irvin W. Rybicki was born in 1922 in Detroit. He joined GM in February 1944 as project engineer at the Milford Proving Grounds. It was in September 1945 that he was transferred to GM Styling Staff as junior designer, and began what was to become his chosen career.

He was chief designer of the Oldsmobile studio from December 1957 to February 1962, when he went to Chevrolet as chief designer. In July 1965, he was named group chief designer for Chevrolet. Five years later, he was executive in charge of exterior design for Chevrolet and Pontiac. It was in July 1977 that he succeeded Bill Mitchell as vice president in charge of the GM Styling Staff.

Apart from the fins and tubes and rockets, the overall impression was one of glass. The roof metal was cut back and the glass extended everywhere. Total glass

The overall shape for the Linear Look of the 1959 models was essentially defined as early as March 1957. Front end treatment and wheel covers are still tentative, but the roofline and rear fenders were final.

Various rear bumper and taillamp designs were tried out for the 1959 models. This version was still in the running in April 1957, but subsequently rejected. Details of it were later picked up by Buick and Cadillac.

1959 Oldsmobile Dynamic 88 two-door sedan. This series was built on a 123-inch wheelbase, and the car was more than ten inches longer than the previous year's, at 218.4 inches. It weighed 4,364 pounds.

area had been increased by up to thirty-six percent over the 1958 models. The windshield angle was made faster, moving the base farther away from the A-post, so that the new Vista-Panoramic windshield (as it was called in Olds publicity) had 570 square inches more glass area than on the preceding models. Electric windshield wipers, moving in a wider arc, were standard equipment (in place of the former vacuum wipers).

The cars looked considerably wider, too, but the actual difference was only about an inch. Shoulder room was increased by up to four inches, however, making three-abreast seating a less crowded experience.

The oval was completely gone from the front end by this time. The grille frame curved around the outer units in the four-lamp headlight arrangement, with a rectangular-mesh grille deeply recessed under the hood lip, and set back from the edge of the bumper. New, circular parking lamps were located between each pair of headlamps. Bold, block letters spelled Oldsmobile right across the center of the grille, perhaps a necessity, for there were no other obvious trademarks or identification. Trunk space was increased by up to sixty-four percent.

A new Safety-Spectrum speedometer was introduced on the 1959 Oldsmobiles. The speed was indicated not by a sweeping hand but by a moving band of color that was green up to 35 mph, orange from 35 to 65 mph and red from there on.

With its 1959 models, Oldsmobile introduced two new body styles. One was the four-door Holiday SportSedan, and the other was called Holiday SceniCoupe.

1959 Oldsmobile 98 Holiday SportSedan. Extreme wrap-around of rear window left a narrow C-post far forward of the rear edge of the roof which extended to provide normal headroom for rear seat passengers.

1960 Oldsmobile Dynamic 88 convertible. Despite the simplicity of its body lines, which stressed length but not bigness, the sheer dimensions of the car left no doubt that it was aimed at the luxury market.

Both were available in all series. Each series also had a convertible coupe and a four-door sedan. The Dynamic 88 and Super 88 series included Fiesta wagons, now with a new tailgate arrangement where the glass descended into the lower panel, which then folded down in the normal way. The only two-door sedan in the program was a price leader for the Dynamic 88.

Engineering changes abounded, starting with the boring out of the engine to 394 cubic inches for the Super 88 and 98-series. The Dynamic 88 retained the 371-cubic-inch engine from the previous year, rated at 270 hp with the two-barrel and 300 hp with the four-barrel carburetor. The 394-cubic-inch V-8 delivered 315 hp at 4600 rpm, with a maximum torque of 435 pounds-feet at 2800 rpm.

Frank Ball and Lloyd Gill did a lot of work on the engines for 1959, but the real credit must go to Gil Burrell. "He was a genius as an engine developer," says an admiring Oldsmobile non-engineer, "He made the 394 so tough there's no way you could ever break it or use it up!"

Lloyd Gill had come to Oldsmobile as a student engineer in 1935 and became a tool designer in 1939. He went on to serve as an engine-design group leader in the 1960's.

Frank Ball joined Oldsmobile in 1950 as a senior clerk in the engineering records department after graduating from Purdue University. He came from Indianapolis and had served in the U.S. Navy in 1945-46. In 1952 Ball was named experimental project engineer and in 1955 became supervisor of the electrical laboratory. His next step up was as a senior project engineer, then he worked as a design analysis engineer, and was promoted to assistant motor engineer under Burrell in 1959.

The high-compression V-8 had been raised to a fine point of perfection by the time its originator, Charles F. Kettering, died at the age of eighty-two in Dayton, Ohio, in November 1958.

Brakes had suffered for four years, while the chemists tried to come up with better and better lining materials, more and more resistant to heat. The 1959 models had air scoops on the drums for better cooling but brake fade was still a problem for anybody who tried to hurry through traffic.

The New-Matic Ride was thrown out, and the leaf-spring rear suspension system restored. An improved power steering system became optional, and the front springs were reworked for better progressivity of action. A new split choke system on the 1959-model carburetors helped cut fuel waste during the warm-up period.

Durable acrylic-base paints developed by DuPont became standard on all 1959 Oldsmobiles with Magic Mirror finish, and an improved heating and ventilation system became standard on all models. The 1959 models were off to a promising start.

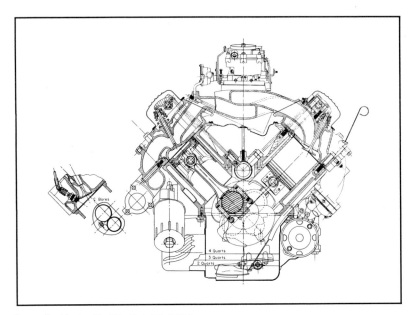

Cross-sectional drawing of the 394-cubic-inch Rocket V-8 shows the clearance situation in the crankcase, where connecting rods and counterweights narrowly miss the piston skirts.

The heavy V-8 engine, pushed further into the nose of the frame (as it had been for 1959) did indeed provide the Oldsmobile with an unwavering down-the-road stability.

The 1959 models did not have shortcomings in performance, but they became known as being heavy on the gasoline—an inevitable consequence of increasing their size and weight, and gearing them so that performance would not be lost. For 1960, therefore, Oldsmobile tried to lighten the cars and alter the gearing so as to get lower fuel consumption. Wheelbases could not be changed except at great expense, so they were left at 123.0 and 126.3 inches, respectively, for the 88- and 98-series.

But the sheet metal was cut back, shortening the Dynamic 88 and Super 88 to 217.6 inches and the 98 to 220.9 inches. Curb weights were brought down to 4,351 pounds for the Dynamic 88 four-door sedan, a saving of forty-five pounds. An impressive seventy-one pounds were taken out of the Super 88, which tipped the scales at 4,370 pounds. The 98 shed a full seventy-five pounds, for a curb weight of 4,518 pounds.

Axle ratios were lowered, to slow down the engines relative to road speed, across the board. This improved fuel economy and reduced noise, but exacted its toll in the form of lost performance. Chief engineer Harold N. Metzel had been blamed for the poor fuel consumption of the 1959 models; he was going to do better in that regard for 1960, even if it meant slower acceleration.

On the 98, the 3.42:1 axle ratio was exchanged for a pinion and ring gear giving a 3.23:1 reduction. Hydra-matic was standard on the 98, and for Super 88's with automatic transmission, the axle ratio was lowered from 3.23:1 to 3.07:1. At the same time, its tire size was reduced from 9.00-14 to 8.50-14. An even greater step was taken on the Dynamic 88 with Hydra-matic, which had used the 3.07:1 axle in 1959. Now it was reduced to 2.87:1. For cars with synchromesh transmission, the axle ratio became 3.42:1. It had previously been 3.64:1.

It cannot really be said that the styling was refined, for it was too vague in Oldsmobile identification. The abrupt styling changes made since 1956 had broken the earlier continuity. In the search for new themes and the establishment of new evolutive forms, nothing was found in the old model that was worth carrying over into the new one, and when that happens year after year, the car ends up showing a bewildering lack of ancestry.

Some of the ideas on the 1960 Olds were picked up by Mercury five years later (the grille pattern, the darts on the fenders). Oldsmobile also borrowed an idea from Ford in adopting an optional rear-facing third seat in the 1960 Fiesta wagon. It was accessible through the tailgate, like Ford's, but had the advantage of being folded in a single, swift, one-handed motion, while the Ford needed a two-step operation.

What the 1960 models could have accomplished in sales volume during a normal year will never be known, for production was suspended on October 30, 1959, due to a national steel strike. When the assembly lines began rolling again, nearly 50,000 sales had been lost. It was no comfort to Wolfram that things were

"I wrapped that program up with the team—and then we did the '60—the '61—and I left the studio during the development of the '62," recounted Irv Rybicki.

Other personnel changes were also to have an effect on the division's fortunes. One general sales manager, V. H. Sutherlen, retired in 1958, and was succeeded by S. F. Mehring. At the end of 1960, Mehring was replaced by Emmett P. Feely, another old-timer, born in St. Louis, Missouri, and educated at St. Louis University. He had joined General Motors in 1925 in the sales end, and made quite a career at Oldsmobile. Was he going to be able to turn the tide and get people to buy Oldsmobiles again? He would certainly be helped by many product changes.

Extensive sheet metal changes had been made on the 1960 models. Tailfin direction was changed from vertical to horizontal; whatever aerodynamic advantage that might have been gained in terms of high-speed stability would thus be lost (or perhaps it was a way of saying that the car did not have a stability problem, and an admission that tailfins were only a styling gimmick after all).

1960 Oldsmobile 98 Holiday SportSedan. The extreme look of the year before was moderated, and the linear concept strengthened. Wheelbase was unchanged at 126.3 inches, but overall length was cut back over two inches.

1960 Oldsmobile Super 88 Fiesta station wagon. This year the Fiesta no longer had hardtop construction but was based on the four-door sedan. Rearmost roof section was slightly raised.

getting tougher for medium-class cars in general, though he was probably pleased to see two of Oldsmobile's direct competitors bite the dust. In November 1959, barely into the new model year, Ford dropped the Edsel, and ten months later Chrysler Corporation phased out the DeSoto.

Oldsmobile's sales statistics for 1959 and 1960 show what happened, and are part of the historical record.

	1959	**1960**
Total market (millions)	6.0	6.6
Olds sales	360,525	355,798
Olds rank	6th	7th
Olds market share	6.0%	5.4%
GM market share	42.1%	43.6%

Buick had fallen hopelessly behind, and Oldsmobile was hurting—its drop from sixth to seventh position was caused by Dodge's rise. Pontiac managed fourth place in 1959, only to lose it to Rambler the following year.

The medium class was not a good market to be in, for the buying public was now demanding smaller cars that cost less and were cheaper to run, as well as more fun to drive. In misguided optimism, Jack Wolfram was eagerly looking forward to the day when his F-85 could go on sale.

After four difficult years, he did not have too much faith in the big cars. And yet, the 1961 models were practically all-new cars. Metzel and his engineers had come up with a new chassis, Burrell had found a few extra horses in his Rocket V-8 and Rybicki's new styling was strikingly different.

The frame was a new perimeter design, with the side-members brought out to the doorsill area inside the wheelbase, and joined to the narrower-base sections by torque boxes. This frame was more flexible than the one it replaced, but not, of course, structurally weaker. What was happening to body and frame design philosophy was a result of GM's new experience with unit construction (X-body).

Other bodies, intended for mounting on frames, were improved in various ways, using the lessons from monocoque shell construction, with the result that their torsional stiffness increased considerably, with a small increase in weight. These new bodies demanded far less support from the frame, and needed fewer body mounts. A reduced number of body mounts meant fewer potential paths for transfer of noise and vibration from the road to the passenger compartment, and new techniques in body-mount composition began to evolve. Frames were allowed to

First proposal (left) for the 1961-model front end. The picture was taken in March 1959. Vertical/oval parking lights were discarded, but the rest was refined into a final design. Front fender line for the 1961 models had not yet emerged by February 1959, when this mockup (middle) was shown. On the other hand, the rear fender treatment had already found its final shape. Rear end panel proposal (right) for 1961 was smooth but trunk lid opening and decor posed manufacturing problems. This design dates from February 1959.

1961 Oldsmobile Dynamic 88 four-door sedan. Return to normal A-posts was made step by step. The A-post still stands on the door and not on the main body structure. Overall length was cut back to 212 inches.

flex more, almost to the point of serving as an extension of the springs, while the body became increasingly undeformable.

New suspension systems were designed and developed. Key men connected with this project were C. M. Scholfield, senior project engineer for chassis, and James H. Diener, chassis engineer. Diener had graduated from Purdue University in 1938 and joined Oldsmobile in 1940. He had worked as a senior project engineer since 1954, and had been involved with all major developments in chassis and body engineering.

Leaf-spring rear suspension was abandoned for 1961, and Oldsmobile could once again offer an all-coil ride. The new rear-axle suspension had a four-link system, basically similar to those of the 1958 chassis and the new F-85 compact, with vertical coil springs and nylon-sleeved telescopic shock absorbers. "Twin-Triangle Stability" was assured by this new axle-locating system, which restricted axle movement to one single plane. The links carried heavy rubber isolation to prevent transfer of noise and harshness.

Changes in front suspension were merely evolutionary, the redesign having been caused mainly by the change to a new type of frame. It was advertised as Pivot-Poise with Counter-Dive, in combination with Dual Center Control Steering.

Saginaw had a new steering gear ready, working on the recirculating-ball principle, which became standard across the board. It was used singly on cars with non-assisted steering, or in combination with the Roto-Matic power steering (which

was standard on the 98 and optional on the other series). Power brakes were also standard on the 98, and all models featured the pedal-operated parking brake, first introduced on the 1960 Oldsmobiles.

Hydra-matic had a new feature advertised as Accel-A-Rotor action. Behind this clever term was hidden a major engineering change: A separate torque converter was inserted next to the fluid coupling. It was arranged to function only in first and reverse gears, providing high torque multiplication by hydraulic means at low vehicle speeds, and thereby easing the stress on the mechanical gearing. Because it extended the torque multiplication range, it was claimed to serve as an extra low gear for livelier getaways, whose action gradually blended with that of the fluid coupling as the car gained speed. This fact enabled Hydra-matic Division to take out one speed of the planetary gearing, making the unit a three-speed.

Engine displacement remained at 394 cubic inches, but the marketing people at Olds could not resist playing with new names. Only the baseline engine was called Rocket. It was standard in the Dynamic 88 series and came equipped with a

Rocket V-8 engine in 1961 edition, with four-barrel carburetor and Hydra-matic transmission. The division had made its four-millionth V-8 in 1960 and completed the fifth million in 1963.

1961 Oldsmobile Super 88 Holiday coupe. New, sleek C-post design was reserved for two-door models. The Linear Look has been made to accommodate a rocket theme. This model weighed 4,175 pounds.

Rochester Econ-O-Way two-barrel carburetor having a two-stage automatic choke and 8.75:1 compression. Maximum output was 250 hp at 4400 rpm, with a peak torque of 405 pounds-feet at 2400 rpm.

When equipped with a Rochester Multi-Jet four-barrel carburetor and pistons, raising the compression ratio to an even 10.0:1, the same 394-cubic-inch V-8 was called Skyrocket. With its extended speed range, it delivered 325 hp at 4600 rpm and generated a maximum torque of 435 pounds-feet at 2800 rpm. In their name-changing spree, the marketing department had added the word Classic in front of the number 98, apparently motivated by pity for its loneliness, ending the cruel days when it was forced to stand alone, underprivileged against the lower-ranking 88 which had long been accompanied by such splendid appellations as Dynamic and Super. And the lowly four-door sedan, whose popularity had been dwindling under the assault of the four-door hardtops, was renamed Celebrity sedan, in an effort to upgrade its standing.

Celebrity sedans were offered in the Dynamic 88 and Super 88 series, but not as a Classic 98. Instead, the Classic 98 series included a new six-window Holiday sedan to accompany the six-window town sedan, four-window SportSedan, Holiday coupe and convertible coupe.

Strangely, the Fiesta name disappeared from the station wagons, which continued in two- and three-seat versions in both the Dynamic 88 and Super 88 series. Both 88-series also included Holiday coupes and Holiday sedans, as well as convertible coupes. A two-door sedan continued in the Dynamic 88 series only, playing the role of price leader. The 88's continued on a 123-inch wheelbase, while the Classic 98 was pulled back to a 126-inch wheelbase (from 126.3 in 1960).

Side sculpturing was the main styling trick on the '61's. A full-length torpedo with a blunted nose was set in relief, running right through the door panels, from fender to fender. Lower fender skirts, outside of the wheelbase, were splayed outward to give an impression of a wide stance. No vestige of tailfins was to be seen. The fender line followed the torpedo contour, coming to a point, and the deck lid was curved to match this tapering streamline.

The deck lid had chrome-lined crescents cut out of it near the lower corners to accommodate the circular taillights, which had been moved inboard of the fenders.

The greenhouse was much modified, the most notable innovation being the return to a near-normal A-post after so many years of panoramic windshields. The 'dogleg' A-post had not made a whit of difference to the driver's view, but it certainly reduced the impact strength of the roof structure, offering only about one-fifth the resistance of a normal A-post in a rollover accident.

In January 1960, the Oldsmobile styling studio prepared this mockup as a proposal for 1962. Its main features were adopted for production.

1961 Oldsmobile Starfire 98 convertible coupe. It was built on a 126-inch wheelbase and weighed 4,356 pounds. Its 394-cubic-inch V-8 delivered 325 hp and pulled a 3.23:1 axle ratio.

The new A-post had a slightly baroque curve at its base, as if to give a visual reminder of the previous dogleg design. At the back end, the SportSedan and Holiday sedan roof was pulled out to form an eave-like projection above the backlight, which was wrapped around the corners to meet a narrow C-post. Holiday coupes had a very smooth roofline and extremely slim C-posts.

Finally, the grille. "It looked pushed-in, as if the car had been in an accident," was the reaction of a designer from another GM studio. "I couldn't believe they were serious about using that on a production model."

Inside Oldsmobile, criticism was muffled at the time, but an engineer later said of the 1961-model front that "it looked like what's left of your teeth after Sonny Liston put his fist in your mouth."

"The idea might have been good, but it didn't come off right," explained a member of the Oldsmobile sales staff. "We wanted to get away from the old face with the assertive chromed grille as the center of attention. We were looking for an air-intake effect, with the headlamps at the outer ends. And instead of using a chrome frame around the grille, we curved the bumper ends into the fender tips, forming a wide U-shape or an oval with an open top."

Did the consumers like it? "No, you might say they were afraid of it. They seemed to shun Oldsmobile that year. I don't know if it was the grille in particular that scared them off, but our design was certainly a weakness at a time when Pontiac, above all, was developing a strong front end, and Buick, Chrysler and even Mercury were doing grilles which added something to their cars' appearance."

Wolfram must secretly have begun to doubt his own capacity for understanding the Oldsmobile market. Looking back over his experience, he searched for ideas for a hype. "We'll bring back the Starfire," he told his staff one morning. The new Starfire convertible came out in January 1961, with its own specific version of the 394-cubic-inch Skyrocket engine, console-shift Hydra-matic and bucket-seat interior.

It had the 123-inch wheelbase of the Super 88, but the 98 grille and rear end, with special side ornamentation, so as to constitute the first of a separate series. It weighed 4,240 pounds.

The Starfire was aimed at the Thunderbird market, and the convertible was followed by a hardtop in 1962. This time, Wolfram had followed Pontiac's formula for attacking the T-bird, as evidenced in the Grand Prix, by using standard body parts, while Buick went to a unique body for the Riviera in 1963 (as Olds was to do with the Toronado some years later).

Somehow Wolfram became convinced that the Classic label was counterproductive to selling the 98, and ordered it dropped for the 1962 model year. At the same time, he reinstated the Fiesta name for the Dynamic 88 and Super 88 station wagons. The Dynamic 88 two-door sedan had also been a headache rather than a help, and it was struck from the program. To avoid conflict with the Starfire, the convertible coupe was eliminated from the Super 88 series (but allowed to continue as a 98, carrying a profit margin similar to the Starfire's).

Wolfram told the stylists he needed a completely new look for 1962, and would accept whatever tooling costs became necessary. He began to spend more time in the styling studio, sometimes barging in unannounced for a personal check on the progress of this or that. And he didn't go alone. He asked his top engineers to

1962 Oldsmobile 98 Holiday sports sedan. Its engine was called Skyrocket, rated at 330 hp. Power steering and power brakes had become standard on the 98-series.

1962 Oldsmobile Starfire coupe. The two-door hardtop roof was done in very conservative taste, and the rear end and side treatment conform closely to the proposal.

come along, and his sales executives were also asked to make judgments on styling ideas.

Whether it was because of Wolfram's closer supervision or not we cannot say, but the results were eminently satisfactory. The 1962 Oldsmobile 88's and 98's were a fine blend of harmonious lines and simple, attractive ornamentation. You could say they were pretty, if cars of that size can be called pretty. The fact is that without basic body changes—but a wholesale renewal of outer sheet metal, front and rear ends, and rooflines—Oldsmobile had acquired a unity of style with certain characteristic elements that would constitute a basis for evolution and reinstate a theme of continuity in Oldsmobile design.

The torpedo sculpturing was downplayed and turned into horizontal accent lines. A low chrome-plated grille, with a number of discreet horizontal bars protruding to form a vertical ridge at the center, formed a pleasant new face.

Technically, the 1961 models had been quite satisfactory, and the number of engineering changes made for 1962 was kept to a minimum. The main difference in the chassis was the adoption of factory-sealed lubrication, putting an end to the regular greasing interval. The engine program, however, underwent something of a revision.

The Rocket engine had its compression ratio increased to 10.25:1, output climbed to 280 hp and torque to 430 pounds-feet, with retention of the two-barrel carburetor. It continued as standard for the Dynamic 88. A regular-fuel 260-hp Rocket with an 8.75:1 compression was optional at no extra cost. The Skyrocket engine was used in the 98 and Super 88, and with its new 10.25:1 compression ratio, power output was raised to 330 hp and torque to 440 pounds-feet. The Skyrocket

engine was fitted with special pistons giving a 10.5:1 compression ratio when installed in the Starfire, renamed the Starfire engine, with a rated output of 345 hp.

Styling reform, model-program reform, and a reform of market philosophy were to pay off very well for Oldsmobile. During 1962, sales began to recover. Starfire sales soared to 39,229 (while only 8,624 had been sold in 1961), and the number of 98 registrations climbed from 45,464 to 64,389 cars. Sales of the Super 88 remained static, while the Dynamic 88 leaped ahead, from 133,979 to 171,806 cars. The total picture of the division's standing at the start of 1963 includes the F-85:

	1961	**1962**
Total market (millions)	5.9	6.9
Olds sales	328,586	440,995
Olds rank	5th	4th
Olds market share	5.6%	6.4%
GM market share	46.5%	51.9%

Despite its decline in 1961, Oldsmobile had moved up in the rankings, mainly due to a catastrophic drop in Plymouth and Dodge sales. The following year, Olds moved ahead of American Motors (Rambler).

CHAPTER 11

Gathering Momentum

JACK WOLFRAM WAS FEELING GOOD. He had realized a coup in getting Oldsmobile turned around, and like any good general, he knew he had to press his advantage and exploit the victory. That meant relentless pursuit, with no time for resting on laurels. Even in the depths of adversity, Wolfram had never lost his fighting spirit, or his nerve. He authorized spending for new and ambitious programs, when the prospects of benefiting from them were bleakest.

"In Wolfram's days, Oldsmobile was not so much related to engineering as his management style was related to marketing," said Jim Williams, who worked in the Oldsmobile public relations department from 1964 to 1971. "Pontiac had crept ahead of Olds, and they were fighting for third position in the market place."

Now that things were improving, Oldsmobile should use its momentum to make further advances, Wolfram believed, and make his preparations pay off. Oldsmobile's new engineering center had been completed in August 1962, and doubled the division's drawing-office and laboratory capacity.

In the spring of 1963 Oldsmobile announced a major reorganization that would affect over seventy percent of the division's manufacturing operations. The plan was to be completed in time for 1964-model production startup, and involved integration of the F-85 and full-size-car assembly lines, the addition of a new paint shop, plus new machinery for the engine and stamping plants. Plans for a new administration building were announced in August 1963, and Oldsmobile's new home was completed by mid-1965.

At the start of the 1964 calendar year, Oldsmobile was producing 1,400 cars every day at the Lansing plant, and GM assembly plants elsewhere completed another 1,000 Oldsmobiles daily.

Business was good, and Oldsmobile was going from strength to strength. Then Wolfram retired on June 6, 1964, due to ill health. He could look back with pride on having built a strong organization, but he had been a very lonely man all those years he held the reins of Oldsmobile. He was perhaps respected, but certainly not loved, and not greatly admired by the people who had worked for him.

"He was a bloody tyrant," some said.

"A super-egomaniac," others described him.

"He was very strong, and he ran a one-man show."

"He was very conservative, and all his actions were predictable."

Opinions clashed sometimes, converged sometimes, always leaving a little doubt. We knew Wolfram only superficially from brief meetings in his office, and cannot dispute these statements.

"Wolfram, in some circles, was not a particularly popular man," we were told by one who worked in close association with him for several years, "and his management style was certainly criticized by an awful lot of people internally and externally. But he did insist on quality people, and he did seem to have an understanding of what that was, in that he just did not tolerate incompetent people. He was a very demanding man, and working for him was hard training. That helped

1963 Oldsmobile 98 Custom sports coupe. Oldsmobile has now abandoned the oval-theme grille, and the A-post is once again firmly anchored on the cowl structure. Side decor is restricted to doorsill level. The sports coupe was available with front bucket seats and a console-mounted Hydra-matic control stick. Both bumpers were fully integrated in the silhouette.

Oldsmobile an awful lot during the years following his retirement, because these people surfaced now, and they went on to bigger and better things in the corporation.''

From a different source came this statement: ''The people who criticized Wolfram over the years did not understand the strengths that he had. Whether those strengths existed because people feared him, or not, is beside the point—but he knew how to run a tight ship. And he insisted on surrounding himself with people he picked as the best, in every respect. He needed to respect them for their ability. They had to have credentials. They had to look good and they had to sound good. He didn't accept anything that was mediocre in the way of people.''

In his retirement, Wolfram turned to altruistic causes and became involved in research on human relations. He set up the Jack Wolfram Foundation in Lansing, and sponsored research on subjects such as: Does reduced mental activity and loss of work due to retirement cause organic deterioration? Why do some retired people continue to lead happy, successful lives while others turn unhappy and lose self-esteem? He enlisted the help of Wayne State University and Antioch College to

explore an experimental course in what he called 'communicology'—his term for the science of human communications.

Meanwhile, back at the plant, Harold N. Metzel was catapulted into office as general manager, and was succeeded as chief engineer by John B. Beltz. Metzel was an Oldsmobile veteran, and nobody would think of calling him a breath of fresh air, but he did change the atmosphere. He brought about a change in management style and in the general attitude toward the product and marketing.

''Metzel was easy-going, but he sure got a lot done,'' he was praised by a sales department officer.

Jim Williams, who now heads Chevrolet public relations, remembers: ''Metzel was a very quiet, soft-spoken sort of a fellow. Very fair, very conservative. Traditional in most ways, but very likeable!''

Metzel had been responsible for generation after generation of Oldsmobiles and remained close to the product even after his duties were expanded to encompass

Harold N. Metzel (left) had succeeded Jack Wolfram as chief engineer, and later followed him as general manager of Oldsmobile. R. T. Rollis (right) served for many years as general manufacturing manager of Oldsmobile. He played a big part in maintaining quality as production expanded.

1963 Oldsmobile Dynamic 88 Holiday sedan. The 88's were built on a 123-inch wheelbase, and this model weighed 4,156 pounds. The 394-cubic-inch V-8 was rated at 280 hp.

all the division's affairs. He saw the product as the essential reason for everything else's existence, and ran the whole division the same way he had run the engineering staff: quietly, competently and with an outward modesty that covered up a lot of brave decisions and some gambles. In some ways, he had let Oldsmobile fall behind, and in some cases, it really wasn't all his fault. Take the matter of disc brakes, for instance.

Studebaker put disc brakes on the Avanti in mid-1962. General Motors had been working on disc brakes since 1950 but the Engineering Staff under Charles A. Chayne had no thought of getting them ready for production.

General Motors had just finished adding self-adjusters during 1962 (a feature that Mercedes-Benz had introduced in 1936). While AMC put split hydraulic brake circuits on the Rambler American, as Studebaker did on the Lark in 1962, GM hesitantly followed—the Corvette had a dual-circuit brake system in 1962. But not Oldsmobile—not until 1965.

Delco-Moraine had long been trying to develop a disc brake system, and Chevrolet was first to adopt it, for all four wheels of the 1965 Corvette. It was an expensive system, and it took another year before Oldsmobile would even make front disc brakes optional for one of its cars.

Olds had a new brake lining material for the 1963 models intended to give a more positive brake pedal feel. The 1963 models also had improved starter motors, and alternators were fitted across the board. At this time, Pontiac, Ford and Mercury were developing transistorized ignition systems, but Oldsmobile took no initiative in this area.

Positive crankcase ventilation was adopted for all 1963 Oldsmobile engines. AC Spark Plug made the PCV valves for all GM car divisions. On the luxury and convenience front, Saginaw had developed a tilt-away steering wheel that Oldsmobile offered as an option for the full-size 1963 models. Oldsmobile had always been a pioneer in such things, and was among the first to offer six-way power seats.

The performance image earned by the 88 back in the early Rocket V-8 days had worn off by this time, for it was really *quiet* performance and not *rapid* performance that Oldsmobile buyers cared about. Despite their preoccupation with silence, comfort and luxury, which make cars heavy, the Oldsmobile engineers kept their cars' fuel economy up with the best of their competition.

In the 1963 Mobilgas Economy Run, the Oldsmobile 98 delivered 17.18 mpg compared with 16.60 for the Buick Electra and 17.40 for the Chrysler Imperial Custom. The Dynamic 88 recorded 20.01 mpg, compared with 19.38 for the Pontiac Catalina and 17.39 for the Mercury Monterey. Oldsmobile's F-85 was listed

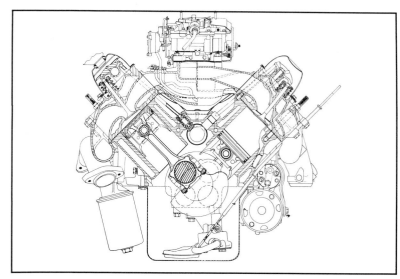

A smaller cast-iron V-8 of 330 cubic inches was introduced in 1963. It became standard in the 1964 Jetstar 88 and replaced the aluminum V-8 in the F-85 and Cutlass.

Cross-sectional drawing of the 330-cubic-inch V-8 shows its basic relationship to the 394 as well as the original V-8 of 1949, but constructional progress is not apparent here.

at 21.10 mpg while the Buick Special V-8 did 23.81 mpg and the Studebaker Lark V-8 got 20.56 mpg.

Oldsmobile was often accused of being content to go its own way, without heed for what the competition was doing. In 1963 Oldsmobile's ads pointed out that the division had produced five million Rocket V-8's, apparently oblivious to the general trend in the market. One direct competitor advertised the "brilliant performance that is now standard in every Mercury—a big Marauder 390 V-8. Team up this engine with Mercury's optional fully synchronized '4-on-the-floor' stickshift transmission and there's a new sense of oneness between you and the car."

Oldsmobile had nothing like it. Competition spilled over even into the terms of warranty. The Dodge was sold with a 5/50 warranty—five years or 50,000 miles. In 1963, Chrysler's Newport and 300 were also aimed at the Oldsmobile market, and had the same warranty period. General Motors did not react to Chrysler's challenge, for the feeling in the Finance Committee was that Chrysler would have to drop the 5/50 warranty when its real cost could be assessed, after two or three years.

At Oldsmobile, Wolfram was still in control, and he just tried to have the right cars for the people he knew as Oldsmobile customers. Trite, perhaps, but it still worked. For 1963 he added two models in the 98-series, a Luxury sedan and a Custom sports coupe, the latter sharing the Starfire's interior package. The cars were technically unchanged. The styling theme from 1962 was, however, developed

further in new designs by Stan Wilen, who had become chief designer of the Oldsmobile studio in 1962, after serving for a period under Rybicki.

The body sides were cleaned up even more, fender lines became crisper, big undecorated surfaces were allowed to remain free of ornaments, though the grilles were still sort of neutral. The A-post once again looked like a perfectly normal windshield pillar, and more formal C-posts were adopted, doing away with the wraparound rear window.

Innovations in the B- and C-body cars for 1964 were not so much in appearance as in labeling. The marketing department had invented a new name it just could not keep bottled up any longer: Jetstar. They thought it was so great that it was used for two new series: Jetstar 88 and Jetstar I.

The Jetstar 88 was a lower-priced series that would normally have revived the Series 68 or 78 designation, but in these days of Celebrity sedans and Fiesta wagons, that just would not do. It shared the 123-inch wheelbase and Fisher B-body with the other 88's, but was powered by a new, smaller V-8 developed for the intermediate-size F-85 and Cutlass.

Newport four-door cost $3,042; a Ford Thunderbird, $4,486; and a Mercury Montclair two-seat station wagon, $3,434.

Body Style	Jetstar 88	Jetstar I	Dynamic 88
Sedan	$2,935		$3,005
Two-door hardtop		$3,603	3,062
Four-door hardtop	3,069		3,139
Convertible	3,318		3,389
Station wagon			3,468

Body Style	Super 88	98	Starfire
Sedan	$3,256	$3,993	
Four-door hardtop	3,483	4,265	
Two-door hardtop		4,188	$4,138
Convertible		4,468	4,753

The engine program for the B-body and C-body cars continued unchanged except for the addition of the new Jetfire Rocket V-8 in the Jetstar 88 series. This unit replaced the Rockette (and killed the turbocharged engine, usurping its trade name without having the slightest link with jets or turbines).

It was called a new engine because it came out of a program in which a completely original design could have been made. Gil Burrell and his assistants prepared and evaluated several new designs of different layout. But in the end it was determined that for the power range in question (220 to 250 hp), the bore centers, camshaft location, distributor drive and oil pump location of the production-type Rocket and V-8 were perfectly suitable.

After considering the probable weight of the vehicles, their axle ratio and tire size, in comparison with performance targets for these vehicles, Burrell calculated that a displacement of 330 cubic inches would be about right. This placed it one-third of the way up from the original Rocket V-8 of 1949, across the gap to the then-current production engine of 394-cubic-inch displacement.

It's interesting to note that after more than ten years' experience with the V-8, Burrell now chose a considerably bigger bore and a shorter stroke than in the original. The 1949 Rocket V-8 of 303.7-cubic-inch displacement had a 3.75-inch bore and a 3.44-inch stroke, while the new 330 used a 3.94-inch bore and a 3.39-inch stroke.

Because of the planned installations in two different sizes of vehicle, the engine needed greater versatility than the old one. Gil Burrell, Frank Ball and Lloyd Gill set to work on refinements that would reduce weight, size and cost without giving up an atom of quality.

Therefore it became inevitable that all major castings would be different from those of the Skyrocket engine. The small block differed in water-jacket arrangement, oil channels, and the cylinder heads had a modified-wedge combustion chamber with a reduced valve angle (six degrees only).

Interior of the 1963 El Torero, based on the 98 Starfire convertible. The folded top was hidden under a plastic cover, and all seats were bucket-type. Sheet metal remained standard.

A whole series of body styles was offered, including the four-door sedan, two- and four-door hardtops and a convertible coupe. The Jetstar I, on the other hand, was built only as one model—a sports coupe—again with the B-body and a 123-inch wheelbase. But it was supposed to be a lower-priced alternative to the Starfire in the ever-growing Thunderbird market, and shared the 345-hp Starfire engine.

Several Oldsmobile people knew at the time this was going to be pretty confusing to the public, but they were powerless. Wolfram agreed, however, to cut back on the Super 88 model lineup, since that series, once his pride and joy, was now definitely on the wane. For 1964, the Super 88 could be had only as a Celebrity sedan or Holiday sedan—no two-door models and no wagons.

The Dynamic 88 series continued with its six separate models, as did the 98-series. The prices remained very competitive, considering that a Chrysler

1964-model Oldsmobile in the mockup stage, photographed in February 1962. It's done as two half-cars, the one on the right (passenger's side) being preferred over the left one.

The same double half-car mockup, seen from the rear. The final design borrowed from both sides. Side panel treatment from the driver's side was accepted.

Due to the use of lightweight components wherever possible, and the advances made in foundry techniques, the 330 Jetfire V-8 was 154 pounds lighter than the 324-cubic-inch Rocket of 1954. Production costs were far lower than they would have been for an engine of different layout, since its manufacture could be integrated with the 394.

It was tuned to put out 230 hp at 4400 rpm for the F-85 on a compression ratio of 9.0:1, and 245 hp at 4600 rpm for the Jetstar 88, with 10.25:1 compression. Both used two-barrel Rochester carburetors and had single exhaust systems. A four-barrel version with 10.25:1 compression put out 290 hp at 4800 rpm. The size of the V-6 had been increased to 225 cubic inches, and its output raised to 155 hp at 4400 rpm.

The Accel-A-Rotor Hydra-matic was retained for all automatic-drive cars equipped with the 394-cubic-inch engine, but an entirely new automatic called Jetaway was used in combination with the 330-cubic-inch engine. It was a development of the 61-05, without the dual-path feature, having instead a torque converter with a variable-pitch stator (based on Buick's pioneering work in this area). It had two-speed planetary gearing.

For new intermediates with manual drive, Oldsmobile adopted an old Chevrolet gearbox (used on its six-cylinder models) with column-shift and synchromesh on second and top gears.

A four-speed all-synchromesh Warner T-10 with floorshift became available for the F-85 and Cutlass. It was a tough unit, with high torque capacity, and almost unbreakable, but it tended to be balky. During 1964 the 'Muncie' gearbox, made by Chevrolet, having a superior type of synchromesh and shift linkage, was used to supplant the T-10.

The new intermediate car, developed by Chevrolet, broke sharply with the construction principles of the compact F-85. Instead of a unit-construction X-body, the new car had a separate frame and carried a new Fisher A-body. The frame was of

the perimeter type, without X-bracing, and contributed little torsional stiffness. Most of the strength was built into the body.

The new F-85 was built on a 115-inch wheelbase, and weighed 3,065 pounds as a four-door sedan with the standard V-6 engine.

It had independent front suspension with coil springs and A-frame control arms, plus a stablizer bar. The rear axle also had coil springs. It was anchored in a four-link system with two lower trailing arms and two upper torque-reaction members splayed at about forty-five degrees from the top of the differential casing.

Tire size was increased to 6.50-14, mounted on five-inch rims, and 9.5-inch brake drums were used all around. Optional tire sizes were 7.00-14 and 7.50-14. Three trim levels were offered: F-85, Deluxe F-85 and Cutlass. The choice of body styles was the same as before, but all bodies were now much roomier, and the car was selling at practically unchanged prices.

Body Style	F-85	Deluxe F-85	Cutlass
Four-door sedan	$2,397	$2,505	
Two-door sedan	2,343	2,537	$2,644
Two-door hardtop			2,784
Convertible			2,894
Station wagon	2,689	2,797	

1964 Oldsmobile F-85 two-door sedan. The F-85 was no longer a compact, but an intermediate. It was not competing against the Mercury Comet, but against the Montego.

Detail of the 1964 Custom Vista-Cruiser station wagon, based on the F-85 chassis. Oldsmobile was to retain this roof as an exclusive, not shared with any other GM division.

The 1964 Vista-Cruiser was built on a longer wheelbase (121 inches) than the regular F-85 station wagon, which shared the 115-inch wheelbase of the sedan.

A unique station wagon style with a raised roof section and skylights was unveiled at the Chicago Auto Show in February 1964. Built on a 120-inch wheelbase, it was added to the production lineup with the label Vista-Cruiser.

For the basic styling of the F-85, Stan Wilen and his boys had done a minimum to set it apart from the Chevelle. It received an Oldsmobile grille (patterned on that used in the Dynamic 88), the angular fender lines of the B-body Olds, plus a remarkable rear-end treatment with the taillights and backup lights forming part of a decorative bar stretching the full width of the panel.

Production was running smoothly, free of quality-control problems, with Bob Cook as production manager and R. T. Rollis as general manufacturing manager. The sales department under Emmett P. Feely was enjoying the rise in the sales curve, but was somewhat at a loss to explain it. Jack Wolfram understood that his sales staff needed some fresh input, more reliable research and more inspired planning and marketing. He began looking around for some talent from outside, and asked careful questions of his peers and others at GM. One day Ed Cole told him about a guy named Worden.

1964 Oldsmobile Jetstar 88 four-door sedan. The Jetstar 88 was a new series which used the small V-8 from the F-85 and the 88-series chassis.

1964 Oldsmobile Super 98 Holiday sedan. Its straight lines emphasized its 215.3-inch overall length, but in general shape, some people said it was just like an 'overgrown Rambler.'

Mack Worden was a graduate of the University of Wichita who had come to General Motors as a parts-and-accessories clerk with Chevrolet's Kansas City branch in 1946. Within three years he was business manager of the Kansas City Zone Office, and in 1953 Chevrolet made him business manager for the division's midwest region. A year later he was transferred to Detroit as assistant national sales promotion manager, rising successively to the posts of national business manager and national owner-relations manager. In 1961 he returned to Kansas City as assistant regional manager for the midwest, where he stayed until Wolfram tapped him for the post of assistant general sales manager in charge of Oldsmobile's marketing, and Worden moved to Lansing.

That was in 1963, and it was generally felt that Worden made a big contribution to the success of 1964. The calendar-year sales results deserve a closer look:

	1963	1964
Total market (millions)	7.6	8.1
Olds sales	474,786	513,134
Olds rank	4th	4th
Olds market share	6.3%	6.4%
GM market share	51.0%	49.1%

In 1963 Pontiac had a lead of 31,000 cars on Olds, with Buick 21,000 cars behind Olds. The following year, Pontiac increased its lead to 175,000 cars, while Buick let the gap widen to 32,000 cars. Among the outside competition, Dodge was ahead of Mercury, with Chrysler running behind Cadillac.

The change to intermediate size for the F-85 had a marked effect on station wagon sales, which nearly tripled, from 9,977 in 1963 to 28,587 in 1964. That's all the more remarkable, since the 1963 registrations included a certain proportion of 1964 models. The total number of intermediates sold in 1964 was 172,071, which boosted the F-85's share of total Oldsmobile sales from twenty-five to thirty-three perfect, at a time when the B- and C-body business slipped by 12,500 cars, or 3.5 percent.

There was practically no difference between Oldsmobile's and Buick's intermediate-car price levels, while the Pontiac Tempest was positioned about $100 lower, and the Chevelle was about $150 under the Pontiac.

Still, the Special outsold the F-85 by 8,000 cars, and Oldsmobile ran sixth among the intermediates, in a market led by the Chevelle (313,000) and Ford Fairlane (253,000). Pontiac was third with 240,000, and Rambler, fourth (232,000).

Metzel, Beltz and Dorshimer had been watching Pontiac's success with the GTO, and concluded that if the muscle-car market was going to develop into

1964 Oldsmobile Starfire coupe. The Starfire had been a series of its own since 1962. By 1964 it had found its identity in using the highest-powered 98-series V-8 in a sports-type body on the 88-series wheelbase.

"The 4-4-2 really was a spinoff of the police package for the Cutlass—and probably styling had something to do with it. There was Beltz again. He wanted a street machine—not a hot-rod," Jim Williams revealed. "Pontiac had been tremendously successful with the GTO, and the 4-4-2 was a way to attract people to an Oldsmobile product of similar type for those who were inclined to buy an Oldsmobile but would otherwise have gone to Pontiac. However, Olds never put the kind of push behind the 4-4-2 that Pontiac gave to the GTO."

The 4-4-2 showed its ability to accelerate from 25 to 70 mph in 5.76 seconds in the 1967 Pure Oil Performance Trials, second only to the Fairlane GT (5.585 seconds). To Beltz's and Dorshimer's delight the 4-4-2 beat the Ford in fuel consumption, with an average of 18.552 mpg against 17.07.

Gil Burrell based the 4-4-2 engine on the tough 394-cubic-inch Rocket V-8. It was developed in record time, for Burrell knew exactly what was needed to meet the output target of 345 hp from a displacement not exceeding 400 cubic inches. A new block was designed, with the bore reduced to 4.00 inches, combined with a new crankshaft having longer crank throws giving a 3.98-inch stroke.

He put in new pistons, with special reinforcements, giving a 10.25:1 compression ratio, and low-restriction exhaust manifolds. A heavy-duty cooling system became part of the 4-4-2 package, along with the dual exhaust system developed for low back-pressure. Bearing dimensions were borrowed from the 394, with a three-inch diameter for the mains and a 2.50-inch diameter for the crankpin journals.

The forged-steel crankshaft and pushrod-and-rocker-arm valve gear were not nearly at the end of their limit at a speed of 4800 rpm, where peak power was delivered. As a result of Burrell's nursing of the torque curve, the engine had extremely good flexibility, and generated a maximum torque of 440 pounds-feet at 3200 rpm. This was no drag-strip engine, but a tremendously strong power unit for an all-around road machine.

Transmissions were almost as important as the engine, and Oldsmobile gave 4-4-2 buyers a choice: a heavy-duty three-speed all-synchromesh gearbox, a close-ratio all-synchromesh four-speed gearbox or the Jetaway 400 automatic. Both manual gearboxes came with heavy-duty clutch and floorshifts, and the Jetaway had a console-mounted selector lever.

Heavy-duty propeller shafts were used with all transmission and axle combinations. Special performance axles for the 4-4-2 were geared at 3.23:1 for cars with automatic transmission, and 3.55:1 for cars with synchromesh transmission.

The frame was beefed up, and heavy-duty suspension systems developed. They differed from the standard Cutlass setup mainly in having higher-rate coil springs, heavy-duty front and rear shock absorbers, a reinforced front stabilizer bar and a rear stabilizer bar that was not used on any other model.

Heavy-duty steel wheels with six-inch rims carried either red-line nylon tires or whitewall rayon tires of 7.75-14 dimension. Metallic brake linings were used, with sintered metal embedded in the friction material. They did a good job of raising the fade-limit temperature, but needed extra-high pedal pressure to produce any decelerative effect when cold.

something of commercial importance, Oldsmobile should have its share of it. In the middle of the 1964 model year, the division's 'me-too' answer to the GTO was far enough advanced to be released to the car-buff press for its reactions. Oldsmobile called it the 4-4-2, a designation derived from its 400-cubic-inch V-8, four-barrel carburetor and dual exhausts. We drove one convertible prototype extensively in the spring of 1964, and found that in comparison with the GTO, it had a better ride, quieter engine, and handling characteristics that were broadly similar but differed in the Olds by having less final oversteer. In a drag race, the GTO would pull away unless the driver was caught with too much wheelspin. In actual road driving, the 4-4-2 was equally quick; and in track-test driving, the variation in lap times for each car fell within the same upper and lower limits. Metzel decided to put it on the market as a sports option for the F-85 Club coupe and any model in the 1965 Cutlass series.

"It's the most alert performer in Oldsmobile's entire model lineup," Metzel told the press, "with three outstanding dimensions of performance: responsiveness, handling and road sense."

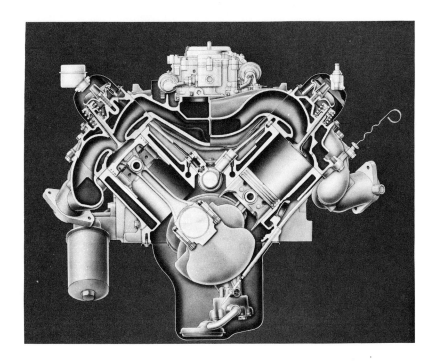

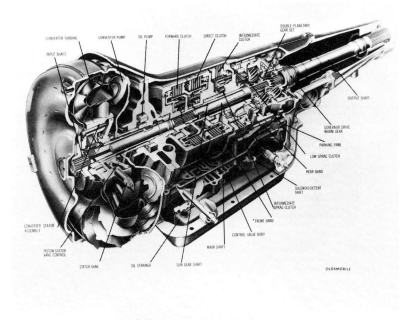

Cross-sectional view of the 425-cubic-inch Super Rocket engine. It benefited from all the advances made in the 330 Jetfire V-8 and was one of the most efficient engines in the industry.

The Turbo Hydra-matic was a combination of the best elements of the old Hydra-matic and Buick's Dynaflow (Super Turbine) transmission, with torque converter instead of fluid coupling, and three-speed planetary gearing.

The 4-4-2 option did not include anything special for the steering, but 4-4-2 buyers had the further option of ordering a heavy-duty manual steering gear (which had a faster ratio but raised the muscle effort beyond normally acceptable levels) or Roto-Matic power steering with a faster-than-standard ratio. A specific instrument panel and steering wheel were part of all 4-4-2 cars, whose exterior identification included a special grille, a louvered hood, simulated air scoops on the rear fenders and special emblems on the rear-end panel.

A new high-performance version of the 330-cubic-inch V-8 was developed for Skylark customers who wanted extra power without going the whole way to the 4-4-2. This new, hot Jetfire V-8 delivered 315 hp at 5200 rpm and was red-lined at 5600 rpm—far above the 4-4-2, which is explained by the difference in stroke between the two engines and Burrell's concern for the torque curve in the 4-4-2 engine. For the high-performance Jetfire engine, low-end torque was sacrificed, and it had its torque peak as high as 3600 rpm (360 pounds-feet).

Oldsmobile's big story for 1965 was, however, the B- and C-body cars. After the frantic, poorly planned body renewals of the late 1950's, which had been extremely costly for Fisher Body Division and the whole corporation, Ed Cole and John F. Gordon had got together to plan a long-term cycle for the A-, B- and C-bodies. Oldsmobile used the A-body for the 1965 F-85 and Cutlass, the C-body for the 98 and the B-body for all models in between.

William L. Mitchell directed the overall styling of the new bodies, fixing their basic proportions. Curved side glass was introduced, in addition to new two- and four-door rooflines. For Oldsmobile, structural changes were few in principle, but nevertheless, a full redesign of the chassis frame and suspension systems became necessary, since the dimensional changes did not permit a simple adaptation of the 1964-model components.

R. W. Perkins, Oldsmobile's chassis engineer, had kept his men working overtime a lot. "It was 1962 when I moved into the chassis group," recalled Dennis

1965 Oldsmobile 98 Holiday sedan. An all-new Fisher C-body was something Oldsmobile shared with the Buick Electra and Cadillac. The engine size was increased to 425 cubic inches.

1965 Oldsmobile Delta 88 Holiday coupe. With its rear fender kickup and very fast roofline, this model became the most copied car of the year.

Condon. "I became the suspension engineer for the full-size cars. That was about the time we developed the forward-mounted steering linkage," Condon went on, "in order to develop what we called compliance understeer. Our philosophy has always been to put understeer into our cars."

Dennis Earl Condon had joined Oldsmobile in September 1952, and worked as a designer for a machine gun program during nine months toward the end of the Korean War. "Then I went into the Air Force for two years and became project officer for the same damn gun I had worked on for Oldsmobile," he said with a grimace. In the fall of 1956, Condon returned to Oldsmobile and was assigned to Andy Watt in the advanced design department.

"I spent four or five years working on transaxles," Condon remembered. "That was a big thing at the time, trying to move the transmission away from the engine, and combining it with the axle. One of the developments that came out of that was the rope-shaft Pontiac Tempest. Oldsmobile and Saginaw were involved with that. But Olds did not use the shaft for its F-85 compact. We did not want vibrations like that, even in our lowest-priced car."

Condon worked in close liaison with the frame and body engineers when the 1965 B- and C-body cars were being prepared. The new frame was, in fact, based on the Chevrolet-designed frame for the intermediate car lines, using C-section side-members rather than the channel-section ones previously favored by Olds.

"We developed a whole series of body mounts," explained Dennis Condon, "where we actually instrumented the cars and measured all the forces that were going between the frame and body through the body mounts. We had triaxial load cells that were actually placed on top of the body mounts, and we were able to measure where all the various loads were going between the body and the frame.

"This project led to body mounts that had different characteristics in all three planes. Olds had a very soft, well-isolated ride, before most of the industry got to that. This involved not only the size and shape of the mounts, but the ability to core body mounts out in certain directions. Our body mount might have a very low rate fore-and-aft, a very stiff rate laterally; and with fourteen or sixteen individual body mounts in the car, we actually tuned each one for particular characteristics depending on where it was located."

Wheelbases remained unchanged, at 123 inches for the B-body models and 126 inches for the C-body cars; but the track was widened to 62.5 inches in front and 63 inches in the rear.

Station wagons were taken out of the big-car series, leaving that market to the intermediate series with two sizes: the basic wagon on the standard 115-inch wheelbase and the Vista-Cruiser on a 120-inch wheelbase. The model lineup was modified, a new Delta 88 appearing to take the place of the superannuated Super 88.

The styling was nothing short of sensational. Stanley R. Wilen, chief designer of the Oldsmobile studio, had brought the standard Oldsmobile from wallflowerhood to stardom. The sleek lines, balanced proportions and the dramatic rear-fender kickup made Oldsmobile the most spectacularly new of all GM's 1965 models. The tucked-under rocker-panel/doorsill lines made the cars look inches lower than those of rival manufacturers, and the very fast roofline of the two-door models created an illusion of speed.

1965 Oldsmobile 4-4-2 convertible. The 4-4-2 was Oldsmobile's answer to the Pontiac GTO, with a 400-cubic-inch V-8 (enlarged from the 330 block), four-barrel carburetor and dual exhausts.

Oldsmobile offered a total of thirty-two different models for 1965, thirteen intermediates and nineteen full-size cars.

Body Style	Jetstar 88	Jetstar I	Dynamic 88
Celebrity sedan	$2,938		$3,008
Holiday sedan	3,072		3,143
Holiday coupe	2,995	$3,602	3,065
Convertible coupe	3,337		3,408

Body Style	Delta 88	Starfire	98
Celebrity sedan	$3,158		
Holiday sedan	3,330		$4,273
Holiday coupe	3,253	$4,148	4,197
Town sedan			4,001
Luxury sedan			4,351
Convertible coupe		4,778	4,493

When it is realized that the faithful 394-cubic-inch engine had been replaced by a new design of 425-cubic-inch displacement for 1965, within a year after the 330 Jetfire V-8 was brought out and developed in parallel with the 4-4-2 engine, one might well wonder whether Gil Burrell and Frank Ball were just code names for whole engineering teams or whether they were individuals who worked around-the-clock.

How they were able to accomplish what they did, with the limited means of a medium-size manufacturer like Oldsmobile, may never be fully known, but their achievement is a feat that commands the highest respect. In 1965 Burrell was promoted to staff engineer in charge of advance engine design, relieving him from the pressures of current-production deadlines and day-to-day management of engine programs. Frank Ball then took over as motor engineer.

R. James Benner was named motor development engineer for Oldsmobile in December 1966, and was to prove his worth in a succession of new engine projects

1965 Oldsmobile Jetstar I. It was built in only one body style, two-door hardtop, and its role was to offer a Starfire-type automobile at a much lower price.

and in connection with a serious new headache for all engine manufacturers: emission-control systems.

Gil Burrell retired on April 1, 1970. "It's been a lot of fun, and it's been a lot of hard work," Burrell remarked as he reflected on his career with Oldsmobile. "Those were exciting years for the industry, just as the years ahead certainly are going to be." If he had said troublesome, he would have been proved to be even closer to the truth.

The 425-cubic-inch V-8 was dubbed Super Rocket by the marketing men. Burrell had created it by keeping the 4.125-inch bore of the 394 Rocket V-8 and adding the bottom end of the 4-4-2 engine with its heftier crankshaft, producing a 3.975-inch stroke.

Many of the lessons from the 330 Jetfire program were applied to this redesign, so that the 425 was substantially lighter than the 394, despite an eight-percent increase in displacement. Novel details included stamped rocker arms and integrally cast valve guides. At 618 pounds complete, the engine weighed only sixty-four pounds more than the 330-cubic-inch V-8!

"With horsepower ratings from 310 to 370, the new engine will greatly enhance the outstanding reputation Oldsmobile has already earned in the performance field," said John B. Beltz, the chief engineer.

The new engine shared the primary dimensions with the 394, so as to avoid tooling changes. Cylinder bore spacing, crankshaft-to-camshaft span, valve-lifter bore spacing, head stud pattern, and so on, remained exactly the same, and were shared with the 330 Jetfire engine, also developed from the same source.

Compared with the 330, the new 425 block had a 1.30-inch-higher deck and one-inch-longer connecting rods (seven inches, center to center).

The 330 engine shared valve sizes with the 394, with valve head diameters of 1.88 inches for the intakes and 1.56 inches for the exhausts. These dimensions, Burrell felt, were inadequate for the 425, so he increased the intake valve head diameter to an even 2.00 inches and that for the exhaust valves to 1.63 inches.

In the adoption of stamped rocker arms, Burrell had taken a leaf from Pontiac's V-8. He was intrigued with the lower cost of the stud-mounted ball-joint principle as an alternative to the rocker shaft, but worried about the risk of the rocker arm going into a swiveling motion and causing the pushrods to rub against the walls of their guide holes in the head. He invented a compromise, using a half-cylindrical base for the rocker arm mounts. It acted as a short section of the rocker shaft, carried on a stud threaded into the head and kept in alignment by a bridge linking the two valve mounts for each cylinder.

Other refinements included chrome plating on certain areas of the hydraulic valve lifters for longer life, and taking the axial thrust on the crankshaft center bearing (instead of the rear one) to eliminate loss of oil past the rear seal.

The 310-hp version was standard in the Delta 88 and Dynamic 88, while the 98 was equipped with a 360-hp version. The 370-hp Starfire version was used in the Jetstar I and Starfire models.

These engines were teamed with a new Turbo Hydra-matic transmission, which differed from the Accel-A-Rotor design in having a hydraulic torque converter with variable vanes (as on the smaller Jetaway). It could be called an enlarged, high-torque version of the Jetaway, but differed mechanically in having three forward speeds in place of two, and water cooling instead of air cooling. Oldsmobile claimed that it gave up to forty percent more torque from a standing start than the Accel-A-Rotor Hydra-matic of 1964.

"In addition," said John Beltz, "Oldsmobile for the first time is offering in all 88's, Jetstar I and Starfire models, a four-speed, floor-mounted manual transmission, fully synchronized in all gears." Oldsmobile's transmission engineer, W. A. Weidman, and his staff had clearly had their hands full while the '65's were being developed.

On the Starfire, the Turbo Hydra-matic was shifted by a T-stick on the console between the front bucket seats. Power steering and self-adjusting power brakes, with wider drums and linings, were standard on all Starfires. The convertible also had power seats and windows as standard. It weighed 4,402 pounds and had a top speed of 124 mph. The lightest of the B-body cars, the Jetstar 88, weighed 3,922 pounds and had a top speed of 115 mph.

Oldsmobile was consciously and deliberately coming out on the performance side, and at the time it was not regarded as a main drawback that fuel economy was suffering. Still, it was widely noticed that Oldsmobile suffered a severe defeat in the 1965 Mobilgas Economy Run from Los Angeles to New York City.

The 98 came fourth in its class (luxury cars) at 15.8 mpg, beaten by the Chrysler New Yorker (17.3 mph), Buick Electra and Cadillac Sedan de Ville. The Dynamic 88 could do no better than seventh in its class with 17.1 mpg, where the top three (Pontiac Catalina, Pontiac Star Chief and Buick LeSabre) averaged better than 19.6 mpg. Even the Jetstar 88, competing in the same class, was only fourth best, at 18.1 mpg, beaten by cars with larger and more powerful engines.

These beautiful but thirsty new Oldsmobiles were coming into a market where the rival models from Chrysler, Dodge, Ford and Mercury also sported new body styling. Dodge had fourteen Polara, Custom 880 and Monaco models, with prices beginning at $2,745. Mercury had fifteen models with horsepower up to 425, and Chrysler had seventeen models with engines up to 360 hp. The Thunderbird came with a 300-hp engine as standard, and a list price of $4,486.

A thirty-nine-day strike against General Motors halted Oldsmobile production from September 25 to November 3, 1964, just as the 1965 models were beginning to come off the line. This gave the competition a picnic, and despite a lot of double-shift working during the winter that followed the settling of the strike, it is doubtful that Oldsmobile ever made up for that loss.

The market expanded to 9.3 million cars and Oldsmobile sold a total of 608,930 cars, increasing its market share to 6.54 percent. The B- and C-body models accounted for 391,413 or 64.3 percent, as the F-85's advance was still faster.

Looking at the individual series, we see that the relative success of the Delta 88 was bought at the expense of the Dynamic 88. The Jetstar 88 declined, while the 98 made a strong advance, and the Starfire held its own. What enabled Oldsmobile to hold on to fifth place in the rankings (after Plymouth had retaken fourth position) was the healthy sales of the intermediates (45,008 wagons and 172,509 others). Still, Buick came within 310 cars of equaling the Olds total, and its Special was running nearly 10,000 units ahead of the F-85.

At the end of the year, R. E. Elliott, the division's controller, was able to report to Metzel that profits were running at a very sound level, and prospects for the rest of the sixties were excellent.

Oldsmobile produced its nine-millionth car on January 21, 1965. R. T. Rollis proudly presents the newcomer alongside the nine-thousandth Oldsmobile, a 7-hp single-cylinder curved-dash model built in 1903.

John B. Beltz

CHAPTER 12

Toronado!

FRONT-WHEEL-DRIVE PROJECTS had been undertaken by Oldsmobile almost at the same time compact car studies began in earnest. Jack Wolfram was general manager in those days, and he must get the credit for providing the funds for them.

Andrew K. Watt, manager of the advanced design section, had been doing a lot of work since 1956 on big-car chassis with front-mounted engines, rear drive and rear-mounted transmissions (transaxles).

When it became clear that none of several designs, no matter how clever and intelligent they were, could pass the cost-accounting exam needed for getting into production, he turned his attention, logically, to the alternative solution for getting better traction in a car with a heavy, front-mounted engine: front-wheel drive. He began talking to his colleagues about it — Metzel, Lewis, Dorshimer, Beltz and others.

At first, they were afraid to consider it as a realistic idea for production cars, because there was a fearsome monstrosity about it. It would so fundamentally change the whole car that a million snags were likely to crop up; sharing components with other models would be difficult; and costs could be, well, prohibitive. Besides, the idea seemed to fall into the domain that the GM Engineeering Staff had staked out for itself: something too experimental by nature, and too vast in its implications, for one of the car divisions to tackle on its own.

The latter consideration prompted John Beltz to ask facetiously: "If they're supposed to be looking into it for us, let's ask Chayne [Charles A. Chayne, GM vice president in charge of the Engineering Staff] how far along they are." Metzel, suspecting that there was nothing going on there in the way of front-wheel drive, smiled one of his patient smiles, and replied: "Why don't you look in the library and see if they have sent us any reports on it?"

That may sound like a careless, light-hearted remark, or perhaps even a put-down, but Metzel was not only too kind a person for that, he was also dead serious about building up his basic knowledge of front-wheel drive. Now, Beltz had probably read every report that Oldsmobile had ever received from the Engineering Staff, and knew full well that none had been issued concerning the engineering of front-wheel drive.

As assistant chief engineer, John Beltz had a lot of engineering management duties and a desk full of other business, but he left a mental searchlight on for front-wheel-drive information. It caught on two things stored in his memory: one was the Universelle, the second, the La Salle II.

The first was a joint project between GMC Truck and Coach Division and the Styling Staff; the other involved Cadillac, GM Styling and the Engineering Staff.

Many variations of the Toronado were designed and evaluated. One feature that ran through all was the prominence of the wheels and the half-circular bulge in the fenders.

In the Oldsmobile styling studio, Dave North directs an assistant making measurements of seating dimensions in the Toronado design.

Artists in the Oldsmobile studio painted a life-size Toronado on the wall to develop a pattern for its final appearance before going into three-dimensional model-making.

The Universelle was an experimental forward-control panel truck, built in 1954 to designs by Maurice Thorne (who had spent many years of his career with Oldsmobile) and Gil Roddewig. It had a V-8 engine positioned behind the front wheel axis, with independent front suspension using torsion bars. Coil springs could not be used in their normal position, as they would have interfered with the front-wheel drive shafts.

The La Salle II was a four-door hardtop, created partly as a show car for the 1955 GM Motorama display, and partly as a feasibility study on front-wheel-drive application to large cars with automatic transmission. The design work was undertaken by the GM Engineering Staff. The V-8 engine was installed in its usual place, with chain drive to the transmission located alongside the oil pan, its output end in front. The power flow went into a final drive unit located below and to the side of the forward part of the block, with shafts to the front wheels on either side. Again, torsion-bar independent front suspension was used.

The drive line was not finished in time for the show, and few people who saw the La Salle II became aware that it was intended to be a front-wheel-drive car, for it went on its display stand without an engine.

It served as a styling prototype, and that was it. No follow-up was undertaken in the way of testing or development. Consequently, GM's Engineering Staff could not say whether the idea was practical or not. The project remained at the theoretical level, though John Malloy wrote in a report: "Some of the advantages offered by the unified power package were potential weight savings and compactness gained by combining the engine, transmission, final reduction gearing, and differential into one package; the elimination of the floor hump; and the opening of new approaches to vehicle styling."

Beltz began developing closer ties with the Engineering Staff with a view to establishing a framework for front-wheel-drive concepts, and he was to become involved with every phase of the experimental projects that followed.

John B. Beltz was born in Lansing in 1926 and attended local schools. After graduating from Eastern High School in 1944, he enlisted in the U.S. Navy and served till the end of the war, attaining the rank of ensign. He kept up his studies as an officer trainee, and in June 1946, was awarded his Bachelor of Science degree from the University of Michigan.

In August 1946, he found a job with Reo Motors in Lansing as a clerk in the engineering specifications department. Six months later he left Reo and joined Oldsmobile as a senior engineering clerk in the engine dynamometer laboratory. He was bright, and he was ambitious, advancing rapidly through various assignments to engineering test supervisor. Metzel named him experimental engineer in 1951, and in 1956 Beltz was appointed assistant chief engineer.

In connection with the front-wheel-drive project, Beltz was at once the overseer and coordinator, its champion and promoter. But it cannot be said that he created the Toronado. If any man can be called 'father of the Toronado,' it must be Andrew K. Watt, who was in charge of advanced design engineering and prototype construction. He was an electrical engineer with a degree from the University of Utah and had about two years' experience working in the industry when he came to Oldsmobile in 1931.

His first job at Oldsmobile was as a test engineer in the product engineering department under John G. Wood. He went on to work as a chassis project engineer and senior project engineer. During the war he was called an ordnance-materials engineer. It is as a transmission engineer that he is best known and remembered among his colleagues, being associated with the development of the Hydra-matic from 1946 to 1956. He was highly versatile, and an inventor with five patents to his credit, in such diverse fields as mechanical linkages, ventilation systems and electrical switches.

Andy Watt became advanced design engineer in 1956 and three years later prepared the first design studies for a front-wheel-drive Oldsmobile. The earliest drawings show a car with unit-body construction, 112-inch wheelbase and the 215-cubic-inch Rockette engine. In other words, a compact car, far smaller and lighter than the production-model Toronado.

Why was the smaller vehicle chosen? And why did it grow into a full-size car? "We had noticed that in Europe, where front drive was popular for small cars, they used rear-wheel drive as soon as the engines got to around 120 cubic inches or so," a veteran Oldsmobile engineer explained. "There was no technological limit to the use of front-wheel drive with bigger engines, as far as we could see, and we believe that the European situation existed entirely for other reasons. Our calculations told us we could use any size engine in the unified power package we were working with. We had no worries about the amount of torque any of our engines would put into the front wheels. Our choice of the smaller engine was based on political considerations.

"The full-size cars were getting pretty full of common components, and the corporation was always pushing us for more integration with other divisions, sharing more and more to get the cost down. We did not think it would be possible to get approval for coming in with a front-drive model in that size, flying in the face of everything they were trying to accomplish.

"We thought we'd have better chances of getting front drive into production if we used it on the compact. After all, Chevy had a rear engine in their X-body car, so if we wanted to do one with front drive, it would be more difficult to find reasons to stop us. So we went ahead and built our first front-drive prototypes on the F-85."

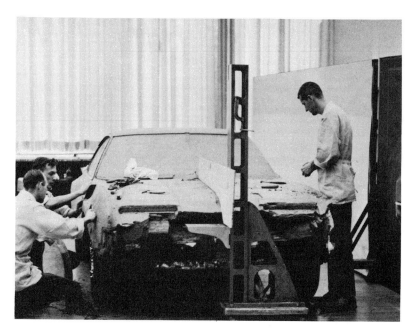

The first clay model of the Toronado was created by copying the shape and proportions of the airbrush painting. Center separation permits development of two versions side by side on the same car.

Watt discussed the technical options with Beltz and Metzel, and they agreed to enlist the services of the GM Engineering Staff in order to avoid spreading the engineering resources of the division too thin.

According to a report, "The division requested that the GM Engineering Staff design and build a two-speed transmission for a package using a chain transfer drive arrangement. This package was of three basic parts—engine, transmission, and final drive—and, when installed in an experimental vehicle, became the first running installation in GM's front drive program."

In this experimental car, the 215-cubic-inch all-aluminum V-8 was mounted transversely, with chain drive in two stages: first from the engine to the transmission, and then a second stage from the transmission output shaft to the differential.

The car was completed in the spring of 1960 and went into a basic test program on the GM Proving Grounds. "It had a unit-construction body with a front stub frame to carry the unified power package," reported A. K. Watt, "The drive

Preliminary clay model of the Toronado was shown to top corporate managers, and got their approval for production. The next step was to build a prototype with seating, instrumentation and controls.

Rear view of the 1966 Toronado chassis shows the utter simplicity of the rear suspension. The frame ended ahead of the axle, and the body structure provided anchorage points for the rear spring shackles.

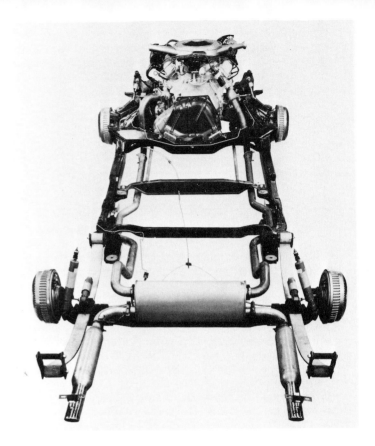

shafts used constant-velocity Rzeppa joints at the wheels and non-constant velocity joints capable of lateral displacement at the differential. The car weighed 3,363 pounds, and its performance and handling characteristics were highly encouraging. It exhibited good directional stability. There were areas where additional development work was needed, mainly in the drive shafts and chains. In July 1960, the test car was rebuilt, and incorporated, among other changes, new upper-control arm bushings and constant-velocity inner universal joints that provided shudder-free drive shaft performance.''

Metzel asked Hydra-matic Division to assist with the development of a silent chain drive, and a supplier, Morse Division of Borg-Warner, became associated with this part of the project.

On their own, Olds engineers tried cogged belts instead of drive chains. But the steel-reinforced belts stretched and wore out, and the cog-type pulleys became noisy. So that was not the answer.

Andy Watt and Jack Wallace also drew up a gear drive system that was built and tested. This design required several precision-mounted bearings to assure low-friction operation and to control the high thrust forces. An idler gear provided the proper rotational direction on the output gear. It was compact, presented simple lubrication needs and promised long life. The noise problem was less than with the initial chain drives, and it looked like the lower-cost solution. But further studies indicated that chain drive, in fact, offered the most advantages.

Jim Lewis came up with the idea of splitting the Hydra-matic transmission in two, with the engine driving through the torque converter to a chain sprocket with cross-drive to the planetary gear trains. This location for the torque converter proved to be the key to successful development of the chain drive, for it became apparent from the results of laboratory testing that when the torque converter was interposed between the engine and the chain, the torque peaks from the engine were sufficiently cushioned to smooth out the input load stresses on the chain. This configuration, therefore, gave more satisfactory noise levels and chain durability.

By January 1963, the first test car was running with this drive train layout. But it was no longer a compact, for outside influences were beginning to bear on Oldsmobile's planning for the use of front-wheel drive.

As early as 1961, Cadillac had expressed an interest in front-wheel drive, and the GM Engineering Staff expanded its work in this area beyond what Oldsmobile

Unified power package for the Toronado shows U-turn in the drive line, between the torque converter and the planetary gear sets. Two-thirds of the engine weight was carried inside the wheelbase.

The drive from the torque converter to the planetary gearing was taken by a Morse chain. This reversed the rotation in the mechanical part, but without causing problems further down the line.

had requested. Later that year, test cars with unified power packages and 429-cubic-inch Cadillac engines were built. This experience was to have some value relative to the outcome of Oldsmobile's work.

While the Olds engineers were plugging away at the front-wheel-drive compact, the sales department started to do some market research. This was at the time the Ford Thunderbird had its greatest success, sales climbing over 70,000 cars a year; and Pontiac launched its Grand Prix as a personal/specialty car market extension of the Bonneville, king of oval-track stock car racing. Both were big cars, with price tags shamelessly out of proportion to their utility.

Now the Oldsmobile studies indicated that people who bought cars of sporty appearance and high power in this price class were more ready than other people to try something as new and different as front-wheel drive.

Consequently, the program was reoriented toward a full-size car, powered by the division's biggest V-8, instead of the smallest. There were certain advantages in this. The Rockette V-8 had been too light to make much difference in traction and down-the-road stability, but the use of the cast-iron Super Rocket engine gave full benefits in these areas.

The existence of the front-wheel-drive car as a distinct project became formalized under the code name XP-784. This designation came from GM Styling where a body design concept that Mitchell wanted to promote for future use had been allocated that number.

Toronado engine and transmission, 1966. A planetary-type differential was used because of space problems. Drive shaft to right front wheel crossed below the oil pan.

Before the two ideas—Oldsmobile's front-wheel drive on one side, and the Styling concept on the other—came together, nobody had much of an idea of the kind of car a front-wheel-drive Olds could be. It is important to realize that the two existed independently.

"The Toronado was developed up in Lansing, and Metzel and Beltz came to Bill Mitchell and said they had this front-wheel-drive vehicle and what could he do around it?" Irv Rybicki recalled.

Moving swiftly, GM Styling prepared full-size drawings to study the mechanical requirements of the car. Seating mock-ups were built to check the car's various dimensions. The project was an exhilarating one for engineers and designers alike, because front-wheel drive offered design proportions and styling freedom beyond what was experienced in conventional cars.

While radical ideas may appear sound on paper, it remains for a three-dimensional examination to determine their final merit. Skilled sculptors set to work building a clay model of the unborn car. Working with micrometer precision, the sculptors prepared a clay-model Toronado complete with actual wheels and tires and detail hardware such as door handles and headlights. Plastic sheets simulated

glass areas, and metal foil was used to create chrome and brightwork on the car's body.

On a cold day in February 1963, the clay model was moved outdoors at the vast GM Technical Center in suburban Warren for evaluation. The reaction was enthusiastic. A further 'go-ahead' was issued.

Ed Donaldson started the interior styling of the car that spring. By January 1964, the interior was modeled in clay, and given tentative approval. Meanwhile, the full-size clay model was continuously being refined and altered, both to meet production requirements and to reflect subsequent engineering modifications as well as styling improvements. At last, when Oldsmobile issued a full approval of the clay model, casting in plaster was ordered.

From these molds, GM Styling's fabrication shop made fiberglass panels. Mounted on a dummy chassis with special frames, these rigid panels were painted, chromed and made to appear real in every detail. The first fiberglass model was reviewed by Oldsmobile and corporate management in mid-1963. Various changes and revisions were ordered. Thus the Toronado progressed along several parallel paths—styling on one track and various engineering programs on other tracks.

For the XP-784 program it was decided that the GM Engineering Staff would spearhead the power-package design and develop the initial frame concept. Oldsmobile and Fisher Body would concentrate on the chassis and underbody engineering. That way, the Fisher Body engineers were allowed greater leeway in seeking the best solutions for adapting a body to a semi-integral frame concept, which Oldsmobile wanted, perhaps due to its experience with the modified X-body prototypes.

The first XP-784 test vehicle was built in 1961 as a Super 88 with a transversely mounted 394-cubic-inch V-8 and the split transmission. It had a planetary differential, purely for space considerations, and not because of any technical advantage, or the particular needs of driven front wheels.

The brake drums were mounted inboard on the drive shafts, and the suspension systems reworked with the coil springs on top of the upper control arm (instead of standing on the lower arm). Later, they went to torsion bar springing, with a short, laminated type of torsion bar linked to the lower control-arm pivot shaft. The torsion bar was only eighteen inches long, again due to space limitations, and not to any search for unusual or advanced solutions. There were problems enough just getting the basic idea to work.

General Motors obtained its first experience with torsion bars when Maurice Olley created a new Dubonnet-type suspension system for the 1939 Vauxhall, using the torsion bars as the main load-carrying element, and letting the hydraulically damped coil spring serve as an auxiliary. Next, GM designed the T-20 tank in 1942, using torsion-bar suspension. This system was subsequently scaled up and applied to the M-26 and other tanks.

About 1947, the GM Engineering Staff, in a joint program with Saginaw Steering Gear Division, prepared a torsion-bar suspension for the front axle of a six-wheel-drive military truck; and in 1952, an independent front suspension system with torsion bars was installed on a prototype 1955-model car, which did not go into production. Because of such exercises, nobody at Oldsmobile had any qualms about using torsion bars, even if it meant a total redesign with a variety of new aspects.

Oldsmobile's engineers had an open mind on all elements of the XP-784. For instance, disc brakes were tried experimentally, both in inboard and outboard mounting positions. But cost considerations, and an incomplete understanding of the actual brake-system requirements of a 4,500-pound front-wheel-drive vehicle, led Metzel to insist on a drum-brake solution.

An early brake design featured drums mounted directly on the wheel hubs, protruding to the outer side for improved cooling. The wheel was a new type, bolted directly to the brake drums with a ten-inch-wide circle of eight bolts near the drum periphery.

Manufacturing complications and unfavorable cost calculations killed that idea—the final design had conventionally mounted drums. They were made of iron for its good heat-sink capacity, had a wide section to provide extra friction surface area and were provided with cast-in cooling ribs along the circumference, as well as on the annular section surrounding the flange.

After a number of modifications had been made to the first car, a redesign was carried out, and new prototypes were made toward the end of 1962. Four bodies were handmade by Fisher Body: three of them went to the GM Engineering Staff, the fourth to Oldsmobile. As test results were reported, Fisher built a second-generation body in five examples.

"The cars," James Diener told us, "were 1964-model Dynamic 88's with bodies converted to flat-floor and integral body construction to simulate the final design, with the hood, grille and fenders reworked to suit the front-wheel-drive mechanism."

These cars had a stub frame where two side-members extended backward from the engine cradle, with no crossways connection between them aft of the rear engine mounts, and carried body mounts at their rear end. The rear suspension was carried directly in attachment points on the body shell.

On the road, test cars demonstrated insufficient torsional and beaming strength on rough road surfaces. Road noise was excessive, and a resonant beaming shake would occur on turnpikes. The complaints were alleviated by extending the side-members to a line below the rear seat, and installing a cross-member, tying their rear points together under the floor.

The front-wheel drive was successful in terms of performance, traction was superb, the steering and handling were safe and surefooted. But there were lots of problems that would have to be sorted out long before it got to the prototype stage. The drive chains were noisy, and the transmission was not free of shudder. The engine rocked under torque reactions, and the universal joints showed abnormal wear.

The transverse engine installation was generally satisfactory. There was a tendency for the engine to rock on its mounts during torque reversals, which could

Pre-production Toronado undergoing tests on the GM Proving Grounds at Milford, Michigan. It was given the most thorough testing of any Oldsmobile ever.

adversely affect both the ride and the steering, but could certainly have been cured in the course of normal development work.

By May 1962, the engine had been turned around to its conventional plane. The major reason for this move was that Cadillac was interested in getting its own front-wheel-drive car, and at this time Cadillac was developing a V-12 engine that would absolutely not fit transversely. In order to enable Cadillac to share the concept and the body, Oldsmobile was persuaded to change the position of the engine.

Of course, Oldsmobile might sooner or later have come around to that decision by itself, without 'help' from the corporation, for it did ease some of the space problems of the installation. It freed more room for the suspension system and eliminated the need for a wholesale change in the cooling system and the use of electric fan drive. The longitudinal-axis engine installation, however, proved far from trouble-free.

Because of the drive train layout, the engine had to be positioned higher up than in the B- and C-body Oldsmobiles using the same engine. This became a problem for the air cleaner installation, since the hood line for the Toronado was lower. To get around this, the engine specialists had to develop a new intake manifold, bent down in the middle, with a lower carburetor flange, and a specific low-profile air filter had to be made. Fast-thinking Frank Ball quickly adapted it from the 1959-model design.

"The runners from the carburetor flange ran upwards into the cylinder head," Frank Ball remembered, "and that meant problems with starting and fuel-mixture distribution. The second problem was the hump we put in the oil pan to get the engine as low as we could."

The engine was installed 1.82 inches off center toward the right, and slightly forward of the front wheel axis (the central main bearing was located about an inch forward of the center line between the wheels).

In the initial drive shaft design, the final drive housing carried an extension to the right, crossing below the crankcase, in front of a shortened oil sump. But this layout did not permit the engine to be mounted as far forward as the vehicle's architecture demanded. An intermediate solution followed, with a full-length oil sump and a welded-in tube running through it, as a tunnel for the right-side drive shaft. Finally, an oil pan shape was developed that permitted the use of an open drive shaft, passing outside the oil sump.

"That hump was towards the back of the oil pan," Frank Ball continued, "and we had to get the oil up over the hump. This was difficult. We put this trough in the side so when the crankshaft was slinging the oil around, the trough would pick it up and bring it back into the pan. It did keep the oil from collecting in front, and the production version was trouble-free."

In February 1964, Oldsmobile demonstrated its Toronado prototype to a group of top GM executives at the Desert Proving Ground in Mesa, Arizona. "Ed Cole wasn't very keen on it at first," recalled a test engineer, "and there was Oscar Lundin to pour cold water on anything that wasn't guaranteed to make money."

Apparently, Metzel did not take a very strong stand in arguing the case for going into production with the XP-784. "It was Beltz who sold the corporation on the program," Harry Lyon recounted. "Beltz was one of a kind. You know how they talk of charisma. John had it. He was a hell of a leader. He could inspire people more than anybody I've ever seen."

With Ed Cole convinced, the rest came easy. Harry Barr was then head of the GM Engineering Staff, and he had worked a great deal of his career under Cole at Chevrolet, and there was a certain similarity of technical thought in the two.

The Engineering Staff also had put a lot into the front-wheel-drive project, and its success could enhance the Staff's prestige within the corporation. Barr became an advocate.

John F. Gordon was close to retirement, and took a neutral attitude toward the project, while, suprisingly, Frederic G. Donner, the chairman, whose background was entirely in finance, welcomed the idea and lent his support. Within weeks, Oldsmobile received approval from the president's office to go ahead with the production and marketing of the XP-784—under certain conditions.

It had to share a new Fisher E-body, then in preparation for Buick's Riviera. Buick was building the Riviera at a rate of about 40,000 cars a year, with a unique body that inevitably turned out to be exceedingly expensive to produce. Replacing it

with a new body, designed to be shared with one or more other divisions, was sure to bring the cost down. Both Buick and Oldsmobile were in favor of the plan, so far. But it nearly came a cropper due to another attempt on the part of the corporation to dictate product engineering. Ed Cole wanted Buick to share the front-wheel drive as well, but Ed Rollert, general manager of Buick, and his chief engineer, Lowell Kintigh, balked.

The whole project was stalled until Buick was able to prove its ability to fit the new E-body on the Riviera's existing cruciform frame and retain the drive line to the rear axle—at minimal cost and no big change in the E-body. The divisional studios turned out strikingly different exterior sheet metal for the two, with the result that they did not even look like sister cars, and could hardly have been more different under the skin. All they shared was the basic underbody, including the floor, wheelbase and cowl structure.

The Toronado was a creation by David North, assistant chief designer of the Oldsmobile studio. It was a fastback sport coupe with a long hood intended for a compact-car chassis. With its heavy front overhang and unique roofline, it was a most visibly different shape from anything Oldsmobile was building at the time. And then there was the fender line, repeating the wheel-opening theme in the fender crown line.

The fender treatment was based on a line that had been 'kicked around a lot' at GM Styling, according to an insider at the time. That statement implies that it did not necessarily originate with the Oldsmobile studio, and also suggests that the several divisions had all been trying without luck to find a suitable car to put it on.

But Leonard Casillo, who took over as chief designer of the Oldsmobile studio in 1971, points out that "Olds was always strongly wheel-oriented. Pontiac has cultivated a venturi shape over the years. Buick has dealt with lines that cross from the front of the car to the rear. Olds goes for wheel-oriented shapes."

A lot of work went into making a wheel opening that conformed to the wheel profile. Filler-plate clearances were established by actual measurements taken on a pre-test car during severe driving maneuvers. The resultant wheel opening line then was given to GM Styling where the line was refined but remained basically unchanged.

"Those wheel flares," Casillo went on, "the concentric, very simple geometrical design wheel opening with the bold flare on top, that has since become one of Oldsmobile's identifying marks."

Terry Tetens of the GM Engineering Staff did wind tunnel tests on Toronado body quarter-scale models, and led the development of the body ventilation system for the XP-784.

Francis E. Smith was head of the Fisher Body program to turn the GM Styling creations into a manufacturable body. His task can be summed up as taking the styling designs and creating a structure inside the styling configuration, working out design criteria and clearing the way for production design. Next, his group had to engineer the tools needed to form the various body parts. Fabrication of individual body components remained the responsibility of Fisher Body Division, as well as assembling the body and delivering it to the car division. The Toronado body was produced at the Euclid plant of Fisher Body in Cleveland, Ohio.

It was still early in 1964 when Metzel decided to get the car ready for production as a 1966 model. That concluded the exploratory phase of the project, and it was taken out of Andy Watt's advanced design section and handed over to the regular design and development groups to handle the intensive work needed to prepare the car for production.

"We considered," John Beltz wrote in a technical paper, "the possibility of maintaining the Toronado as a separate project and pulling specialists from the various groups to work on the car, the thought being that progress could be better followed with the work under the control of one relatively small group of people. This approach was eventually rejected because it was too limiting. We needed to tap the abilities of the entire organization."

All parts that were to be unique for the Toronado had to be redesigned for production. Material specifications had to be determined, production methods considered and decisions made about manufacturing in-house or contracting for parts from outside suppliers. Assembly processes had to be reviewed, and in fact, Oldsmobile found it necessary to set up a separate assembly line for the Toronado!

The period that followed was a highlight in Harry Lyon's career. "It was perhaps the last one-division whole-new-car program," he said, proudly adding, "and Olds did that. Designed the whole car, new from wheel to wheel. It was a significant change for all of us, and the most exciting thing ever."

Lyon was working as a transmission development engineer then, and was involved with the most critical areas of the car. He had joined Oldsmobile in 1959 as a student at the GM Institute in the cooperative engineering program. His first job after graduation was as junior project engineer in the Olds experimental laboratory. In 1961 he became project engineer, advancing to senior project engineer three years later, and by the end of 1965, he held the title of supervisor of test engineering.

Howard Kehrl was also associated with the development of the Toronado drive train, at the design level where Tom Krieg was the key man.

Thomas J. Krieg had joined Oldsmobile in 1953 as a graduate-in-training, after graduation from Tri-State College in 1951 and two years' experience as a methods engineer with Reo Motors in Lansing. His career at Oldsmobile took him from the position of detailer through jobs as test engineer, project engineer and senior project engineer, to assistant transmission engineer by 1963.

Why did the Toronado drive line turn out that way? Tom Krieg explained: "The final drive unit was located on the front of the transmission and on the lower left-hand side of the engine. This had a great deal of influence on the choice of ring gear and pinion design. A spiral bevel design was selected to eliminate the problems caused by pinion offset, for the use of a hypoid bevel, with the pinion either below or above the ring gear center line, would have run the right-hand drive shaft either through the engine crank throw radius or so far down that the ground clearance would have been reduced to an unacceptable degree. The spiral bevel design eliminated these problems and gave a 6.4-inch ground clearance with a five-passenger load in the car."

J. P. Norbye tested the Toronado on the GM Proving Grounds in July 1965. Many of its shortcomings became apparent only after many miles of actual highway driving.

Because of the spatial confinement imposed by the layout, special attention was applied to the differential gears themselves. A completely new planetary-gear differential was designed by the GM Engineering Staff, described as a 'pancake-axle' with minimum width. Oldsmobile, however, had no factory capacity for building it, and its production was farmed out to Buick.

Torque flow entered the differential from the 3.21:1 reduction of the pinion and ring gear. The differential case was provided with an internal ring gear, serving as a track for three planet gears grouped around a central sun gear. By this arrangement the torque was split, half going into the differential pinions and through the planet-gear pinion carrier into the left-side drive shaft. The other half was transferred through the pinion gears to the sun gear, and then to the right-side drive shaft.

During differential action, as for a left turn, the planet pinion carrier ran at a slower speed than the outer ring gear (annulus), forcing the pinions to overspeed the sun gear by a corresponding amount.

The right-side drive shaft was split, with an inboard and running in a fixed position, anchored at its outer end in a bearing carried on a bracket extending from forces for maximum drive-line smoothness.

The final design used a constant-velocity Rzeppa joint at each inboard and outboard position. The joint consisted of six balls in a cage, running between inner and outer races; the balls carrying the torque from the inner to the outer race. The cage kept the balls aligned at an angle that bisected the joint angle no matter where the wheels were pointed, and thereby assured constant-velocity characteristics. There was no slip in the joint because of the curvature on the ball races.

A ball spline was added to the inner joint to provide the necessary freedom for axial-length variations in the shaft, due to the swinging of the suspension arms during spring deflection.

Because of the steering layout, the outer joint needed freedom to move through sixty degrees in steering (thirty degrees each way). It was found that there was overtravel on the outside wheel in turning, which caused joint angles as high as forty-three degrees. On the inner joint, total angularity was kept down to plus-or-minus fifteen degrees.

The front suspension had a stamped A-frame upper control arm with eccentric cam-type caster and camber adjustment, and a lower control arm assembled from heavy box-section stampings. Compression-type lower ball joints were used because they needed less space than the tension type, and therefore were more favorable to front-wheel-drive installation.

Torsion bars extended longitudinally backward from the lower control arm pivot shaft to anchorage points on a stub-frame cross-member under the front seat. Steering knuckles were made with integral steering arms and dual wheel stops, and live wheel spindles were carried in double-row ball bearings.

The front wheel alignment used a negative scrub radius to eliminate drive train and steering linkage vibrations due to torque reactions under wide-open-throttle acceleration.

Due to the high additional costs associated with the drive train, Beltz decided to make the most of the opportunity to simplify the rear suspension and cut costs there; an opportunity that existed because the rear wheels had been relieved of all driving duties, and "were simply along for the ride," as John Fitch phrased it.

The rear axle itself was a simple and lightweight steel pressing. It was carried on two parallel tapered-section, single-leaf springs in an attempt to take maximum advantage of the additional space opened up in the back by driving the front wheels. The springs were mounted with Silentbloc bushings in the front eye at a frame bracket, with rubber bushings in the shackle at the rear eye, mounted directly in the body shell.

Rear shock absorbers were mounted at a shock angle twenty-five degrees forward and inboard from vertical for best control of cushioning and isolation. In addition, there were two horizontal shock absorbers mounted in the fore-and-aft plane to damp out horizontal compliance movements.

"The Toronado ride," according to James Diener, "was developed with two principal objectives in mind. The first was to provide adequate firmness and roll control to satisfy high-performance handling. The second was to produce a

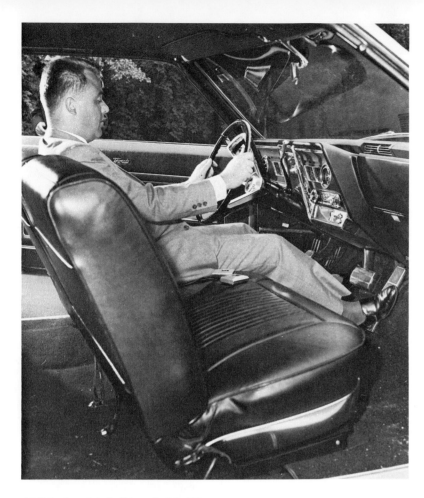

J. P. Norbye demonstrates the driving position in the 1966 Toronado. It had a bench-type front seat with space for three, and ample room for three in the back.

the engine block. This splitting of the shaft made it possible to keep the swinging parts of the shafts to each wheel equal in length. This point was held to avoid problems in the car's dynamic behavior and controllability—an area that was certainly far from fully researched by the time the toronado went into production.

The outboard half of the right-wheel drive shaft was also split in two, with a central connection through a cylindrical rubber damper which cushioned peak comfortable ride with sufficiently slow motions to qualify as a good-riding car, well balanced, and with a minimum of float.''

Beltz wanted the Toronado to live up to its looks, so Frank Ball and Lloyd Gill went to work on getting more power from the Super Rocket V-8. Their target was 385 hp, just ten more than in the Starfire, and a few simple and classic modifications were enough to accomplish that.

A new camshaft was designed, providing higher lift as well as longer opening durations for both intake and exhaust valves. Opening the valves on a steeper ramp gave a considerable increase in breathing capacity, with a corresponding rise in torque and horsepower. An interesting mechanical innovation for the Toronado was a new self-equalizing accelerator cable that operated the carburetor. The simple throttle device included a spring-loaded downshift detent to retain the 'kick-in' feel when passing. The area around the engine, however, needed more attention.

At Oldsmobile's end, body engineering for the Toronado was handled by George T. Jones and Robert J. Schultz. Jones was a prominent chassis engineer, but it was customary for Oldsmobile to move engineers around to different jobs, always rounding out their experience and building up their qualifications for promotion. Lateral moves were made almost routinely, right up to the rank of assistant chief engineer. In Jones's case, he was chassis design engineer when placed in charge of all body activities in 1958, including design of all sheet metal, specifications for all electrical accessories, and liaison with Fisher Body Division.

He had been at Oldsmobile since 1934, fresh from studying for his degree at the University of Pittsburgh, and his first job was making blueprints. Under Youngren and Thorne, he came into the chassis design section, and became a specialist on steering, suspension and brakes.

Compared to Jones, Schultz was a rookie, a 1955 graduate of Michigan State University. He came to Oldsmobile as a graduate-in-training that summer and within two years had been promoted to project engineer. From the post of supervisor—body development—in 1961, he was named body development engineer in 1965.

''The sheet metal for the Toronado was designed to suit specific engineering and styling requirements,'' reported George T. Jones. ''The space requirements of the front-wheel-drive mechanism dictated a longer-than-normal front end, which lent itself well to graceful styling. This long, low style governed the design of the front end structure, and made a retractable headlamp system desirable so that the smooth, flowing lines of the sheet metal could be maintained. The front-wheel drive also created some unusual conditions which had to be considered in the design of the radiator, fender and filler plate areas.''

The car introduced flow-through ventilation, with elimination of the corner-vent windows in the doors. ''There was no real grille on the car,'' Bob Schultz recalled, ''so we had some real cooling challenges.''

It wasn't just the air intake that made changes necessary. Engine cooling became a different problem—when the entire drive train was placed in the same space that was normally allotted to the engine alone, the extra machinery in the engine compartment created a sort of pressure build-up behind the radiator core. To overcome this, the body engineers thought it best to create an area with higher pressure in front of the core, which was done by trapping all of the ram air entering through the grille and bumper by a system of baffles, thereby minimizing the amount of air that by-passed the radiator.

The radiator had to be low and wide to match the style of the car's front end. That was no problem for Harrison Division, which came up with a crossflow core of the right proportions, while also providing better fan sweep coverage and permitting easier air flow paths through the engine compartment to exit vents under the car. The fan was partially shrouded. Without shrouding, the cooling requirements could not be met, but a full-width shroud was found to obstruct the air flow through the radiator at high speeds, resulting in a loss of cooling capacity under those conditions. The solution was to leave a three-inch section along one side of the radiator outside of the shrouded area.

''We also had a shake in the hood, because the hood was so long, and made of a single sheet of steel,'' said Schultz. ''That hood was very long, and I don't think we had it completely licked when we went into production.''

The body shell began at the cowl and extended to the rear bumper. None of the sheet metal used forward of the cowl had any structural duties.

The retractable headlamps were operated by a vacuum system (their mechanism being hooked into the light switch), opening and closing when the lights were turned on and off. A reserve tank connected to the intake manifold permitted about three cycles of opening and closing with the engine turned off.

Each headlamp was mounted on a pivot, with a counterweight cantilevered about six inches off the rotational axis. The hood panels that covered the headlamps were integrated with this assembly, which pivoted through an arc of fifty-six degrees.

The system had to raise the lamps quickly and automatically, with sufficient force to overcome icing conditions. Electrical operation was tried, but required gearing that would be unacceptably slow. The vacuum system was rapid and generally powerful enough. Test drivers reported one unexpected phenomenon: At speeds above 120 mph it was difficult to get the lamps to retract, because the aerodynamic ram force kept them up.

By May 1965, Oldsmobile had a test fleet of thirty-seven pilot-production Toronados. Building them had provided the manufacturing people with advance experience in assembling the car, and gave the development group an additional three months of test experience on the final design.

Finally, in September 1965, production got under way. The car was called the Toronado. Where did they ever get that name? It smacked of Tornado, a name Willys had used for an overhead-camshaft six-cylinder engine. And it contained a Toro, the bull, centerpiece of Spain's favorite spectacle. And there was a little taste of Coronado, scenic bay on the Pacific, named after its Spanish discoverer who explored what is now Costa Rica. Toronado was a coined name which meant absolutely nothing, but it had been registered by Chevrolet, and used on a show car in 1963.

Production version of the Toronado had a striking profile and an exceptionally clean body with extremely discreet use of chrome.

1967 Toronado had a new grille, and the headlight covers were made flush with the hood. Sports-style ventilated wheel covers were optional. Mechanically, the Toronado was unchanged from 1966 specifications.

During 1965, people all over Oldsmobile were desperately looking for a trade name for the XP-784. They had gone through lists of hundreds of possible names, and rejected them all. Metzel was on the phone to the marketing department every day. Sales officials, styling men, engineers and administration personnel, all were searching, making suggestions and tearing them up.

How Oldsmobile ended up with the Chevrolet-coined name was perfectly accidental. As Stan Wilen remembers it, Ed Cole and Bunkie Knudsen, who was then running Chevrolet, happened to walk into the office of Oldsmobile's styling studio one day. Cole asked if they were still looking for a name. Silent nods from around the room expressed the sad fact. Then Knudsen, as casually as he would ask for a cup of coffee, said, "Why don't you call it the Toronado? We're not using it."

General Motors top management decided that Cadillac should be given full use of the Toronado engineering for a specialty car of its own. It was given the name Eldorado and went into production as a 1967 model.

What it borrowed from the Toronado was the concept, and the Fisher E-body. But other than the transmission, it had no interchangeable parts with the Toronado. The Eldorado received certain refinements that were not available in the Toronado in 1967, such as automatic level control for the rear suspension, and variable-ratio power steering. Its subsequent evolution ran closely parallel with that of the Toronado.

1968 Toronado shows major change in the front end, with integrated bumper and grille frame. Engine size was increased to 455 cubic inches, with 375 hp in the standard version and 400 hp as an option.

A forced-air option was offered for the 1968 Toronado. The package included a special camshaft, heat-treated valve spring and damper assemblies, and low-restriction exhaust manifolds. It was rated at 400 hp.

Press reaction to the Toronado was overwhelming in its praise. Shortcomings, when discovered during road testing, were easily forgiven, because the car itself was so exciting and so appealing, and the fact that Oldsmobile had done something so radical made it picayune to criticize. There was a feeling that criticism would have been vulgar, uncouth, as if reports of factual deficiencies in the product were expressions of lack of esteem for Oldsmobile.

Metzel set the stage by claiming: "The Toronado's unique suspension system, and the carefully studied placement of the drive components over the front wheels, make this a car unequaled for road-hugging ability, dramatic cornering, directional stability, powerful, noiseless, vibration-free performance and freedom from the effects of high winds on the open highway. Traction on snow or ice is matchless."

What Metzel said was not untrue, but there was to be a big contrast between our first impressions and our more mature feelings about the car on the completion of a 10,000-mile test.

After the press preview, and driving on selected (by Oldsmobile) tracks of the GM Proving Grounds, Jan Norbye wrote: "When I stepped into the driver's seat of the Toronado, ex-racing driver John Fitch (of Cunningham and Mercedes-Benz fame) sat down beside me. Together we decided to find out exactly what the Toronado would do—and what it wouldn't. My first impression was that it gave no hint of having front wheel drive. Just driving it around was pretty much like driving any old two-pedal control Oldsmobile. This was of course deliberate, because if the Toronado had called for any drastic change in driving methods, its chances in the market place would be severely restricted. However, as I became more familiar with the Toronado and started to take the corners a little faster, used the brakes less and push harder on the accelerator, I began to get an idea of its stability.

"When John Fitch took the wheel, he tried a few diabolical tricks of his own, but failed to get the car out of shape. Imagine a sweeping turn to the right, with undulations large enough to set up a large-amplitude bounce in the car, threatening loss of both traction and steering at any speed over 75 mph. John went sailing through so smoothly that an unsuspecting passenger might never even have noticed the road surface.

"On fast turns, the feeling of stability is most reassuring, and I knew that I had enough power under my foot to pull out of whatever trouble I might get into. But no matter how suddenly I changed lanes, wiggled and woggled, power-on or power-off, at speed, the car remained in perfect control. The rear end never showed any tendency to break away, it just trailed. I have never been in any six-passenger

1968   1969

Comparison between the Toronado steering knuckles of 1968 and 1969. The new steering knuckle was made as a nodular-iron casting. It gave trouble, and Oldsmobile reverted to forged steel. Continuing on the 119-inch wheelbase, the Toronado had its body stretched 3.5 inches for 1969, with a new rear deck and fenders. Front disc brakes were optional.

vehicle that felt so safe and controllable at highway speeds (in the 80s and 90s). Finally, back on a narrow road, I went into a 40-mph left-hander, yanked the wheel over close to full lock, and took my foot off the throttle. The car began to plow, and I would have run out of road if I had not put my foot back on the accelerator. The moment the front wheels were given some driving torque, the car was again fully obedient.''

This sort of behavior in extreme situations was not unusual, and in no way unsafe. What Oldsmobile had concentrated on, was to obtain consistent handling regardless of throttle position.

James Diener summed it up this way: ''Somewhat different torque steer effects, or torque steer interaction, occur in front-wheel-drive vehicles than in rear-drive vehicles. These characteristics are not bothersome in either vehicle design if the chassis components are designed so that their effects during acceleration and deceleration are held to a low magnitude.

''By careful attention to a number of factors, the Toronado chassis design has practically eliminated torque steer interaction. These factors include weight distribution, front and rear roll steer, roll rate, king-pin inclination, steering gear ratio, rigidity of the steering system and tire characteristics.''

If driven like a sports car, the Toronado imposed severe limitations on the pilot. Norbye's report from the proving-ground test drive said: ''It likes to accelerate through the turns, preferably from the moment wheels are first deflected from a straight path. This means that all braking should be over prior to entering the bend, much in the way a motorcycle rider sets his machine up for a turn. Driven this way, the Toronado handles in great style, all wheels firmly on the ground, with remarkably slight body roll.''

Later, after driving the car on Bridgehampton Race Circuit on Long Island, our complaints of the understeer stiffened. It would not take the sharper curves any faster than a Delta 88, despite the greater power available.

The pre-pilot-production test cars had used an 8.00-15 standard-profile tire. They were found somewhat lacking in tractive ability, cornering stability and appearance, which led to the development of a whole new tire design, the TFD (Toronado Front Drive) with its own tread design, on an 8.85-15 carcass in collaboration with Firestone.

The TFD tread pattern gave better traction on wet surfaces, and the carcass had a higher cord angle to make the sidewalls a little stiffer. Uniroyal was also contracted to produce the TFD tire, and later, Goodyear radials were made optional. Front tire wear was a problem with all of them, and Oldsmobile recommended rotating the tires every 6,000 miles to equalize wear.

At a curb weight of 4,496 pounds, the Toronado was the heaviest of all Oldsmobiles, with a front/rear weight distribution of 60/40 compared with the Starfire's 56/44 percent. Front spring rates in the Toronado were ninety percent higher than in the Starfire, rear spring rates sixty percent higher. Yet, the ride was just as smooth, and the Toronado seemed to have better coordination between front and rear springs. Vertical wheel travel is more restricted, and roll stiffness considerably higher.

Zero-to-sixty mph acceleration was a matter of 8.6 seconds, and the car covered the standing-start quarter-mile in 17 seconds flat. It could reach 100 mph from standstill in 24.2 seconds, and 130 mph in exactly 60 seconds. Fuel consumption on the road averaged 12.5 miles per gallon, in calm, unhurried driving under a variety of traffic and road conditions.

Power brakes, very light to the touch on first application, assisted by the rugged look of the wide pedal, instilled a confidence in stopping power that was far beyond the actual capabilities of the car. The combination of fade-prone front-wheel

1970 Toronado. The longer tail gave the Toronado a closer family resemblance to the Delta 88. Headlights were open and framed in the grille, while the front fenders received vertical bumper strips. Air intakes under the bumper were widened.

The 1972-model Toronado broke completely with the original concept. It became a luxury car on a 122-inch wheelbase, without a trace of sportiness.

The whole panel was artistically designed and used only the space right in front of the driver, leaving the area in front of the passengers uncluttered. But with all that room available for useful storage space, the glovebox was ridiculously tiny.

As Leonard Casillo analyzed it: "Now I think the people who like that car like it passionately. And I'm sure it had a regular parade of committed admirers, but it was not a successful car and it certainly did not sell as they had hoped it would. I think the car was probably some years ahead of its time. If I took those same design elements now and tried to work with them in a much smaller package, there are many elements there that would lend themselves quite well to the kind of automobiles we're doing now."

Many sports car enthusiasts liked the looks of the Toronado but were dismayed at its massive size. Some suggested it should have been to 8/10 scale, and even a 6/10 scale was mentioned. Some Oldsmobile insiders began to wish they had stayed with the initial concept, based on the compact F-85.

Despite its 119-inch wheelbase, compared with 123 inches for the Delta 88, the Toronado was roomier than the B-body Holiday coupe, but there was a confusion in the minds of the consumers about what kind of car the Toronado was. Their confusion was just a reflection of that which permeated the management and sales staff at Oldsmobile.

"They were worried about how to merchandize it," an Olds marketing man explained, "They were afraid to sell it on its advantages—traction, handling, and so on. It would do things that other cars just couldn't do, but there was a feeling that advertising the Toronado's strong points might unsell the rest of the line. They just knew they could not sell the Toronado on the strength of front-wheel drive. That would be selling it to the detriment of the most profitable high-volume models."

brakes and a lack of front/rear balance would lead to loss of control in difficult traffic situations. The rear wheels would lock before the pedal pressure had reached the point where the front wheels could do much to help slow the car. The brakes were a sore point with many early Toronado owners, and it became a matter of first priority for Oldsmobile's engineers to make improvements.

Power steering was standard, with a fast-geared variable-rate Saginaw system that gave 3½ turns lock-to-lock. It was excellent, and a tilt-and-telescoping steering wheel was optional.

Among the instruments, only one is worthy of mention: the speedometer. It was a revolving spool with a window in the dashboard (just like the model A Ford).

The 1973 Toronado shows minor styling differences from the preceding and following models. Mechanically the car was unchanged except for safety and emission-control equipment.

The 1974 Oldsmobile Toronado set the all-time record for length at 228 inches. Its weight increased to 4,838 pounds, while emission-control devices reduced power output to 230 hp.

Jim Williams corroborates: "They tried to sell it as a package, more than as a front-wheel-drive car, initially. They more or less disguised the facts of front-wheel drive. They were very cautious about it. In retrospect, you'll probably find people at Olds now who would say that was a mistake."

The selling of the Toronado also stumbled because of certain miscalculations in the sales department. "It was one of the biggest fiascos of car distribution of all time," in the opinion of the sales manager for an important Oldsmobile dealer. "They were too concerned about not having enough business on the West Coast, so they shipped all those cars out there, while dealers elsewhere didn't get the car."

"And when they finally got them," an Oldsmobile zone office manager said, "they were so mad they just let them sit and rot."

The list of possible reasons for the Toronado's failure to reach its sales objectives may be even longer. Product planners in Lansing were driving themselves crazy with unanswerable questions:
—Did people want it to be a different kind of car, more of a luxury model?
—Didn't we put enough emphasis on the front-wheel drive?
—Should we have played up its sporty aspects more?
In any event, Jim Williams's conclusion is inescapable: "I think they felt they had not communicated its character properly to the customer."

The marketing people reversed their view of the trend. "What was thought to be a shift in buyers' attitudes [toward sportier cars] had not really taken place," explained an Oldsmobile sales official, "and so they had to remake the Toronado more in the tradition of the Oldsmobile idiom. They pulled back from the sports-car styling and made a much more formal and luxurious car out of it. And I am not so sure that when they were making those decisions, they were wrong."

Jim Williams takes the opposite view: "When they first came out with the car, the styling was controversial. I have a feeling that if they had only held on to the original styling, it would have come on like the Camaro did—but they went ahead and changed it."

There wasn't time to make any big changes for the 1967 model year. Because of the brake problems, front disc brakes were made optional, and a proportioning valve was added to prevent premature locking of the rear wheels. Why weren't discs made standard? There were thousands of Toronado owners who used the performance capabilities of their car so sparingly that they never noticed the inadequacies of the brakes. Oldsmobile concluded that customers who needed better brakes would have the sense to order discs and be ready to pay extra for them.

The disc brakes were made by Delco-Moraine, and consisted of 11.3-inch ventilated rotors with two-piston calipers, adapted from the Corvette four-wheel system. Power front disc brakes with single-piston calipers were not standardized till the 1970 Toronado came out, and the proportioning valve was eliminated.

With the 1969 disc brake option came a new nodular-iron steering knuckle, cast as one single piece, including disc brake mounting brackets. It was found to have superior reliability in proving-ground tests, but gave trouble in consumer hands, so Oldsmobile quickly changed right back again to the 1968 version.

The main styling change for 1967 was the adoption of an egg-crate-pattern grille. Sales fell to 22,094 that year. "Sales were going bad, and continued to get worse," reported an Olds middle-echelon executive, "and then we came out with those ugly ones with the fat bumper-grille on them in 1968-69. They were turkeys.

The news in the 1975 Toronado was mainly the rectangular headlamps, which blended well with the jutting, squared-off look of the front end.

1977 Oldsmobile Toronado brougham. New grille (unsplit!) and straight bumper are fitted onto the 1971-78 body shell. A 200-hp 403-cubic-inch V-8 was now standard in the Toronado.

Around that time, the Riviera was a very clean-looking car, very nice indeed. And it started killing us on sales.''

A full-height oval grille with dual headlamps inside the frame and a vertical center bar was integrated with the massive bumper, and made the front end look heavy. For 1969, the rear fender line was raised, and a vinyl top was adopted. These two changes completely broke up the unique roofline of the older models and increased the resemblance to the two-door B-body cars.

The low production volume increased the pressure on the engineering department to cut the cost of the Toronado in every possible way. Somehow they found space for a conventional bevel-gear differential which replaced the planetary one for 1968. At the same time, cheaper Delta-type three-ball inner-end universal joints were fitted on the drive shafts.

The engineers were also toying with ideas for variations in body types, to widen the appeal of the Toronado. Several station wagon prototypes were made, making astonishingly good use of the low, flat floor, and presenting a very attractive silhouette. Beltz was very serious about getting it into production, and for a while thought he was going to succeed. By this time he was general manager. But someone higher up in the corporation, Rollert or perhaps Ed Cole, made it impossible: ''No more front-wheel-drive models until you have learned to sell the one you've got,'' he was told.

Toronado sales reached 25,536 in 1968 and 26,766 in 1969, far behind the Riviera's 45,000 and 47,000. Ford's T-bird sales, incidentally, came down from 65,000 to Riviera level in 1969.

Then came 1970, with practically no visible change in the Toronado, and sales dropped to 16,554 for the calendar year. By this time, however, a major redesign was prepared for 1971.

It was restyled as a luxury car, and built on a 122.3-inch wheelbase, its curb weight climbing to 4,557 pounds. There were major engineering changes in the chassis. ''The frame got a little bigger every year,'' Bob Schultz remembered. ''We were trying to get more insulation, a little better construction, and finally we said, 'Ah, let's make it a full frame.' ''

The Toronado was put on a shortened version of the 98-series frame, which also meant going to a new rear axle and coil-spring rear suspension. Spring rates were lowered; the ride became extremely soft, with increased body roll; and handling precision suffered greatly. Because the parts were shared with other models, the cost of building the Toronado came down a bit, but the sticker price soared to $5,457.

Toronado sales climbed to 38,721 in 1971 and 44,118 in 1972. The division was not losing money on it any longer, but many felt that the whole purpose of building the car with front-wheel drive had been sacrificed on this gamble for a new clientele. It paid off for Oldsmobile, but in the opinion of one insider, it was not entirely due to its own efforts: ''Suddenly Buick made the Riviera ugly in 1971 and that helped us.'' The car continued with minor technical and styling changes through the 1978 model year.

CHAPTER 13

The Metzel Years

AFTER A SEASON LIKE 1965, the auto industry began thinking in terms of the twelve-million-car year. Oldsmobile had had its best year ever in 1965, with sales of over 600,000 cars, and Harold N. Metzel steered the division into 1966 with great expectations. There was a new excitement about Oldsmobile, no doubt chiefly due to all the publicity around Toronado.

"Toronado was the car that put us on the map, you know," said an ex-Olds sales staff member. "You ask, 'did it change the image of Olds?' I don't think it changed the image so much as it started a more open attitude up there about things that were new and different in the market place—about how to go after younger-aged buyers. You know, they were more willing to try to go after new markets after that. It seems fairly obvious now, but until then their image had been so conservative, and so was their attitude about automobiles."

Of course, the Toronado was just the most visible part of what was happening. There was also the 4-4-2, and the fresh new styling that had begun with the 1965 models. For 1966, Stan Wilen adapted the B-body styling theme to the A-body cars (F-85 and Cutlass), which started the intermediates on a spectacular climb toward prestige and popularity. They had a similar grille and face, and a very stylish rear-fender kickup which made the rest of the car look lower.

The model lineup was narrow, but effective, and prices were quite low, considering what it would cost to get a Chevelle or a Tempest equipped to comparable levels of refinement, comfort and convenience.

Body Style	F-85	Deluxe F-85	Cutlass	Vista-Cruiser
Four-door sedan	$2,401	$2,497	$2,673	
Two-door sedan	2,348		2,633	
Four-door hardtop		2,629	2,846	
Two-door hardtop		2,513	2,770	
Convertible			2,965	
Station wagon	2,695	2,793		$2,935

The baseline engine was called the Action-Line Six. It was a 250-cubic-inch in-line engine made by Chevrolet; much longer, taller and heavier than the small Buick V-6. But Buick had taken the V-6 out of production and sold the whole machining line to Kaiser Jeep in Toledo, leaving Oldsmobile without a six.

The F-85 was so big and heavy that there was no real gain in fuel economy by using a six, but it was needed for price-structuring reasons.

Among the luxury options was a new Cutlass Supreme treatment of the four-door hardtop, a very high-style car with specific trim and decor. Here, Olds was stepping out in front of the other divisions with something new—an intermediate-class car that looked every bit as classy as the 98. It started a trend which Oldsmobile was to exploit successfully for many years.

1967 Oldsmobile 98 Luxury sedan. The Fisher C-body was restyled again, and the Oldsmobile designers smoothed out the sheet metal to an unprecedented degree.

Among the 1966-model B-body cars, Oldsmobile discontinued the Jetstar I, and added a new convertible in the Delta 88 series.

Body Style	Jetstar 88	Dynamic 88	Delta 88
Four-door sedan	$2,927	$3,013	$3,160
Four-door hardtop	3,059	3,144	3,328
Two-door hardtop	2,983	3,069	3,253
Convertible		3,404	3,588

Body Style	Starfire	98	Toronado
Four-door sedan		$3,966	
Luxury sedan		4,308	
Four-door hardtop	$3,564	4,158	$4,617
Convertible		4,443	

1966 Oldsmobile Delta 88 convertible. Exterior changes for 1966 were minimal. Technical changes were important, with a new rear axle (and optional limited-slip differential).

1967 Oldsmobile Delmont 88 Holiday sedan. The Delmont series was born from a desire to provide a vehicle that would move customers up from the intermediate class to the full-size car.

On the technical side, things were quiet. There had been a rash of quality problems during the catch-up period after the strike at the start of the 1965 model year, but that was entirely due to lack of quality control during those hectic days. No design flaws or miscalculations cropped up, and all resources were concentrated on the Toronado program.

1967 Oldsmobile Delta 88 Custom Holiday sedan. Vinyl tops were an extremely popular option at this time, affording a look that was closer to the real convertible than the regular hardtop.

1967 Oldsmobile 98 Holiday sedan. Built on a 126-inch wheelbase, the 98 was 223 inches long and weighed 4,413 pounds (considerably less than the Toronado). The engine was a 365-hp 425-cubic-inch V-8.

During 1966, Oldsmobile went to a new, fully automated electronically controlled crankshaft-balancing system as part of a new crankshaft machining line.

Rochester supplied a new four-barrel carburetor design named Quadrajet which became standard on the Super Rocket V-8. It had been developed jointly with Oldsmobile engineers. Olds managed at the same time to go into the axle business and manufacture its own final-drive gears and a new type of limited-slip differential for its B- and C-body cars.

A molded-plastics department was installed in another building, and a new process was adopted for application of a very thin nickel coating called Dur-Ni nickel strike, directly beneath the final chromium surface on 1967-model Oldsmobile bumpers.

All 1966-model cars going to California were equipped with emission-control systems, using fan-belt-driven air pumps to inject air into the exhaust manifolds.

Automatic speed control became optional on 1966 F-85's with automatic transmission. The system was made by Perfect Circle, while Pontiac and Buick used one developed by AC Spark Plug (which was eventually forced on Oldsmobile as well).

The competition was not sitting still while Oldsmobile was making its moves. Chrysler released its hemi-head 426-cubic-inch V-8 for use in 'street version' production models, outgunning all high-performance rivals in terms of brute power. Chevrolet produced the Chevelle SS 396, undercutting everybody else's muscle-car prices.

Ford introduced two-way tailgates on all station wagons except the Falcon for 1966, and Pontiac brought out a new overhead-camshaft six as the standard engine for the Tempest and Le Mans.

On the luxury-car front, Mercury was advertising the Park Lane "with a look that's pure, classic, unique. With a ride that's restfully quiet and solidly exciting." At the same time Dodge launched a new full-size fastback called Charger, Pontiac kept hammering away at the Wide-Track theme and Chrysler screamed about its five-year 50,000-mile warranty.

None of them could get the kind of attention Oldsmobile was enjoying, and the publicity men cherished their day in the limelight. "Look to *Olds* for the NEW," said the advertisements from the Lansing-based division.

For 1967, GM B-bodies received a substantial facelift, and Stan Wilen developed the existing lines in careful, subtle ways, maintaining strict continuity, while getting a little bolder in fender shapes, grille frames, taillights and side moldings. The lackluster Jetstar 88 and the venerable Dynamic 88 were unceremoniously dropped and a new series called the Delmont 88 appeared.

"They were in a name-switching act then," Jim Williams recalled. "They came out with a new car and it was an attempt to move people up into the 88-series. The name, however, never flew."

"The Delta 88 became known as sort of a mid-priced big-car version," an Olds sales official recounted, "and we were trying to introduce something just below it. We wanted something solid that had a family-car notion to it. But I honestly don't know where the name Delmont came from."

With the Toronado in the lineup, there was no longer any justification for the Starfire, so that name was quietly shelved.

Ralph Nader's book, *Unsafe at Any Speed*, was published in 1965, and during 1966, the U.S. government introduced legislation to impose safety standards for motor vehicles.

The 1967 Oldsmobile range had collapsible steering columns, dual-circuit hydraulic brakes and warning lights for brake-system malfunction. They also had four-way emergency flashers, padded steering wheel hubs, non-overriding door handles, soft window-handle knobs, tread-wear indicators in the tires, low-profile instrument-panel knobs, while front seat shoulder belts became optional. Non-

1968 Oldsmobile 98 Holiday sedan. Along with the new split-grille front end, the 98 featured concealed windshield wipers (a development borrowed from Pontiac). Engine displacement was increased to 455 cubic inches.

1968 Oldsmobile 98 convertible. Rear end panel was practically the same as in 1967. The license-plate notch in the trunk lid became typical of Oldsmobiles from this period.

reflecting wiper arms were standard on the F-85, which also had a breakaway mounting for the inside mirror. Front disc brakes became optional on all 1967-model Oldsmobiles.

In anticipation of coming emission-control regulations, Oldsmobile introduced its Controlled Combustion system, which included an arrangement to preheat the carburetor air to a constant one hundred degrees Fahrenheit by an exhaust-heated stove. Oldsmobile also offered the new Delco capacitive discharge ignition system for 1967. (Pontiac also had it, along with GMC trucks.)

But Oldsmobile was not keeping up with everything its sister divisions were doing. Pontiac stole a march on everybody by introducing recessed wipers, resting off the glass, under a lip on the hood, on its 1967-model B-body cars. Buick offered automatic level control for the Riviera, and Cadillac made it standard on the Eldorado; while Olds shied away from that, as if still embarrassed over the failure of the New-Matic Ride in 1958.

Expansion projects during 1967 included 91,000 square feet of additional floor space at the Lansing plant. In addition, a new building for paint inspection and repair facilities with 57,000 square feet of floor space was set up to free equivalent space next to the final assembly lines. At the same time, Oldsmobile completed a new stamping plant on West Saginaw Street, and began an extension of the parts warehouse.

Mack Worden was being groomed for the top spot in the Oldsmobile sales department, but Metzel tactfully waited till Emmett Feely reached retirement age before giving Worden the title of general sales manager in 1966. Bill Buxton, who had been regional manager for the southwest, was transferred to Lansing in 1967 as assistant general sales manager.

As a former Chevrolet salesman, Worden knew the importance of the youth market. A year or two after the introduction of the 4-4-2, Toronado and Vista-Cruiser, the average age of the Oldsmobile buyer was still over forty-five. He began to cultivate a more youthful image for Olds, with Beltz and Wilen to support the new image with hardware keyed to sport, leisure and the sales department's overall concept of youth activities.

For 1967, the division began an ad campaign featuring Youngmobiles. Phrases like "swing with the youth movement" were used. "A whole lineup of new Oldsmobile models that have "young" written all over them!" read a banner headline. Showrooms were full of similar slogans, often punning with the Olds name and its antonyms. Did it work? Just look at the figures:

	1966	1967
Total market (millions)	9.0	8.4
Olds sales	580,550	551,274
Olds rank	5th	6th
Olds market share	6.44%	6.60%
GM market share	48.1 %	48.5 %

What happened? Olds slipped one place in the rankings despite advancing its penetration by 0.16 percent in a declining market, simply because Buick came from behind and jumped in front. Pontiac was running a solid third, and Plymouth, fourth.

Oldsmobile's strength was the A-body car, and its weakness scattered evenly over all other series. Inexplicably, the 98 fell back from 88,000 in 1966 to 79,000 the following year. The Delta 88 took a severe dip, from 90,000 to 84,000, and the Delmont, despite its newness and the strong advertising push behind it, did not get far beyond 107,000.

In contrast, the intermediate series advanced from 40.6 percent to forty-seven percent of Oldsmobile sales, the total rising from 235,618 units in 1966 to 259,569 in 1967. That placed the F-85 family ahead of Buick's Special, and less than 40,000

1968 Oldsmobile Cutlass S Holiday coupe. The Cutlass S was not related to the Supreme, but a semi-sports model selling at a moderate price. Power and chassis options from the 4-4-2 were available on the S.

1968 Oldsmobile Delmont 88 Holiday sedan. Despite the logic of its packaging and merchandizing, the Delmont 88 never caught on with the public, and the series was discontinued after the 1968 model year.

1968 Oldsmobile Delta 88 Custom Holiday coupe. More fastback than notchback, the two-door B-body was highly successful for all divisions that used it.

cars behind the Tempest, putting the Olds fourth among all intermediates regardless of price.

All GM intermediates were due for a total change, and Ed Cole had developed a master plan to build the A-body in two sizes: a long wheelbase for four-door models and a short wheelbase for two-door ones.

This stemmed from the reasoning that in coupe bodies, the faster rooflines necessitated moving the back seat forward to assure normal head room in the rear.

Keeping the same wheelbase for the two-door bodies, then, brought no real advantage. The gain in trunk space was illusory, and the extra length meant extra weight, which not only cost more, but was bad for performance.

Cole had been serving as executive vice president in charge of the Operations Staff since 1961, and in October 1967, acceded to the presidency of GM. At the same time, James C. Roche succeeded Frederic G. Donner as chairman. Roche was a Cadillac man, and so was Harold G. Warner, who replaced Cole as head of the Operations Staff. Donald L. Boyes was named vice president in charge of the Car and Truck Group. He was an MIT engineer who had joined GM in 1928 and worked his way up through parts-and-accessories.

These changes in top-level management did nothing to improve the situation for Oldsmobile, but cannot be considered to have hurt Metzel's division in any

1969 Oldsmobile Vista-Cruiser. Split grille adopted for the 1968 models was refined for 1969, which also got recessed windshield wipers. Two-piece tailgate was retained from 1964-67 design.

1969 Oldsmobile Delta 88 Royale two-door hardtop. The Royale was a new sub-series, aimed at upgrading the Delta name. New sheet metal was adopted, with a sharp tuck-under at the hip line. Vinyl top was standard on Royales.

measurable way. All divisions were subject to the same corporate dictates, with exceptions always made for Chevrolet because of its sheer size, and for Cadillac because of its prestige.

The new A-body program evolved under the direction of Harry Barr at the GM Engineering Staff, up to the point where the car divisions and Fisher Body were called in. That's not because the heads of the GM Engineering Staff felt that Oldsmobile lacked competence in all areas and could not be trusted. On the contrary, it was because Oldsmobile had its hands full with the Toronado, unofficially spearheading the corporation's work on front-wheel drive.

For the new A-body cars, the engineering tasks were mainly linked with the body and frame. Fisher Body did most of the body engineering, in association with Chevrolet for structures and Pontiac for body mounts.

Power trains, brakes, suspension and steering systems were largely carried over from the 1964-67 models, so the new setup for long-range engineering was not really to come into effect until the 1971-model B-, C- and E-body programs. But it was a definite step in the irreversible chain of events draining power from the divisions and concentrating it at the corporation.

Like all other GM A-body cars, the 1968 F-85 and Cutlass had four-door models on a 116-inch wheelbase and two-door models on a 112-inch wheelbase. The Oldsmobile studio, under Stan Wilen, had come up with a very curvacious shape, having the fashionable short-deck/long-hood proportions promulgated by Ford's Mustang.

The styling people had been trying to develop a face of its own for the F-85, distinct from the B-body cars. The feeling was that they succeeded with the 1968 models, both in creating an attractive front end, and in establishing a base they could build some continuity on.

Bob Schultz told us, ''The design staff was trying very hard to come up with a visual heritage for all the division's cars, and we were looking for something that could become identifiable as an Olds. We were all very enthused about a grille design that had wide-spaced vertical bars and separate apertures on each side. It was a very gutty-looking car and, I think, one of the cars that helped evolve what was to become a strong Cutlass theme. At the time, of course, no one said 'that's a look we're gonna hang on to for a long time.' ''

In 1968 Oldsmobile also introduced the two-door Cutlass Supreme, destined to be a great success.

According to Irv Rybicki: ''On the 1968 A-body cars we went from a notchback to a fastback. The Cutlass had the fastest roofline of them all, at that time. When we developed that car Beltz came into the studio one day. 'You know what I'd like you fellows to do for me? Let's take that roof panel and see if we can create a notchback and give me a little Eldorado around the rear quarter-panels and I'll sell the hell out of that damn thing. I'll knock off all the other A-cars.'

'' 'All right, John, we'll take a look at it.' So we taped up this car and it looked pretty good and we tore up the clay model that had been released as the fastback and did this notch, and Olds went to the corporation with this project, and they were out there first with a notchback approach. Which got them started.''

According to Jim Williams, the original idea was not Beltz's own, but came from the marketing people: ''Beltz became convinced—he wasn't convinced to begin with—that they should put a formal-roof model in a coupe style into the Cutlass line.

''Pontiac and Chevrolet elected to go the other route, with a separate series using modified A-bodies [known as G-bodies] for the Grand Prix and Monte Carlo. And at Olds, they were well aware of the chances of gaining momentum in the A-car line at the expense of Chevrolet and Pontiac.

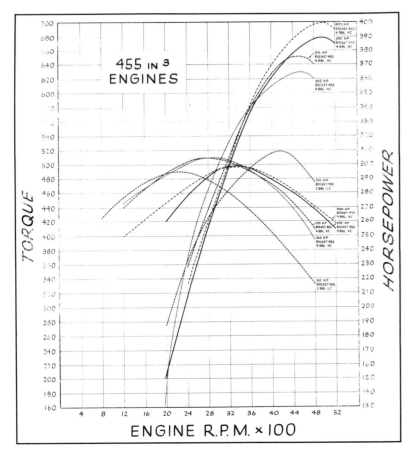

The four versions of the 455-cubic-inch engine for 1969 had considerable differences in the speed at which peak torque was generated, but maximum torque was nearly the same in all.

New single-piston disc brake with floating caliper was adopted for 1969, in replacement of former double-piston design. Drum brakes continued as standard on all models.

"They made all their decisions in that light—how to increase their penetration against Chevrolet and Pontiac. This is partly due to the fact that Oldsmobile had so many dealers that were dualed with Chevrolet. The Cutlass Supreme was assigned a top-of-the-line role and probably drew from the intermediate sedan market more than from the specialty car market."

What did Olds hope to gain?

"I think they wanted to get the young affluent kind of buyer into an Olds, first of all. They wanted to give the public a choice and hoped that they would have a car that was more competitive in the Olds car line than the Grand Prix and Monte Carlo were to Pontiac and Chevrolet."

The Vista-Cruiser continued, its wheelbase one inch longer than before at 121 inches. The 4-4-2 continued as a two-door coupe, two-door hardtop or two-door convertible on the 112-inch wheelbase.

Oldsmobile took the lead in the use of new materials by its adoption of polypropylene front wheel housings for all F-85 1968 models. The plastic wheel housing weighed half of the previous part made of steel and, in addition, would not rust. Fisher Body engineers pointed out that the plastic wheel housings improved appearance, reduced lead time and provided greater design flexibilty. It could also cut costs, since several metal parts could be combined into one plastic part.

"That plastic fender liner was a first for Olds," recalled Bob Schultz, "and it was a pretty major step in the use of plastics. Olds developed it strictly on its own, and it was later taken up by the other divisions."

All 1968-model Oldsmobiles were equipped with buzzers that sounded an alarm whenever drivers left their cars with the ignition key in its lock.

On the 1968 B- and C-body cars, Oldsmobile introduced a split grille and adopted recessed windshield wipers (shared also with the A-body cars). Both had been Pontiac developments.

"Pontiac dropped the ball on the split grille," said an Oldsmobile designer. "They had it first, and it was pretty successful. We started using it in 1968 and that down-the-road appearance has been very successful. It has good road identity. It is recognizable as an Oldsmobile in motion, at a glance. We still use it. It's the biggest single styling thing we've got going for us."

It spread to the F-85/Cutlass/4-4-2 series in 1969. Other styling changes were slight in the A-body, while B- and C-bodies had all-new skin. The wheelbase was stretched to 124 inches for the 88's and 127 inches for the 98.

"We removed all side moldings above doorsill level and added a coke-bottle effect by flaring out the fenders around the wheel arches," said a body engineer. "The belt-line kickup was kept on the two-door models, while the four-door versions borrowed a trick from Cadillac, sweeping upwards to meet the descending line from the window frames at the C-post."

The model program was streamlined by the elimination of the Delmont 88, while splitting the Delta 88 line into two levels: Delta and Delta Custom. In addition, there was a new option in the Custom series, the Royale, available only as a hardtop coupe.

Most noticed of the engineering changes for 1968 was the enlargement of the 330-cubic-inch V-8 to 350 by boring out the cylinders to 4.06 inches, and the 425 Super Rocket V-8 to 455 cubic inches, by increasing the stroke to 4.25 inches. The bore could not be increased any more within the existing design, so there was no other way to get bigger displacement than to lengthen the stroke. Pontiac and Buick were going to 455 cubic inches, and Oldsmobile could not let itself fall behind.

The long stroke imposed a new 200-250 rpm lower rev-limit of 5200 rpm, which was more than made up for in the form of increased low-range torque.

The 350-cubic-inch engine delivered 250 hp at 4400 rpm, on a 9.0:1 compression ratio with a two-barrel carburetor. Its maximum torque was 355 pounds-feet at 2600 rpm. It was used in the F-85, Vista-Cruiser and Delta 88.

The 4-4-2 engine was reworked for 1968, getting the new long-stroke crankshaft and bottom end from the 455-cubic-inch V-8. It used the new, big block with a bore reduced to 3.87 inches, so that the displacement remained constant at 400 cubic inches. Running with a 10.5:1 compression ratio and a single four-barrel carburetor, it delivered 350 hp at 4800 rpm, with a maximum torque of 450 pounds-feet at 3200 rpm.

The 455-cubic-inch V-8 delivered 375 hp at 4600 rpm with a compression ratio of 10.2:1, and produced a peak torque of 510 pounds-feet at 3000 rpm. It was also available in a 320-hp version for the B-body cars, 365 hp for the 98, and 385 hp for the Toronado.

Other engine changes for 1969 were external only, such as an improved choke on two-barrel carburetors and a revised shape for the heated-air ducts to shorten warmup time.

1970 Cutlass Supreme Holiday coupe. Split grille and semiformal roofline were the highlights of the intermediates from Oldsmobile that year. The two-door models were built on a 112-inch wheelbase, with power train options up to 320 hp.

A-body cars powered by V-8 engines were given a new automatic transmission, with three speeds. It was called Turbo Hydra-matic 350—a smaller, lighter version of the 400 unit used in combination with the 455-cubic-inch V-8.

The 1969 model year will also be remembered for some of the following changes Oldsmobile made. The ignition key was moved to the steering column, where it was hooked up with the gearshift mechanism and steering shaft to lock the transmission (in park) and the wheels (pointing whichever way the driver left them).

Variable-ratio power steering became standard on the 98, optional on the Delta 88. Rear-axle drive pinions were reinforced and made to run more quietly under heavy loading. Single-piston floating-caliper front disc brakes and fiberglass-belted bias-ply tires become optional for all Oldsmobiles. The B- and C-body chassis was partially redesigned, with new rear suspension geometry for a more level ride and a reduction in the fore-and-aft forces fed into the body.

The 1969-model Oldsmobiles came on the market in the year when Chrysler went to its fuselage look, the Dodge on a 122-inch wheelbase and the Chrysler on a 124-inch wheelbase. Chrysler ads proclaimed "the roomiest car built in America today" and informed its dealers of a favorable trend in the market: "Almost one-third of present Chrysler owners have moved up from the lower price class."

That added up to a threat Oldsmobile had to take seriously. At the same time, Mercury unveiled the new Marquis, "the most dramatically styled automobile since the Continental Mark III," in eight models, including hardtops, stations wagons and a convertible, aimed right up against the Olds 98.

About halfway into the 1969 model year, a momentous change occurred at Oldsmobile. Metzel reached retirement age and left the division on April 30, 1969. His successor as general manager was John B. Beltz, taking office on May 1.

CHAPTER

Beltz and Beyond

BELTZ WAS METZEL'S CHOICE for the post, and if the divisional general managers were elected by popular vote among the personnel, Beltz might have carried it off unanimously. He was that popular.

"He was a personality. Everybody liked him, and he typically would involve himself with people who were middle-management," said an admiring official of medium rank.

"He would go into the plant," said a production engineer. "He paid as much attention to people at the bottom of the ladder as he did to those at the top."

Public relations man Jim Williams appreciated his capacity to lead: "Beltz was just a natural-born leader. He was probably the most respected division head and had a way all his own to run meetings. He could sit in a meeting and get to the issue faster than anybody I've ever seen—and do it with a certain amount of flair."

Chief engineer at thirty-eight, Beltz became general manager at forty-three, the youngest GM vice president and head of a car division—a full year junior to John DeLorean, who was now running Chevrolet after a brilliant career at Pontiac.

How did Beltz see his new task? "I try to approach it from the point of view that a general manager who tries to continue being chief engineer is going to create problems where none existed before. The new chief engineer has responsibility for the engineering. As I see it, we get a better job if he sticks to that and I stick to general managing," Beltz told Jim Wargo, a reporter for McGraw-Hill (*Product Engineering,* September 14, 1970).

The new chief engineer was Howard Kehrl, who had been involved with transmission development for the Toronado and held the title of assistant chief engineer since 1964. He was three years older than Beltz, and was regarded as a Chevrolet man by his colleagues at Oldsmobile.

Kehrl was a native Detroiter who had attended Wayne State University and graduated from the Illinois Institute of Technology. As part of the Naval Officers Training Program during World War II, he went through the Midshipmen's School at the University of Notre Dame in 1944. He stayed on at Notre Dame after the war, teaching some engineering subjects while continuing his studies, graduating in 1948 with a Master of Science degree in engineering mechanics.

Kehrl joined GM that same year as a graduate-in-training with the Research Laboratories, and a year later became research engineer. From 1951 to 1954 he worked as a senior project engineer and later assistant staff engineer at Cadillac's tank plant in Cleveland, and then he was transferred to Chevrolet. There, he worked his way up through the ranks, from development engineer to design engineer and finally, director of the Chevrolet Engineering Laboratories.

A wave of reassignments allowed his appointment as chief engineer of Oldsmobile, and we'll deal with that side of the business as we examine the technical evolution of the Oldsmobile car under Kehrl's leadership.

"Kehrl came to Olds from Chevrolet," remembered Bob Schultz, "and it was sort of a surprise, for Olds did not have much interdivisional traffic in engineering personnel. It was great news to us at Olds, for he was a great engine guy. He really knew what he was talking about in engines. He got into the body/chassis end of the business at Olds and rounded out his experience."

Experimental Oldsmobile 455-cubic-inch V-8 with turbocharger had aluminum cylinder block and heads.

Cro-Sal Can-Am racing engine in front view. The space taken up by the turbochargers and fuel-injection system more than doubled the package size of the basic engine.

1971 Oldsmobile Delta 88 Royale two-door hardtop. Oldsmobile B- and C-body cars had new frames and completely new body structures this year. The split-grille design came to maturity on these cars.

After many years' absence, the full-size wagon came back to Oldsmobile in 1971. The Custom Cruiser was built on a 127-inch wheelbase and shared the front sheet metal with the 98-series. It introduced a clamshell tailgate.

Beltz, meanwhile, threw himself into his new responsibilities with characteristic energy and enthusiasm, always with clear ideas, from marketing to government relations, from financial control to automation. But the product never left his field of attention for a moment. Product planning received particular emphasis.

"Beltz was obsessed, I think, with the need to make the car designs more attractive to the consumer," said an Oldsmobile marketing man, "and to proliferate the model mix with cars that were not volume leaders but contributed something in image appeal."

"Beltz was the perfect sales-promotion type of guy," opined a sales staff member. "He was willing to do all kinds of crazy stuff." That refers to Beltz's open manner with the dealers, the press and the public, and his readiness to take any new proposal for making Oldsmobile better known throughout the whole spectrum of the auto market, no matter how far-fetched it might sound, under serious consideration.

The sales staff man added, "He was an engineer and as such he was super. And he was strong, of course. By far the best man we've ever had around here. But he could be hard to deal with. He was very demanding."

In the sales department, Bill Buxton had taken over from Mack Worden, who was tapped for a corporate office, serving first as director of the Marketing Staff, and since 1969 as vice president in charge of the Marketing Staff. J. M. Fleming was named marketing director for Oldsmobile. Oldsmobile continued its upward march in the face of determined and prosperous competitors, and a fairly static total market.

Lynn Townsend, chairman of Chyrsler Corporation, predicted new-car sales at the level of 9.6 million for 1969. He missed by over 150,000 cars, and Chrysler's corporate sales figure declined by 100,000 cars. Its challenge had fizzled. So had

1972 Oldsmobile Cutlass S hardtop coupe. Because of the strike in 1970, the 1972 models were delayed one year, and the production car for 1972 carried on the sheet metal from 1971.

1972 Oldsmobile Delta 88 Royale hardtop sedan. Revisions in the bumper and grille arrangement were not totally fortunate. Sheet metal remained unchanged from 1971.

Mercury's, whose sales declined by 15,000 cars. The picture for Oldsmobile was healthy, with a cloudless outlook:

	1968	1969
Total market (millions)	9.4	9.45
Olds sales	624,262	642,889
Olds rank	6th	6th
Olds market share	6.64%	6.81%
GM market share	46.7 %	46.8 %

Sales of the 98 advanced from 94,000 to 111,000 and the Delta 88 (all lines) from 209,000 to 224,000. The division's A-body cars were holding their ground relative to their rivals in the intermediate market, with a slight decline. The Tempest was taking a bad beating, and the Buick Special/Skylark, still behind the F-85, paralleled its downtrend. The A-body cars' share of Oldsmobile sales slipped from 47.3 to 43.8 percent, a most welcome adjustment, since the bigger cars had higher profit margins.

GM spent a total of $1.044 billion to build and equip new plants and modernize existing facilities during 1969. Oldsmobile's share was quite minimal, but plant capacity increases at Oldsmobile were budgeted for 1970 and 1971. Pontiac got most of the money allocated to the car divisions in 1969, for such projects as a five-story administration building, a bigger assembly plant in Pontiac, a new emissions test lab.

Product development at Oldsmobile progressed within the confines of the new directives issued by the top corporate management. All-new B- and C-bodies were planned for the 1971 model year, with a total renewal of the A-body for 1972.

"There are essentially five marque studios," explained former GM Styling Staff member Stan Mott in *Car* magazine, September 1969. "There are also four body studios in which the A, B, C, and E bodies are designed . . . although any empty studio can be turned overnight into a special project studio if management so needs."

Beginning in 1968, the duties of the GM Engineering Staff were formulated this way: "Engineering Staff develops forward engineering policies, and coordinates the product programs of the divisions. It also carries out engineering studies of new products and developments which are beyond the basic research stage." Harry Barr was then vice president in charge of the Engineering Staff.

In 1971-72 Oldsmobile was given responsibility for steering, in coordination with Saginaw. Chevrolet had to share its responsibility for suspension design with Pontiac, since that division was placed in charge of handling (vehicle dynamics), which also impinged on Oldsmobile's area, since steering cannot be separated from handling.

Buick retained control of brakes, in coordination with Delco-Moraine; and Cadillac's responsibility for driver vision was divided between the division and the Styling Staff. Chevrolet was given the added responsibility of front-end structures, which meant bumpers and impact-absorption by the car as a whole, or 'energy management' as the studies of the diffusion of impact forces into specific elements of body and frame were sometimes called.

Despite all this central direction and integration, people at Oldsmobile still retained a feeling of independence. "Corporate control over product planning and design may have hit Oldsmobile last," said a former Oldsmobile engineer. "The distance from the GM Building in Detroit to Lansing may have helped delay the process." Of course, Buick was just as far away, up in Flint, so the theory probably is not valid. But there are other differences that set Oldsmobile apart from the other divisions.

1973 Oldsmobile Cutlass Colonnade hardtop sedan. In the new A-body, a B-post was included, but Oldsmobile publicity insisted on calling the sedan a hardtop.

1974 Oldsmobile Cutlass Salon Colonnade hardtop coupe. The fender lines from the 1970 styling mockup got into the 1973-model A-body. Despite its 112-inch wheelbase, overall length was 210.6 inches.

Jim Williams explained: "Oldsmobile was structured quite differently from Chevrolet, for instance, where product planning was carefully coordinated between sales and marketing, on one side, engineering and production on the other. At Oldsmobile, the engineering department made a lot of decisions that perhaps, today, they would not make."

A retired Oldsmobile sales official told us: "Oldsmobile's engineering department was very much in control of what the division did in terms of product. They released it, and engaged their responsibility for it. Olds engineers seem to have a more unilateral attitude than in other divisions. Whenever they were ready, they released the hardware, independently of the sales department."

A prominent engineer admitted: "At Olds the engineering department made all the product decisions—and took all the lumps. We did not have so much to do with the numbers of everything that was produced; but in terms of what the designs were like, we were in control. Oldsmobile's product planners did not have the same sophisticated 'clinic' activities going on in those years that we have now."

A man who worked in the Oldsmobile exterior styling studio in 1969-70 shed further light on the situation: "The general manager was supposed to have the final say-so over styling but it was the engineering department that appropriated that right. The engineers spent more time in the styling studios and had more to say about styling than the sales people or the manufacturing people."

A manufacturing engineer had his own theory: "Our engineers prided themselves on the quality of the Oldsmobile car. There was always a heavy emphasis on reliability. Perhaps that had a part in making the engineering management so strong. You kind of got the impression when you were working here that Oldsmobile was leading the industry in reliability."

Jim Williams corroborated his opinion: "Olds had a ton of pride in quality. There was a feeling of superiority which rubbed off on the customer. Oldsmobile enjoyed tremendous owner loyalty. People who bought an Olds had such a good car

they came back for the next one. Of course, Olds had a good advantage in the work force. It was a stable force. People went to work at Oldsmobile and never left. Olds had workers who cared, and workers who held leading positions in the community. You never heard anyone say anything against Oldsmobile in Lansing."

A service department official from Olds recalled, "When they started building the Vega at Lordstown, they had all the most modern equipment and a plant full of young people. They boasted they were going to do one hundred cars an hour, and I guess they did. We all know about the quality problems and callbacks they ran into. Well, at Olds in Lansing, for years we had been doing 100 to 110 cars an hour much bigger and with more parts and more varieties of options than you could get in the Vega, and with a fine quality record. That's the way Oldsmobiles were made, and everybody worked together to keep it that way."

Beltz was looking beyond merely maintaining the best parts of Oldsmobile. He was looking to the future, and was always looking for ways to get the idea across to young people that Oldsmobile just plain knew more about cars than other car makers. He sought to impress them with Oldsmobile's engineering ability.

As an example, he thought it might be important to attract future buyers, that Oldsmobile should demonstrate its ability to outdo the rest of the industry in engine design and development. The hardware that was created in support of this idea was indeed outstanding.

Beltz had actually started some engine projects shortly after becoming chief engineer. Gill Burrell laid out an experimental single-overhead-camshaft version of the 330-cubic-inch V-8 in 1966, and Harold M. Haskew and P. L. Francis developed it to a high degree of refinement, with a specific power output about ten percent above the hottest production version.

In 1967-68, Frank Ball was working on a four-valves-per-cylinder version of the 4-4-2 engine. Doubling the number of valves opened the way for increasing the gas flow mass while cutting back on valve overlap, thereby increasing power and torque while reducing fuel consumption and exhaust emissions.

Each bank was given a hemi-head with two camshafts operating four valves per cylinder. All four camshafts were driven by a train of spur gears from the crankshaft, an arrangement that is known to give extremely accurate valve timing—with the drawback of being noisy, especially at idle.

Both of these designs were pursued as candidates for production. Others were started as design exercises or to seek the glory of racing victories.

In 1969, Oldsmobile agreed to cooperate with Gene Crowe and Ralph Salyer in the creation of an engine for their proposed four-wheel-drive Can-Am racing prototype called the Cro-Sal. Target output was in the area of 700 hp.

The job was given to Gil Burrell. As John Beltz explained to Ray Brock, editor of *Motor Trend*, "He is in charge of our advanced engine designs. He has no worries at all about current problems and he has a great mind—purely a creative designer. All he has to do is tinker with new ideas. It's his responsibility to keep us ahead."

Burrell dusted off his turbocharging know-how and put a turbocharger on each bank of the 455-cubic-inch V-8. The units were TRW 375 E10, and the system allowed boost pressures up to 10½ pounds per square inch. The cylinder compression ratio was lowered to 8.4:1, well within safe limits of overall pressure, and a Lucas fuel-injection system was adapted.

Though the block followed the production-model design, it was cast in aluminum to save weight. The heads were also aluminum castings, of standard design, with the runners reworked to give more efficient gas flow.

A lot of hot-rod parts were used inside, such as Forgedtrue pistons, Dykes rings, Bruce Crower camshaft and valve springs. TRW came up with special valves, and Oldsmobile made its own forged-steel crankshaft with a three-inch main-bearing diameter. Dynamometer tests made in the spring of 1969 showed that the engine put out 647 hp at 5500 rpm and 659 hp at 6250 rpm. As the Can-Am season began, the Cro-Sal was anything but raceready, however, and this very interesting project was abandoned. Oldsmobile kept on fiddling with the engine for a while to test the effects of low compression on emission control, but nothing new came out of that.

A second racing engine concept was created to study, as Burrell phrased it, 'the top efficiency potential of the 350-cubic-inch V-8.' The cast-iron block was bored out to give a displacement of 389 cubic inches, and the standard heads were modified for improved breathing. The standard camshaft was replaced by a flat-tappet design made by Iskenderian. Each cylinder had its own exhaust pipe, the four for each bank merging into one large-diameter pipe at a point calculated to give optimum extractor effect. An experimental manifold was created, cast in aluminum, with headers to form flanges for four two-barrel Weber Type IDA downdraft carburetors, each fitted with short ram pipes. This was a high-compression engine (about 11.5:1), tuned to deliver 500 hp. It was installed in a Cutlass and taken to the Bonneville Salt Flats where it established a new international Class C speed record.

In 1970 Oldsmobile revealed that Burrell had been working on a low-profile dual-fan Toronado engine. The accessory drive was rearranged to carry two smaller fans instead of the single standard big one, driven by V-belt from an automatic clutch on the nose of the crankshaft. This was done in preparation for future Toronado installations with a lower hood line. The area of the two fans corresponded well with the planned radiator outline, giving more efficient air flow and better cooling,

without the need for fan shrouding. Tests indicated that the dual-fan combination drained less power from the engine and produced less fan noise, but it was pushed aside as redundant when the 1971 Toronado was designed.

What did get into production was much tamer, conceptually, but had all the power that the cars could possibly use. For 1969, Oldsmobile introduced W-Machine options for the Cutlass S and 4-4-2.

The Cutlass S engine was designated W-31 and was a 350-cubic-inch V-8 with 10.5:1 compression and a performance-calibrated Quadrajet carburetor, delivering 325 hp at 5400 rpm. But the W-31 package was more than the engine, borrowing some suspension reinforcements from the 4-4-2 and including a plastic hood with functional air scoops, as well as specific ornamentation in the form of paint stripes and W-31 chrome lettering on the front fenders.

The 455-cubic-inch engine was made standard in the 4-4-2, with a rating of 365 hp at 5000 rpm. Those willing to pay for more received the W-30 version, with a hotter camshaft and select-fit engine parts, putting out 370 hp at 5200 rpm. But the effect fell short of expectations, even within the hot-rod and dragstrip market, and it is doubtful that it had any long-term benefit for the Oldsmobile image. For the overall car market, the effect was assessed as negligible.

More significant, in practical terms, was the introduction of valve rotators on all V-8 engines—350, 400 and 455—for 1970. Valve rotators, giving the valve stem a part-turn every time the valve opened, were common in heavy-duty truck engines; especially on exhaust valves, because of their effects in equalizing valve-head to valve-seat wear, maintaining a better seal and higher heat flux, all of which resulted in longer engine life and longer intervals between valve jobs. Oldsmobile put valve rotators not only on the exhausts but on the intake valves as well, putting Oldsmobile engines truly in a class of their own.

Since 1970 production engines were the responsibility of Bob Stempel, for Kehrl had taken Frank Ball out of that group and promoted him to assistant chief engineer in charge of sheet metal and advance design. Bob Dorshimer continued as assistant chief engineer for the motor, transmission and chassis group.

Robert C. Stempel had been assistant motor engineer since the end of 1966, when Lloyd Gill retired. Born in Trenton, New Jersey, Bob Stempel got his engineering degree from the Worcester Polytechnic Institute, graduating in 1955. He served two years in the U.S. Army and came to Oldsmobile in 1958 where he was put to work as a senior detailer in the chassis group. After a variety of assignments, he became transmission design engineer in 1963.

Bob Stempel was universally respected, and many of his colleagues regarded him with awe, if not reverence. "Stempel would work night and day to learn everything he could possibly learn about a car," said Bob Schultz, "and when Bob had the story together you could be pretty well satisfied that it was the complete story. He is an excellent engineer."

"Stempel's biggest strength was engine development, and more specifically, emission controls," a high-ranking Oldsmobile executive explained. "He got in on emission controls early, and that's what gave him his start on the way up. But he's a man who'd say 'don't get in my way—I'm in a hurry to get there.' "

From among his engineering colleagues, we were told things like: "He is a very astute man, and a hell of a hard worker. I mean, you can't keep up with him."

"There's just one word for Stempel—gangbusters. He's on the job night and day, and he's a super talker. He's got all the answers, and he's got them right."

"He's a very good leader, and a hard worker with tremendous energy and drive."

Among other personnel changes that Kehrl ordered, almost as soon as he became chief engineer, was to appoint Tom Krieg as chassis engineer and move George T. Jones over as body engineer. At the same time, Bob Schultz was named head of product-planning engineering.

Beltz fully approved of these changes, and explained the philosophy behind them to Jim Wargo (*Product Engineering,* September 14, 1970): "Engineers must be moved horizontally, all people need to be moved horizontally. In anyone's career, it's impossible to move rapidly enough to suit his needs for variety and experience if each move must be a promotion. At Olds, a man may be moved from suspension or ride and handling, or developing the F-85, to a position where he can become expert in, for example, wheels and tires. The purpose is to keep him interested. If he's interested, he keeps learning, and you keep developing people."

At the corporate management level, John Beltz also found changes in personnel, and at first it looked great. At Boyes's retirement, Pete Estes was promoted to group vice president in charge of the Car and Truck Group. Estes had been an Oldsmobile engineer before he was offered the post of chief engineer for Pontiac in 1956. But in 1970, Estes was sent off to Europe as head of GM's overseas subsidiaries, and a colorless bureaucrat, Richard Terrell, who had formerly been group executive for non-automotive and defense activities, took over the Car and Truck Group.

A parallel upheaval in personnel in the GM Styling Staff had actually preceded the reshuffle at Oldsmobile. In February 1968, Stan Wilen was transferred from chief designer of the Oldsmobile studio to the same office for the Cadillac studio. Stanley Parker, who had run the Cadillac studio for six years, took over at Oldsmobile.

Bill Mitchell, vice president in charge of the Styling Staff, had always had a small number of personal assistants, whose duties were never spelled out. Suddenly, their assignments were formalized. Irv Rybicki was named executive in charge of the divisional exterior studios; Clare MacKichan became executive in charge of advanced automotive design and engineering; and Vincent D. Kaptur, Jr., chief engineer of automotive body development. Jack Humbert was made group chief designer for the Pontiac, Oldsmobile, Buick and Cadillac studios, forming another layer separating the creative area from styling management.

On arrival in the Oldsmobile studio, Stanley Parker outlined some of his ideas to Joe Callahan (*Automotive News,* October 28, 1968). "Our design trends are toward cleaner looks, more simplicity and less clutter. For several years, all of us were guilty of torturing metal, but you can't save a design by loading on tons of chrome," Parker declared.

Work on the 1970 models was in full swing when Parker was given the Oldsmobile studio. That was a year for slight change, since the big overhaul of the B- and C-bodies was coming on the 1971 models. Their main dimensions and outline were fixed by the end of 1968, and it's in the 1971 Delta 88, 98 and Toronado that we first see the true Parker treatment.

The 88's and 98's for 1971 were longer and lower, with faster windshield angles and side glass curved to continue the sheet metal contour. The roof structure was cantilevered on the C-post to permit the widest possible front and side visibility.

New split grilles appeared, standing in big rectangular frames extending downward into the bumper area, where the main rail was lowered. The side-by-side dual headlamps were set in rectangular bezels to match the squared-off look of the grille. On the Delta Royale, the grille was made of fabricated aluminum, while all others had chrome die-cast grilles.

The convertible disappeared from the 98-series, while the Town sedan and Luxury sedan were replaced by four-door hardtops.

Oldsmobile brought back the full-size station wagon as a 1971 model called Custom Cruiser. It shared the front-end sheet metal and grille with the 98, but was a B-body vehicle. Chevrolet, Pontiac and Buick had the same body shell. One feature of the wagon was the clamshell tailgate, stemming from a patent by Edward N. Cole. The rear glass retracted up into the roof, and the lower tailgate panel slid down under the floor.

Prices were still relatively uninflated:

Body Style	Delta 88	Delta 88 Custom	Delta 88 Royale
Four-door sedan	$3,749	$3,940	
Four-door hardtop	3,867	4,108	
Two-door hardtop	3,805	4,033	$4,291
Convertible coupe			4,299

Body Style	Custom Cruiser	98	Luxury 88
Four-door hardtop		$4,852	$5,159
Two-door hardtop		4,790	5,065
Station wagon	$4,518		

Power steering and power front disc brakes were standard throughout, but buyers of the 88 or even the Custom Cruiser had to pay $243 extra for automatic transmission.

Passenger-car models had coil-spring rear axle suspension, while the station wagons had rear axles mounted on multi-leaf semi-elliptics. This was not done out of any need to increase carrying capacity, but for reasons of space utilization. If the four-link coil-spring suspension had been used, the optional third seat would have been too high for the roofline. The third seat was forward-facing, with entry from the front, by folding half of the regular back seat. The Custom Cruiser was built on the same 127-inch wheelbase as the 98, while the 88's had a 124-inch wheelbase.

All B- and C-body models had a new front suspension, based on the Buick-developed Accu-Drive, which had the control-arm geometry arranged so as to maximize stability during bump deflections on the straightaway, at the cost of increasing roll-understeer.

All engines had lower compression ratios to enable them to operate on low-octane, regular-grade gasoline. This was done throughout the industry, and therefore did not put Oldsmobile at any particular disadvantage.

Just as the 1971 models went into production, a one-hundred-day strike laid Oldsmobile completely idle. It has been calculated that GM lost more than one million cars due to that strike, with a loss of about 180,000 cars suffered by Oldsmobile. Although it was 1971-model cars that were involved, the greater part of the loss shows up in the 1970 calendar-year registrations.

	1970	1971
Total market (millions)	8.4	9.8
Olds sales	461,732	661,380
Olds rank	7th	5th
Olds market share	5.5%	6.8%
GM market share	39.7%	45.2%

Under the effect of the strike, GM's 1970 penetration dropped to the lowest point since 1935. Pontiac managed to hang on to fourth place, but Dodge got ahead of Buick and Oldsmobile. The following year, Olds climbed above both Dodge and Buick.

These gains were won mainly on the strength of the B- and C-body cars. The intermediates (no longer called F-85, but only Cutlass) were basically unchanged since 1968, and it was clever packaging and merchandizing that kept them strong—well ahead of both the Buick Skylark and the Pontiac Le Mans.

Though Cutlass sales moved up in numbers from 1970 to 1971 (237,418 to 290,772), their share of the division's business went down from 51.4 percent to forty-four percent (by number of cars—not in dollar volume). The 98 enjoyed a strong revival of popularity, going from 63,000 to 113,000 cars; the Toronado came out ahead of the Riviera for the first time; and the 88's, including the Custom and Royale, outsold Pontiac's lower-priced Catalina (including the Brougham and leftover Executives).

Another effect of the strike was the postponement of the new A-body program, scheduled for 1972, but set back by one whole year, as GM stopped tooling orders and deferred a maximum of spending till the cash flow had been reestablished.

The 1972-model Cutlass was given a facelift, consisting mainly of a new split grille of bolder design, with horizontal bars. Power trains were simplified, with elimination of the Chevrolet six-cylinder engine, so that every Oldsmobile was

1975 Oldsmobile Cutlass Salon Colonnade hardtop coupe. It started out with a 350-cubic-inch V-8 as standard in 1973; two years later, the standard engine was a 250-cubic-inch Chevrolet six rated at 105 hp.

powered by a V-8 made by the division itself. New brake drums for the Cutlass were four pounds heavier, for greater heat-sink capacity, and had cast-in ribs.

In the B- and C-body cars, styling changes for 1972 were minimal. However, Oldsmobile took an important step in the area of body structure, with the adoption of a one-piece plastic front-end panel—lightweight and corrosion-free.

Olds was not the first to use plastics in this application, for Pontiac had tried it on the GTO two years earlier. "But Pontiac went through a horrible experience," recalled Bob Schultz, "and word went around the corporation that nobody would ever do that again. But we had been working on it and felt pretty good about it, and it was about a year after Pontiac had stopped using plastic front-end panels that Oldsmobile got into it in a big way, using a shell-molding compound. The first year we bought them outside. Then we put in our own compression-molding equipment and next we got our own mixing equipment." Oldsmobile was in the plastics business to stay.

While the new A-body cars were being designed, Leonard M. Casillo succeeded Stanley Parker as head of the Oldsmobile studio. He had been assistant chief designer under Parker since 1968, and had a hand in the 1971 Toronado and other models. Casillo had started out with Chevrolet in 1961, and then did a stint in the Oldsmobile studio. After two or three years, he left Oldsmobile to work in the Advance Studio, and came back to Olds in the number two spot.

Engineering personnel changes included naming George T. Jones executive engineer and moving W. A. Weidman up as transmission engineer. It was on the personnel front that Oldsmobile was to be struck by the worst of all imaginable tragedies: In the spring of 1972, John Beltz succumbed to cancer.

He knew it was coming. It was in 1970 that the doctors had told him it was terminal, and during the two years that followed, he continued to lead Oldsmobile

Division, competently, cheerfully, never letting on to outsiders that anything was wrong with his health—right to the end. Sorrow of his death was widespread. And suddenly, Oldsmobile Division was like a ship without a rudder.

"After Beltz, Olds was confused and its image shattered," an engineer expressed his opinion. It was almost a reflex on the part of Ed Cole, then president of GM, and John Z. DeLorean, vice president for the Car and Truck Group, to move the chief engineer into the general manager's office at Oldsmobile. That was a tradition in Lansing.

But this time, the appointment was received with mixed feelings. The new general manager was Howard M. Kehrl, who had been chief engineer for three years and with Olds for eight years. It is true that Kehrl, succeeding Beltz first as chief engineer and then as general manager, was up against 'a tough act to follow.' The men in the engineering ranks never praised him without some barbs: "He impressed us with his vast knowledge, but he was so slow in making up his mind it's like he thought the time would stand still for him," said one.

"Kehrl was a good engineer, but, oh so conservative, and I don't think he did any good around here," we heard from another.

"He had an open mind and was ready to be convinced we ought to do this or that, but if he had any strong opinions himself he hid it well, and he never gave us a feeling of leadership," a third engineer stated.

It was his superiors rather than his subordinates that Kehrl impressed most; his invariably calm appearance and carefully phrased comments and softly spoken arguments gave him the stamp of executive quality. Promotions came his way with shorter and shorter intervals. After a year and a half as general manager of Oldsmobile, Kehrl was appointed group vice president in charge of the Car and Truck Group.

A former staff member does not rate him highly for his contribution to Oldsmobile: "Beltz infused all of us with a new kind of enthusiasm, and gave us unequaled leadership. Then they ran Howard Kehrl in there after him. He was an old fuddy-duddy and the whole thing fell apart in his hands. We lost the spirit."

In 1975 Kehrl was given responsibility for the Design, Engineering, Manufacturing and Research Staffs, and since the start of 1981, he holds office as vice chairman of General Motors. When he left Oldsmobile, he had nothing to do with picking his successor.

John D. Baker was the chairman's choice. Richard G. Gerstenberg admired his performance as head of GM of Canada, and Ed Cole agreed to let him have a chance to run Oldsmobile. Baker had come up through Delco-Remy Division, having joined GM at the age of twenty-three in 1940. But within a month of moving to Lansing, Baker died.

Kehrl then acted to get an Oldsmobile man at the helm, and Terrell and Cole quickly gave their approval for the promotion of Robert J. Cook as general manager of Oldsmobile. Cook had joined GM as an engineering student at the GM Institute in 1940, and was assigned to Oldsmobile where he worked his way up through a number of production and purchasing posts. He served as general manufacturing

manager from the start of 1972, as Rollis went into retirement and Bob Truxell was transferred to purchasing.

"Now Oldsmobile has the right man in the right place again," claimed Fritz Bennetts, public relations director of Oldsmobile, shortly after Cook's appointment. But there is no unanimity inside the division about Cook's way of doing things.

A marketing official told us, "He's good in money. He's good in production and product quality. But he's just too stodgy."

And this from an engineer: "Cook's a nice guy, but hopelessly conservative."

Bob Stempel was named chief engineer of Oldsmobile in May 1972, but left the division in June 1973, to serve as special assistant to the president of GM (Ed Cole). When Cole retired in the fall of 1974, Stempel went to Chevrolet as engineering director, and in November 1978, he was named general manager of Pontiac.

Bob Dorshimer moved up as chief engineer of Oldsmobile in June 1973, and it was a wise and popular choice. "Dorshimer is a super engineer," said one of his assistants. "He's smart. Great guy to work for. And the best chief engineer in General Motors."

Another engineer said: "Bob Dorshimer is his own man. He's not flashy. He just gets things done—year after year after year."

Another engineer succeeded Cole as president of the corporation—Pete Estes, who had been identified with Olds before he went to Pontiac in 1956.

In the Oldsmobile product lineup for 1973, the addition of the compact Omega was overshadowed by the all-new Cutlass. The Omega was not built by Oldsmobile, but by the GM Assembly Division, to Chevrolet design, sharing the body, chassis and basic power unit with the Nova. Modifications made to give it an Oldsmobile appearance were mainly confined to the grille. It was built as a sedan, coupe and hatchback on a 111-inch wheelbase, with the Chevrolet six as the base engine, and Oldsmobile's 350-cubic-inch V-8 as optional.

This sharing of complete cars among several divisions was the result of rising costs. Even more typical was the splitting up of the car into various areas of responsibility. "It's a matter of where the resources are," explained an Oldsmobile engineer. "You go after the group that gives you resources in certain areas, and the components and systems of the car are divided up among a number of activities assigned to separate divisions, coordinated by the corporate staff."

The new Cutlass was a corporate design, in which Oldsmobile's main contribution was the steering gear and linkage, engineered in collaboration with Saginaw and Delco. Saginaw made the steering gear, and Delco produced a hydraulic vibration damper to filter out road shocks from the steering linkage.

The brake system was developed by Buick and Delco-Moraine, and was noted for using front discs as standard, without power assist. Power brakes were standard for station wagons and high-line models—an extra-cost option for the rest of the line.

A new perimeter frame was designed by the GM Engineering Staff and developed by Chevrolet, while the body design and engineering were done by the

Styling Staff in liaison with Fisher body. Pontiac was involved with the body-mounting system and designed the coil-spring rear suspension, while Chevrolet developed the front suspension (based on Buick's Accu-Drive geometry).

The dual-wheelbase principle was continued, with the same 112-inch wheelbase for the two-door and 116-inch wheelbase for the four-door models. But the number of body styles was drastically reduced. There were no hardtops and no convertibles. "The convertible was eliminated primarily because of safety," said Bob Schultz, "and though the NHTSA rules had provision for convertibles, we felt we were still not on solid ground with regard to product liability."

"Convertibles were probably loss-makers, anyway," stated an official in the sales department.

Body Style	Cutlass	Cutlass S	Cutlass Supreme
Four-door sedan	$3,137		$3,395
Two-door sedan	3,049	$3,159	3,245

All A-body station wagons were Vista-Cruisers, with prices starting at $3,789.

The B- and C-body range continued with minimal alterations. A Regency four-door hardtop was added to the 98-series, but the 88 lineup was unchanged. The division's engine program included only two sizes, 350 and 455 cubic inches, of the same basic V-8.

The sales picture improved substantially after the introduction of the Omega, which meant sheer plus-business for Oldsmobile dealers, and the new intermediates, which gained twenty-three percent in sedans and coupes but lost 38.5 percent in station wagons. In return, Custom Cruiser sales climbed by twenty-six percent. The B-body car was static overall, though the Royale was stealing sales from the plain Delta 88, and the C-body models slipped by a few percentage points.

Cutlass sales accounted for 45.5 percent of Oldsmobile's unit sales in 1973, up from 43.5 the previous year.

The model lineup had few changes for 1974. The 4-4-2 was dropped in the wake of the fuel crisis, but the Cutlass line was expanded by adding the Salon above the Supreme.

Bob Dorshimer made some reassignments and conferred assistant chief engineer titles on Jim Lewis and Bob Schultz (Frank Ball was already holding that title). W. L. Freiberg was appointed power train engineer and T. R. Fernand chassis engineer, while G. T. Jones became executive engineer and Ted Louckes body engineer.

Oldsmobile added an extra 45,000 square feet to its Lansing plant between the end of 1973 and the spring of 1976. These expansions were connected with assembly facilities for the Cutlass and the new B-body cars due as 1977 models. At the same time, Fisher Body started an 85,000-square-foot expansion of its Lansing plant to serve Oldsmobile's growing needs. This added a new paint shop, a new facility for interior trim and a railhead extension. It was completed in 1977.

1976 Cutlass Supreme Colonnade hardtop coupe. Basically a 1973 model, the Cutlass was not to be downsized until the 1978 model year. New rectangular headlamps were a handicap rather than a plus for the styling.

In 1974 the engine plant was retooled to add a smaller V-8 of 260-cubic-inch displacement, which became standard for the 1975-model Cutlass Salon, and optional for other Cutlass and Omega models. It was essentially a 350 block with smaller bore. The 250-cubic-inch Chevrolet six was standard in Omega and Cutlass, while the 350 V-8 became standard in the Delta 88 and Royale. The Custom Cruiser was given the 400 V-8 as standard, so that only the 98 and Toronado carried the 455 V-8 as standard. At the start of 1975, Oldsmobile was making 182 engines an hour.

Engine	Production Per Hour
260 V-8	35
350 V-8	95
400 V-8	12
455 V-8	40

All Oldsmobile engines for 1975 had exhaust systems with catalytic converters. From 1970 through 1974, meeting the increasingly stringent emission standard had caused a big drop in the gasoline mileage of all Oldsmobile models. The use of catalytic converters made it possible to restore some of the lost fuel economy by allowing the engines to run more efficiently but with dirtier exhaust, which the converter then cleaned up.

"Oldsmobile was instrumental at the time when the catalytic converter project was started," claimed Bob Dorshimer. "Olds became involved with all sorts

1977 Oldsmobile Starfire SX sport coupe. The Starfire name was out of production from 1966 to 1976. The new Starfire was a subcompact with the HS-body derived from the Chevrolet Vega/Monza.

1977 Oldsmobile 98 Regency sedan. With wheelbase cut down from 127 to 119 inches, the car was over 700 pounds lighter than the preceding model. Standard engine was a 170-hp 350-cubic-inch V-8.

of questions. What sort of converter should it be? Where should it go? We were dealing with a new piece of stuff for six millions cars a year. It was a traumatic two-year-long battle of wits. Olds did it. Bob Stempel was our top engineer on that. Even Ed Cole was involved.''

Since Chevrolet was introducing the Monza coupe for 1975, Oldsmobile was given its own version of the HS-body car. Nobody knew what to call it, and finally Cook settled on the Starfire name, thus transferring a name formerly associated with the most powerful, luxurious and prestigious models to the smallest (but not the cheapest).

The new Starfire was built as a two-door coupe only, conforming to a basic shape evolved under Chuck Jordan's direction. The car was built at Lordstown, Ohio, and was powered by a Buick V-6 engine, so that Oldsmobile's involvement was mainly as a selling agent.

A low-budget restyling of the X-body for 1975 resulted in a dramatically more modern look, especially for the Omega four-door sedan. The Omega line was split in two trim levels—Omega and Omega Salon.

Changes in the intermediates and full-size cars were absolutely minimal. They were all to be replaced as soon as possible, continuing only to keep the assembly lines busy and the showrooms filled until new and more economical cars could be developed and put into production.

The corporation's downsizing program led to the creation of task forces for each car size, with priority of timing so as to replace the biggest cars first: the new B- and C-bodies for 1977, the new A-body for 1978 and new X- and E-bodies for 1979.

Why were the Delta 88/98 downsized before the Cutlass? It wasn't Oldsmobile's decision; it was a corporation decision. ''We are trying to pull our biggest ones down first. The serious problem is—and I hate the damn word—the gas guzzlers. They are the ones we have to get rid of first,'' said Pete Estes in an interview published in Forbes magazine, August 15, 1975.

Several little dramas were played out to prolong the lives of the moribund 'gas-guzzlers' and make them more competitive by modest spending on styling changes. One example was the 1976 Cutlass S Colonnade hardtop coupe, built on the A-Special body. ''We tried it out in a clinic,'' recalled Irv Rybicki. ''I think it was in Dallas.

''Four cars were in it—Monte Carlo, Grand Prix, Buick Regal and the Cutlass S, which had the first real lean-back nose. We got the results here three weeks later and when the computer had sorted it all out they placed the Grand Prix on top, and the Cutlass Supreme was way down here on the bloody bottom!

''That was nine months before it went on sale. Oldsmobile panicked and asked us to change it. In the time available, it was impossible to make any big changes. I tried to analyze the information and decided it could have been nothing more than the color they reacted unfavorably to. I put my finger on the color and nothing else, for we were confident, all of us who had anything to do with that design, that the car was a real winner.

''The battle went on. We took a firm position in favor of the car, and the division finally backed down. 'OK, we'll go with it.'—Well, hell, it was the hottest thing we put out that year.''

At the start of the 1976 model year, GM Chairman Thomas A. Murphy forecast that the corporation would make 4.6 million cars in the year ahead. The divisional general managers furnished individual make-by-make breakdowns which put Oldsmobile's target at 691,000 cars, ahead of Buick (at 650,000) but behind Pontiac (700,000). Cadillac was expected to make 275,000 cars and Chevrolet 2,295,000.

When the year was up, Oldsmobile had sold 867,485 cars, nearly eleven percent above the prognosis. Pontiac barely exceeded its goal, while Cadillac and Buick moved ahead by considerable margins. Only Chevrolet fell far short. Would this be reflected in a more equitable balance between Chevrolet and the other car divisions? Not at all. To the corporate accountants, Chevrolet is the mass market, and the division is supported to the hilt.

Oldsmobile's sales performance, however, was so phenomenal that the Cutlass outsold the lower-priced Chevelle by a 1.75:1 ratio. The intermediate-car share of Oldsmobile sales jumped in one calendar year from 53.66 percent to 57.2

Model	1975	1976
Starfire	28,072	27,545
Omega	37,672	54,806
Cutlass	324,610	495,976
Delta 88/Royale	103,261	143,627
98/Cruiser	91,666	122,585
Toronado	19,601	22,946

Oldsmobile 88's of 1977 vintage underwent a storm of litigation in the following year or two. It turned out that a number of such cars were sold with Chevrolet V-8 engines—a combination that did not exist in any catalogue, which was never advertised, and of which no notice was given to the buyers. When it was revealed in the press, Oldsmobile came under a barrage of lawsuits from owners who wanted an Oldsmobile engine when they bought an Oldsmobile car.

"It was not intended to bamboozle the public." explained an Oldsmobile engineer. "The prior year—1975—we had engine capacity up to bazoo, and we were sitting here trying to find new outlets for our V-8's. The marine market took about 10,000. Then Bob Hoyne, one of our manufacturing people, negotiated with other divisions and got Buick and Pontiac interested in the 350-cubic-inch V-8. Olds engines had a super reputation, and they wanted them. We made commitments to Buick and Pontiac for a quantity of 350-cubic-inch V-8's with four-barrel carburetors."

A Pontiac spokesman recalled: "The decision was made somewhere in General Motors. It was part of a general trend towards corporate engines. The main reason was emission-control certification. The divisions were getting ready for downsizing, and had too many power-train combinations in production. The corporation undertook a volume-planning exercise. They decided the market was good for X number of four-barrel V-8's. That number met Oldsmobile's capacity, and Chevrolet's production schedule was cut back correspondingly. In the corporate view, the B-O-P market was more sensitive to four-barrel availability than the Chevrolet market."

That statement is corroborated by sources within Oldsmobile, and an Olds sales official amplified the exlanation: "Suddenly our sales took off. It was unbelievable. We couldn't even supply ourselves with engines—and we couldn't

back out of our commitments because of the special requirements for the V-8's we were making for Buick and Pontiac. So there we were, with a fantastic sales potential, and not enough engines. The engineering department was really upset when they were told 'Chevrolet has the capacity and we'll just have to use their engines.' That's what happened. The Chevy 350 began appearing in the 88. And the dealers weren't notified."

Of course, it wasn't the first time Chevrolet engines were used in Oldsmobile cars. The F-85 has used the Chevy six since back in '66, and the Cutlass had it again from 1974 onward, as did the Omega. And it is certain that no Buick or Pontiac buyers protested if they found out they had Oldsmobile power under their hoods. "It was an inevitable decision," according to an Oldsmobile spokesman. "It probably would have happened in the next year or so, anyway. The biggest mistake was we didn't have a press conference."

The matter certainly would not have been blown up to the same extent if it had been handled differently. Several sources have reported a story about a newspaperman talking to an Oldsmobile official at some preview, saying, "I notice that's a Chevy engine in there . . ."

"Shhhh," was the only answer he got from the factory representative. And that would be enough for any reporter to know he had a story to tell.

Not that there was anything wrong with the Chevy engine, but it seemed wrong that Oldsmobile had something to hide. "Of course, there was the Rocket image," explained Jim Williams. "People grew up with the Rocket V-8. A guy bought an Olds, found he didn't have a Rocket engine, and . . . he thought he had *lost* something." Settling the case cost Oldsmobile about $45 million. Owners settled for $200 a car and a five-year engine warranty.

The 400- and 455- cubic-inch V-8's were discontinued at the end of 1976, and Oldsmobile began producing a new 403-cubic-inch V-8 in September 1976. It was made with the same stroke and crankshaft as the 350- and 260-cubic-inch V-8's. All three shared the same bore centers and deck height. Deck height was unchanged from 1949 specifications. The basic layout of these engines stems from the 330-cubic-inch V-8 introduced in 1964. It had evolved into a 350 for 1968, and the 260 was added in 1975.

For 1977, the engine picture at Oldsmobile became truly corporate. The division had only three versions of its V-8 in production: the 260 (LV-8), the 350 (L-34) and the 403 (L-80). The 403 was standard in the Toronado, and the 350 (by Olds or Chevrolet) in the 98-series. The Chevy 305-cubic-inch V-8 was used in the Omega, Cutlass and Delta 88 as an option above the 231-cubic-inch Buick V-6.

Finally, Chevrolet's Vega engine, the 140-cubic-inch overhead-camshaft four, was standard in the Starfire. It was replaced the following year by Pontiac's 151-cubic-inch pushrod ohv four-cylinder engine.

But the big news for 1977 was the downsized B-body cars. On August 21, 1975, General Motors Chairman Thomas A. Murphy stated in Detroit that his company was planning to spend $15 billion over a six-year period to convert its entire model range to smaller, lighter and more fuel-efficient designs.

1978 Oldsmobile Cutlass Supreme brougham. The down-sized prestige-model intermediate featured a molded-plastic front end and weighed 3,200 pounds.

This was just the first wave in downsizing. The B-body program had been started in 1974, with William T. Collins, a former assistant chief engineer at Pontiac, as program manager. Convertibles were eliminated. The Delta 88 was put on a 116-inch wheelbase (and so was the Custom Cruiser), while the 98 was given a 119-inch wheelbase. They were actually smaller but roomier than the Cutlass, as well as lighter, but still big cars in every sense. The Oldsmobile styling was done by Leonard Casillo, on a basic design developed by Irv Rybicki.

Cutlass sales continued to increase in 1977, but the Delta 88 Royale enjoyed the most spectacular climb, from 111,000 to 156,000 units.

The following year, the A-body cars were downsized in a corporate program directed by Edward L. Mertz, an engineer who had worked under Donald McPherson, Jim Musser and Lloyd Reuss at Chevrolet (where he made his mark). Wilson West, assistant chief engineer of Fisher Body, was attached to the A-body project to handle the body-engineering and production matters, while Irv Rybicki took a very personal hand in the styling.

The new car line was to replace not only all the former A-body models but also those having the G-body (Pontiac Grand Prix and Chevrolet Monte Carlo). The new Cutlass was built on a 108.1-inch wheelbase in three body styles: four-door sedan, two-door coupe and station wagon.

The decision showed excellent continuity of style and detail with the former Cutlass. Leonard Casillo explained: ''Olds has a special ability to pull an Oldsmobile out of a corporate design package, say, the A-body, where we have so much shared metal with the other divisions and we're left with front end sheet metal, taillights and bumper graphics, to make the face on the car particularly *ours*. On both A- and B-bodies the Olds studio has come up with some upper-body designs that have been picked for all-divisional use.''

The existence of a diesel-engine program at Oldsmobile was revealed on September, 19, 1975, by GM Chairman Thomas A. Murphy. It had then been going on for two years—for it was in 1972 that Bob Dorshimer ordered a study made on 'What's the next engine Oldsmobile ought to produce?' and got the answer, 'A diesel.'

At that time, Chevrolet and the men in the top technical positions were making big plans for the Wankel rotary engine. But in the Oldsmobile engineering department, the diesel looked like it offered a better long-range potential. Preliminary studies began before the fuel crisis occurred.

''Future emission rules were an overriding consideration in the diesel program,'' stated Frank Ball. The diesel is known to run more economically than gasoline engines, but has totally different emissions.

''We did not know the first thing about how to make a diesel engine,'' Ball went on, ''but we knew we had to avoid new tooling. We had to convert an existing engine to diesel operation. We began by taking a GMC V-6 to test with pre-chambers. At first we used Mercedes-Benz pre-chamber inserts, flown over from Stuttgart. It was noisy. Not good. But it ran! And surprisingly well.''

Diesel engines from Opel and Nissan were installed experimentally in Oldsmobile cars for evaluation. Then Harry Lyon went to work on redesigning the Olds 350-cubic-inch V-8 for diesel operation.

''They said it couldn't be done,'' recalled Lyon gleefully, ''but we really took the standard engine and its machining line, and ran a diesel down that same line. That was extremely critical from the standpoint of being able to afford to do it.''

Harry Lyon came to Oldsmobile straight from college in 1959 and became a tester in the laboratory. He worked mainly in power trains, and then was assigned to emissions, under Stempel, in 1967. By 1972 he was Oldsmobile's top man on emissions. Two years later, priorities had changed, and fuel economy was on top. He was Dorshimer's choice for spearheading the diesel program.

''There were big modifications,'' admitted Frank Ball. ''We went to a swirl chamber, but not the Ricardo type. It ran well. We were surprised. But it still had noise, smoke and emission problems.

''We developed a new laboratory technique to change the combustion chamber in one cylinder only, and measure emissions. That way we could go through a lot of combinations in a relatively short time. Just measure one cylinder instead of eight. It worked perfectly. A lot of people work with single-cylinder test engines, but that way you don't get the dynamics of the V-8 or whatever the real engine is to be—exhaust and intake pulses, etc. Also it's easier to use a real engine than to build a single-cylinder test unit.''

Why did they tell Harry Lyon it couldn't be done? ''Specifically, they said the block wasn't strong enough,'' Lyon recounted, ''and that the deck heights were wrong. I went to see diesel people outside GM. They all said you can't do it.

''Sure we had metallurgical difficulties,'' Lyon went on. ''The heads had to be changed, and the block had to be beefed up. We maintained the bolt pattern and the bore centers. The biggest change was in the head. And we had to do some work in the main-bearing area. Why we were successful, well, you can go right back to one guy, Kelly Thurston, he put the first one together. Kelly is a pretty good combustion

guy, and used to work for me in advanced engines. He came out of Ethyl. Worked at Ethyl for years. Interesting guy.''

Another who should not be forgotten is Art Sundeen, who invented the quick-start system for the diesel. ''It uses some electronics,'' said Harry Lyon casually, ''nothing really unique, but ingenious.'' Art Sundeen was working in the electrical group and had nothing to do with the diesel project. But after a chance conversation with Lyon, he had this idea, designed the circuit and sent over a drawing. Lyon looked at it, grasped the principle immediately, and said out loud, ''We'll do it this way.''

The Olds diesel became optional for the 1978-model Delta 88, 98-series, Custom Cruiser, and released for Chevrolet's pickup trucks. A 260-cubic-inch version was added in 1979 but abandoned in 1980. Meanwhile, the 350 had spread to Cadillac for use in the Seville, in which the carburetor-version Olds 350 was standard.

In 1979 Olds began development work on a pure-diesel V-6, and broke ground for a new plant that will make diesel engines exclusively on a 280-acre site in Delta township near Lansing. Production capacity is planned for about 400,000 engines a year.

The days of Oldsmobile's gasoline-fueled V-8 are not necessarily over, but a truly new design will be needed if the V-8 is to survive. The rest of the engine program centers on fours and sixes, and is being coordinated at the corporate level. But Oldsmobile will continue indefinitely as an engine manufacturer. ''Jim Benner now runs our engine group,'' explained Harry Lyon. ''He's really excellent, an outstanding engineer who knows what he's doing.''

Oldsmobile sold 1,006,344 cars in 1978, and Robert J. Cook announced a goal of 1,050,000 for 1979. The Cutlass retained its title as the nation's best-selling intermediate (now smaller than the X-body compacts, but not for long), accounting for 520,279 sales. Delta 88 and Royale sales advanced to 273,384 while the 98-series reached 123,431. The Omega was disappointing, dropping to 42,860 cars, and the Starfire could not get beyond 18,350. Even the Toronado, still on its 122-inch wheelbase, did better (28,039).

1980 Delta 88 Royale brougham. Standard engine was a 231-cubic-inch Buick V-6. The 1980 models were about 20 pounds heavier than the '79's but had about eight percent lower aerodynamic drag.

1980 Oldsmobile Toronado. The effort to save weight continued after the downsizing—the 1980 model had shed an additional 147 pounds compared with the 1979 model.

A new, smaller Toronado was planned in 1975 and went into production in the fall of 1978 as a 1979 model. GM had developed new E-bodies with unified chassis design for the Buick Riviera, Cadillac Eldorado and Oldsmobile Toronado. As a result, the Riviera was changed to front-wheel drive. The Toronado received a new independent rear suspension system with coil springs, designed and developed by Cadillac.

Engines for the Toronado were either the 307-cubic-inch Chevrolet LV 2 or the Olds 350-cubic-inch L 34 V-8. The drive train layout was basically unchanged, with automatic transmission only. Wheelbase was brought down to 114 inches, length to 205.6 inches and curb weight to 3,900 pounds.

Styling the car was a difficult task, as Irv Rybicki explained: ''The first problem we faced was the fact that the designers for many years were involved in this game of adding inches and making it lower and wider—and the proportions got a little longer and a little slicker. They played that game for fifteen years and then suddenly we're resizing all our vehicles and making them shorter and lighter.

''So, the big problem was to find a way to take this big car, 228 inches long, cutting it down to 204, and come up with a reasonable proportion. It's fine if you can bring the roof down six inches. That would give reasonable proportions, but we had to maintain torso room. As a matter of fact, we set a goal for ourselves to increase rear knee room by at least three inches. That was necessary, because the big car never did have adequate knee room in the rear seat.

''We spent months blocking out the car and getting the silhouette right— hood length to upper length to deck length to width, so that on the road it was a pleasing proportion. We set goals for ourselves: like flush windshields and flush

1980 Oldsmobile Omega brougham coupe. With the downsizing of the X-body, the Omega also switched to front-wheel drive. The car went into production in April 1979.

doing some full-scale testing in the Lockheed-Georgia wind tunnel at Marietta, Georgia, but to little effect. Styling still determined the shape of the 1977 B-cars, 1978 A-cars and 1979½ X-cars on the basis of esthetics, not aerodynamic efficiency.

The next-generation Oldsmobile, due in 1982-83, will no doubt prove to have considerably lower aerodynamic drag, as well as being lighter and more efficient throughout.

General Motors is the world's number one car manufacturer, and is likely to hold on to this position in the future. Oldsmobile has a role to play in the GM scheme, and the division has the freedom to develop this role in response to changes in the market and motoring conditions in general.

"I think there are two things about Oldsmobile that puts it on top of all the GM divisions," said Bob Dorshimer proudly. "First, it's the willingness as a moderately sized division to take on *really* new projects—like the diesel engine. It's a special willingness to look ahead. Secondly, it's the quality and solidity of the product. I like to believe that that's something unique that we've got: A really top-quality car, whichever line we're talking about."

backlights, to set these E-body cars apart from the rest of GM's line. Hopefully those innovative ideas will come down through the system and finally reach the Chevette."

GM had planned the new X-body compacts as 1979 models, but the program was delayed several times, and they were finally announced in April 1979. The new Omega came out of a corporate project directed by Robert J. Eaton, who later in the year became Oldsmobile's assistant chief engineer for experimental operations and chassis design and development.

The new Omega was a drastic departure—a small family car on a 105-inch wheelbase, with unit-construction bodies built as a four-door sedan and two-door coupe. The Pontiac 151-cubic-inch LW 9 four-cylinder engine was standard, and the Chevrolet LE 2 173-cubic-inch V-6 optional. In either case, the engine was mounted transversely, driving the front wheels. A four-speed floor-shift was standard with the four, and a column-shift automatic standard with the V-6.

It had all-coil, all-independent suspension with MacPherson spring legs in front and trailing arms at the rear. Aerodynamic drag was claimed to be ten percent lower then for the 1978 Omega, but a big part of that was due to smaller frontal area, not to a lower drag coefficient. Oldsmobile, along with the rest of General Motors, has held a rearguard position in aerodynamics all along.

In 1972 GM announced plans for a full-size wind tunnel, but they were canceled in March 1974, due to a liquidity crisis at the corporation. The wind tunnel plan had to rest till 1978, and it was not completed and calibrated until 1980.

No big use of wind tunnel testing was made until the Camaro body was developed in 1964-66, and then mostly in one-fifth scale. After 1970, GM began

Appendix I   Model Year Output, 1946-1980

Year	66	68	76	78	98	88	Super 88	TOTAL
1946	30,554		53,466	20,953	14,364			119,337
1947	55,610	17,956	49,711	33,963	37,148			194,255
1948	41,993	16,614	29,167	20,651	65,235			172,852
1949			95,556		93,478	99,276		288,310
1950			33,257		106,220	268,412		407,889
1951					100,519	34,640	150,456	285,615
1952					76,244	18,617	118,558	213,419
1953					100,330	32,800	201,332	334,462
1954					93,325	72,861	187,815	354,001
1955					118,626	222,361	242,192	583,179
1956					90,439	216,019	179,000	485,458
1957					79,693	172,659	132,038	384,390
1958					60,815	146,567	88,992	296,374

Year	Dynamic 88	Super 88	98	F-85	Starfire	Jetstar 88	Jetstar I	TOTAL
1955								583,179
1956								485,458
1957								384,390
1958	146,567	88,992	60,815					296,374
1959	194,102	107,660	81,102					382,864
1960	189,963	97,985	59,417					347,365
1961	137,459	53,236	43,022	76,446	7,804			317,967
1962	188,737	58,147	64,154	94,568	41,988			447,594
1963	199,315	62,770	70,308	118,811	25,549			476,753
1964	167,674	37,514	68,254	177,918	16,163	62,505	16,084	546,112
1965	119,497		92,406	212,082	15,260	55,437	6,552	591,701
1966	95,834		88,119	229,573	13,019	30,247		586,381

Year	F-85 Cutlass	Delmont 88	Delta 88	Toronado	Omega	98	Starfire	TOTAL
1965	212,082		90,467			92,406		591,701
1966	229,573		88,626	40,963		88,119		586,381
1967	253,960	108,356	88,095	21,790		76,189		548,390
1968	275,129	66,624	102,505	26,454		91,747		562,459
1969	280,966		252,087	28,494		116,408		677,955
1970	309,273		203,431	25,433		95,844		633,981
1971	264,091		182,537	28,980		83,291		558,899
1972	334,582		253,661	48,900		121,568		758,711
1973	405,519		278,699	55,921	60,363	138,468		938,970
1974	333,251		137,509	27,582	50,280	70,556		619,178
1975	319,531		134,150	23,301	41,807	78,850	31,081	628,720
1976	500,129		175,129	24,304	58,159	104,479	29,159	891,499
1977	632,742		246,408	34,085	63,984	139,423	19,091	1,135,909
1978	527,606		277,181	24,815	50,117	118,765	17,321	1,015,805
1979	563,751		291,587	50,056	40,225	127,651	20,299	1,068,155
1980	484,994		165,678	43,440	134,323	73,635	8,237	910,306

Appendix II Model Specifications, 1946-1980

Year	Wheelbase (inches)	Overall Length	Overall Width	Overall Height	Weight (pounds)	Std. Engine	HP	Axle Ratio	Tire Size
SPECIAL 66/DYNAMIC 66									
1946	119	205	75.5	63	3,445	238 L-6	100	3.90	6.00-16
1947	119	205	75.5	63	3,445	238 L-6	100	3.90	6.00-16
1948	119	205	75.5	62	3,445	238 L-6	100	3.90	6.50-15
SPECIAL 68/DYNAMIC 68									
1946	119	205	75.5	63	3,461	257 L-8	110	3.73	6.00-16
1947	119	205	75.5	62	3,461	257 L-8	110	3.73	6.50-15
1948	119	205	75.5	62	3,461	257 L-8	110	3.73	6.50-15
DYNAMIC CRUISER 76									
1946	125	212	75.5	63	3,450	238 L-6	100	3.90	6.50-16
1947	125	212	75.5	63	3,450	238 L-6	100	3.90	6.50-16
1948	125	212	75.5	62	3,450	238 L-6	100	3.90	6.50-15
FUTURAMIC 76									
1949	119.5	207	76.5	61.5	3,520	257 L-6	105	3.90	7.10-15
1950	119.5	207	76.5	61.5	3,520	257 L-6	105	3.90	7.10-15
DYNAMIC CRUISER 78									
1946	125	212	76.5	63	3,500	257 L-8	110	3.73	6.50-16
1947	125	212	76.5	63	3,500	257 L-8	110	3.73	6.50-16
1948	125	212	76.5	63	3,500	257 L-8	110	3.73	6.50-16
FUTURAMIC 88									
1949	119.5	207	76.5	61.5	3,560	303 V8	135	3.73	7.60-15
1950	119.5	207	76.5	61.5	3,560	303 V8	135	3.73	7.60-15
DELUXE 88/GOLDEN ROCKET 88									
1952	120	204	75.7	62	3,770	303 V8	145	3.64	7.60-15
1953	120	204	77	62	3,827	303 V8	150	3.64	7.60-15
1954	120	205.3	78.3	61.5	3,858	324 V8	170	3.42	7.60-15
1955	122	203.4	77.8	61.5	3,927	324 V8	185	3.42	7.10-15
1956	122	203.3	77.6	61.5	4,028	324 V8	230	3.64	7.10-15
1957	122	208.2	76.4	61	4,236	371 V8	277	3.64	8.50-14
SUPER 88									
1951	120	204	76	62	3,679	303 V8	135	3.64	7.60-15
1952	120	204	75.7	62	3,804	303 V8	160	3.64	7.60-15
1953	120	204	77	61.8	3,864	303 V8	165	3.64	7.60-15
1954	122	205.3	78.3	61	3,900	324 V8	185	3.42	7.60-15
1955	122	203.4	77.8	60.5	3,940	324 V8	202	3.42	7.60-15
1956	122	203.3	77.6	60	4,061	324 V8	240	3.23	7.60-15
1957	122	208.2	76.4	58.2	4,339	371 V8	277	3.64	8.50-14
1958	122.5	208.2	78.5	57	4,272	371 V8	305	3.64	8.50-14
1959	123	218.4	80.8	56	4,441	394 V8	315	3.64	9.00-14
1960	123	217.6	80.6	56.1	4,370	394 V8	315	3.42	8.50-14
1961	123	212	77.2	55.8	4,225	394 V8	325	3.42	8.00-14
1962	123	213.9	77.9	55.8	4,033	394 V8	330	3.23	8.00-14
1963	123	214.5	77.9	56.3	4,202	394 V8	330	3.23	8.00-14
1964	123	215.3	78	55.9	4,194	394 V8	330	3.23	8.00-14
DYNAMIC 88									
1958	122.5	208.2	78.5	57	4,249	371 V8	265	3.64	8.50-14
1959	123	218.4	80.8	56	4,396	371 V8	270	3.64	8.50-14
1960	123	217.6	80.6	56.1	4,351	371 V8	240	3.42	8.50-14
1961	123	212	77.2	55.8	4,186	394 V8	250	3.07	8.00-14
1962	123	213.9	77.9	55.8	4,173	394 V8	280	3.23	8.00-14
1963	123	214.5	77.9	56.3	4,172	394 V8	280	3.23	8.00-14
1964	123	215.3	78	55.9	4,152	394 V8	280	3.23	8.00-14
1965	123	216.9	80	55.5	4,092	425 V8	310	2.73	8.25-14
1966	123	217.0	80	55.5	4,121	425 V8	300	3.23	8.25-14
JETSTAR 88									
1964	123	215.3	78	55.9	3,905	330 V8	245	3.23	7.50-14
1965	123	216.9	80	55.5	3,905	330 V8	260	3.23	7.75-14
1966	123	217	80	55.5	3,965	330 V8	260	3.23	7.75-14
JETSTAR I									
1964	123	215.3	78	54.2	4,345	394 V8	345	3.42	8.00-14
1965	123	216.9	80	54.1	4,154	425 V8	370	3.23	8.25-14
DELTA 88/ROYALE									
1975	124	226.9	79.9	54.5	4,594	350 V8	170	2.73	HR78-15
1976	124	226.7	80	54.5	4,515	350 V8	170	2.73	HR78-15
1977	116	217.5	76.8	55.7	3,602	231 V6	105	2.73	FR78-15
1978	116	217.5	76.8	55.2	3,613	231 V6	105	2.73	FR78-15
1979	116	217.5	76.8	55.2	3,649	231 V6	115	2.73	FR78-15
1980	116	218.4	76.3	54.7	3,470	231 V6	110	2.73	P205/75R15
DELMONT 88									
1967	123	217	80	55.5	4,955	330 V8	250	3.23	8.55-14
1968	123	217.8	80	55.5	4,090	350 V8	250	3.23	8.55-14
CUSTOM CRUISER 98									
1946	127	216	77.4	64.2	3,715	257 L-8	110	3.63	7.00-15
1947	127	216	77.4	64.2	3,715	257 L-8	110	3.63	7.00-15
1948	127	216	77.4	64.2	3,715	257 L-8	110	3.63	7.00-15
FUTURAMIC 98									
1948	125	213.5	77.5	61.3	3,880	257 L-8	110	3.73	7.00-15
1949	122	210	77.7	61.1	3,818	303 V8	135	3.56	7.60-15
1950	122	210	77.7	61.2	3,815	303 V8	135	3.56	7.60-15
CLASSIC 98/STARFIRE 98									
1951	122	208	80	62.5	3,942	303 V8	135	3.90	7.60-15
1952	124	213	76	62.6	3,923	303 V8	160	3.64	7.60-15
1953	124	215	77	62.2	3,975	303 V8	165	3.64	7.60-15
1954	126	214.26	78.26	61.5	4,012	324 V8	185	3.42	7.60-15
1955	126	212.4	77.8	60.5	4,032	324 V8	202	3.42	7.60-15
1956	126	212.3	77.6	60.5	4,211	324 V8	240	3.42	7.60-15
1957	126	216.7	76.4	58.2	4,522	371 V8	277	3.42	8.50-14
1958	126.5	216.7	78.5	57	4,580	371 V8	305	3.42	8.50-14
1959	126.3	223	80.8	56	4,593	394 V8	315	3.42	9.00-14
1960	126.3	220.9	80.6	56.1	4,518	394 V8	315	3.23	9.00-14
1961	126	218	77.2	56.6	4,370	394 V8	325	3.23	8.50-14
1962	126	220	77.9	56.6	4,235	394 V8	330	3.07	8.50-14

SERIES 98

Year	Wheelbase (inches)	Overall Length	Overall Width	Overall Height	Weight (pounds)	Std. Engine	HP	Axle Ratio	Tire Size
1963	126	221.7	77.9	57.1	4,413	394 V8	330	3.08	8.50-14
1964	126	222.3	78	56.5	4,403	394 V8	330	3.08	8.50-14
1965	126	222.9	80	55.8	4,382	425 V8	360	3.08	8.55-14
1966	126	223	80	55.8	4,368	425 V8	365	3.08	8.55-14
1967	126	223	80	55.8	4,413	425 V8	365	3.08	8.85-14
1968	126	223.7	80	55.8	4,347	455 V8	365	2.56	8.85-14
1969	127	224.4	80	55.8	4,436	455 V8	365	2.56	8.85-15
1970	127	225.2	80	55.8	4,397	455 V8	365	2.56	J78-15
1971	127	226.1	79	54.6	4,620	455 V8	320	2.73	J78-15
1972	127	227.2	79.6	54.6	4,567	455 V8	225	2.73	J78-15
1973	127	230.2	79.6	54.7	4,662	455 V8	225	2.73	J78-15
1974	127	232.4	79.8	54.2	4,778	455 V8	210	2.73	J78-15
1975	127	232.4	79.8	54.7	4,883	455 V8	190	2.56	JR78-15
1977	119	220.4	76.8	56.6	3,985	350 V8	170	2.41	GR78-15
1978	119	220.4	76.8	55.5	4,124	350 V8	170	2.41	FR78-15
1979	119	220.4	76.8	55.2	3,942	350 V8	160	2.41	FR78-15
1980	119	221.4	76.3	54.7	3,924	307 V8	150	2.41	P215/75R15

STARFIRE

Year	Wheelbase (inches)	Overall Length	Overall Width	Overall Height	Weight (pounds)	Std. Engine	HP	Axle Ratio	Tire Size
1962	123	213.9	77.9	54.7	4,335	394 V8	345	3.42	8.00-14
1963	123	214.5	77.9	55	4,343	394 V8	345	3.42	8.00-14
1964	123	215.3	78	54.2	4,345	394 V8	345	3.42	8.00-14
1965	123	216.9	80	53.3	4,154	425 V8	370	3.23	8.25-14
1966	123	217	80	54.1	4,204	425 V8	375	3.23	8.25-14

STARFIRE

Year	Wheelbase (inches)	Overall Length	Overall Width	Overall Height	Weight (pounds)	Std. Engine	HP	Axle Ratio	Tire Size
1976	97	179.3	65.4	50.2	2,983	231 V-6	105	2.56	B78-13
1977	97	179.3	65.4	50.2	2,793	140 L-4	84	3.42	A78-13
1978	97	179.3	65.4	50.2	2,806	151 L-4	85	2.73	B78-13
1979	97	179.6	65.4	50.2	2,736	151 L-4	85	2.73	B78-13B
1980	97	179.6	65.4	50.2	2,765	151 L-4	90	2.73	A78-13B

TORONADO

Year	Wheelbase (inches)	Overall Length	Overall Width	Overall Height	Weight (pounds)	Std. Engine	HP	Axle Ratio	Tire Size
1966	119	211	78.5	52.8	4,496	425 V8	385	3.21	8.85-15
1967	119	211	78.5	52.8	4,494	425 V8	385	3.21	8.85-15
1968	119	211.4	78.8	52.8	4,465	455 V8	375	3.08	8.85-15
1969	119	214.8	78.8	52.8	4,481	455 V8	375	3.07	8.85-15
1970	119	214.3	78.8	52.8	4,498	455 V8	375	3.07	J78-15
1971	122.3	219.9	79.2	54.7	4,670	455 V8	350	3.07	J78-15
1972	122	220.3	79.8	54.7	4,672	455 V8	265	2.73	J78-15
1973	122	226.8	79.8	53.2	4,794	455 V8	250	2.73	J78-15
1974	122	228	79.5	53.3	4,838	455 V8	230	2.73	J78-15
1975	122	227.6	79.5	53.3	4,787	455 V8	215	2.73	JR78-15
1976	122	227.6	79.7	53.3	4,761	455 V8	215	2.73	JR78-15
1976	122	227.6	79.7	53.3	4,761	455 V8	215	2.73	JR78-15
1977	122	227.5	80	53.2	4,747	403 V8	200	2.73	JR78-15
1978	122	227.5	80	53.2	4,767	403 V8	190	2.73	JR78-15
1979	114	205.6	80	54.2	3,852	350 V8	165	2.41	P205/75R15
1980	114	205.6	80	52.5	3,730	307 V8	150	2.41	P205/75R15

F-85/CUTLASS

Year	Wheelbase (inches)	Overall Length	Overall Width	Overall Height	Weight (pounds)	Std. Engine	HP	Axle Ratio	Tire Size
1961	112	188.2	71.6	52.6	2,726	215 V8	155	3.08	6.50-13
1962	112	188.2	71.6	52.6	2,726	215 V8	155	3.08	6.50-13
1963	112	192.2	73.7	52.7	2,747	215 V8	155	3.08	6.50-13
1963	115	203	73.8	54	3,075	225 V6	155	3.23	6.50-14
1964	115	203	73.8	54	3,263	330 V8	230	3.08	7.00-14
1965	115	204.4	73.8	54.5	3,320	225 V6	155	3.23	6.96-14
1965	115	204.4	73.8	54.5	3,341	330 V8	250	3.08	7.35-14
1966	115	204.2	75.4	54.5	3,146	250 L6	155	3.08	6.95-14
1966	115	204.2	75.4	54.5	3,369	330 V8	250	3.08	7.35-14
1967	115	204.2	76	54.4	3,162	250 L6	155	3.08	7.75-14
1967	115	204.2	75	54.4	3,365	330 V8	250	3.08	7.75-14

OLDS TWO-DOOR A-BODY (F-85/Cutlass)

Year	Wheelbase (inches)	Overall Length	Overall Width	Overall Height	Weight (pounds)	Std. Engine	HP	Axle Ratio	Tire Size
1968	112	201.9	76.2	52.8	3,265	250 L6	155	2.87	7.75-14
1969	112	201.9	76.2	52.8	3,265	250 L6	155	2.78	7.75-14
1970	112	203.2	76.2	52.8	3,771	250 L6	155	2.78	F78-14
1971	112	203.6	76.8	52.9	3,288	250 L6	145	2.73	F78-14
1972	112	203.6	76.8	52.9	3,499	350 V8	160	3.23	F78-14
1973	112	207	76.5	53.3	3,837	350 V8	180	3.23	F78-14
1974	112	210.6	76.5	53.4	3,984	350 V8	180	2.73	F78-14
1975	112	211.7	76.7	53.4	3,773	250 L6	105	3.08	FR78-15
1976	112	211.7	76.2	53.4	3,751	250 L6	106	2.73	FR78-15
1977	112	209.6	76.2	53.4	3,904	260 V8	110	2.73	GR78-15

FOUR-DOOR A-BODY (F-85/Cutlass)

Year	Wheelbase (inches)	Overall Length	Overall Width	Overall Height	Weight (pounds)	Std. Engine	HP	Axle Ratio	Tire Size
1968	116	205.6	76.8	53.5	3,362	250 L6	155	2.78	7.75-14
1969	116	205.9	76.8	53.2	3,300	250 L6	155	2.78	7.75-14
1970	116	207.2	76.8	53.5	3,361	250 L6	155	2.78	F78-14
1971	116	207.6	76.8	53.5	3,330	250 L6	145	2.73	F78-14
1972	116	207.6	76.8	53.5	3,547	350 V8	160	3.23	F78-14
1973	116	211	76.5	54	3,905	350 V8	180	3.23	F78-14
1974	116	214.6	76.5	56.1	4,040	350 V8	180	2.73	F78-14
1975	116	215.7	76.7	54.1	3,845	260 V8	110	2.73	FR78-14
1976	116	215.7	76.7	54.1	3,960	260 V8	110	3.08	FR78-15
1977	116	215.2	76.2	54.1	3,760	231 V6	105	3.08	FR78-15

CUTLASS

Year	Wheelbase (inches)	Overall Length	Overall Width	Overall Height	Weight (pounds)	Std. Engine	HP	Axle Ratio	Tire Size
1978	108.1	197.7	71.9	54.2	3,158	231 V-6	105	2.93	P185/75R14
1979	108.1	200.1	71.3	53.5	3,172	231 V-6	115	2.93	P185/75R14
1980	108.1	199.1	71.9	53.2	3,161	231 V-6	110	2.93	P185-75R14

OMEGA

Year	Wheelbase (inches)	Overall Length	Overall Width	Overall Height	Weight (pounds)	Std. Engine	HP	Axle Ratio	Tire Size
1973	111	197.5	72.4	53.8	3,290	250 L6	100	3.08	E78-14
1974	111	199.5	72.8	52.4	3,334	250 L6	100	3.08	E78-14
1975	111	199.6	72.9	53.4	3,518	250 L6	105	2.73	FR78-14
1976	111	199.6	72.9	54.3	3,382	250 L6	105	2.73	E78-14
1977	111	199.6	72.9	54.7	3,199	231 V-6	105	3.08	E78-14
1978	111	199.6	72.9	54.7	3,250	231 V-6	105	3.08	E78-14
1979	111	199.6	72.9	53.2	3,271	231 V-6	115	3.08	E78-14B
1980	105	181.8	69.8	51.9	2,496	151 L-4	90	3.34	P185/80R13

Appendix III Engine Specifications, 1946-1980

	Carb.	Comp. Ratio	HP-RPM	Torque-RPM	Remarks
140 L-4					
1977	1-2V	8.0	84-4400	117-2400	Starfire
151 L-4					
1978	1-1V	8.3	85-4400	123-2800	Starfire
1979	1-1V	8.3	85-4400		Starfire
1980	1-2V	8.2	90-4400	128-2400	Starfire
173 V-6					
1979	1-2V	8.6	115-5100	145-2400	opt. in Omega
1980	1-2V	8.5	115-4800	150-2000	opt. in Omega
215 V-8					
1961	1-2V	8.75	155-4800	210-3200	std. in F-85
1961	1-4V	10.25	185-4800	235-3200	opt. in F-85
1962	1-2V	8.75	155-4800	210-3200	std. in F-85
1962	1-4V	10.25	185-4800	235-3200	opt. in F-85
1963	1-2V	8.75	155-4800	210-3200	std. in F-85
1963	1-4V	10.25	185-4800	235-3200	opt. in F-85
1963	1-4V	10.0 +Turbo	215-4600	300-3200	std. in Jetfire
225 V-6					
1964	1-1V	9.0	155-4400	225-2400	std. in F-85
1965	1-1V	9.0	155-4400	225-2400	std. in F-85
1966	1-1V	8.5	155-4200	240-2000	std. in F-85
231 V-6					
1975	1-2V	8.0	110-4000	175-2000	std. in Starfire
1976	1-2V	8.0	105-3400	185-2000	std. in Starfire
1977	1-2V	8.0	105-3400	185-2000	std. in Omega
1978	1-2V	8.0	105-3400	185-2000	std. in Omega, Cutlass Salon, and Delta 88; opt. in Starfire
1979	1-2V	8.0	105-3400	185-2000	opt. in Starfire
1980	1-2V	8.0	110-3800	190-1600	opt. in Starfire
238 L-6					
1946	1-1V	6.5	100-3400	190-1400	Series 66, 76
1947	1-1V	6.5	100-3400	190-1400	Series 66, 76
1948	1-1V	6.5	100-3400	190-1400	Series 66, 76
250 L-6					
1966	1-1V	8.5	155-4200	240-2000	std. in F-85, Cutlass
1967	1-1V	8.5	155-4200	240-2000	std. in F-85, Cutlass
1968	1-1V	8.5	155-4200	240-2000	std. in F-85, Cutlass
1969	1-1V	8.5	155-4200	240-2200	std. in F-85, Cutlass Six
1970	1-1V	8.5	155-4200	240-2200	std. in F-85, Cutlass Six
1971	1-1V	8.5	145-4200	230-2000	std. in F-85, Cutlass Six
1973	1-1V	8.25	100-3600	175-1600	std. in Omega
1974	1-1V	8.5	100-3600	175-1800	std. in Omega
1975	1-1V	8.25	105-3800	185-1200	std. Omega, Cutlass 2-Door
1976	1-1V	8.25	105-3800	185-1200	std. Omega, Cutlass 2-Door
257 L-6					
1949	1-1V	6.5	110-3600	212-1600	Futuramic 76
1950	1-1V	6.5	110-3600	212-1600	Futuramic 76
257 L-8					
1946	1-1V	6.5	110-3600	210-2000	Series 78, 98
1947	1-1V	6.5	110-3600	210-2000	Series 78, 98
1948	1-1V	6.5	110-3600	210-2000	Series 78, 98, Futuramic 98
260-V-8					
1975	1-2V	8.0	110-3400	205-1800	std. in Omega, Cutlass 4-D
1976	1-2V	8.0	110-3400	205-1600	std. in Omega, Cutlass 4-D
1978	1-2V	7.5	110-3400	205-1800	std. in Cutlass Supreme; opt. in 88 and 98
1979	1-2V	7.5	105-3400	195-1600	opt. in Cutlass
1980	1-2V	7.5	105-3400	195-1600	opt. in Cutlass
260 V-8 Diesel Injection					
1979		22.5	90-3600	160-1600	opt. in Cutlass
301 V-8					
1979	1-2V	8.2	135-3800	240-1600	opt. in Delta 88
303.7 V-8					
1949	1-2V	7.25	135-3600	253-1800	88 and 98
1950	1-2V	7.25	135-3600	253-1800	88 and 98
1951	1-2V	7.5	135-3600	253-1800	88 and 98
1952	1-2V	7.5	145-3600	255-2000	Deluxe 88
1952	1-4V	7.5	160-3600	265-2000	Super 88, Classic 98
1953	1-2V	8.0	150-3600	255-2000	Deluxe 88
1953	1-4V	8.0	165-3600	275-2200	Super 88, 98
305 V-8					
1977	1-2V	8.5	145-3800	245-2400	std. in Omega V-8
1978	1-2V	8.5	145-3800	245-2400	std. in Omega V-8, std. in Cutlass Wagon; opt. in Starfire, Cutlass
1979	1-4V	8.5	160-4000	235-2400	std. in Cutlass Wagon; opt. in Cutlass
1979	1-2V	8.5	130-3200	245-2400	opt. in Starfire
1980	1-4V	8.6	155-4000	240-1600	std. in Cutlass Wagon
307 V-8					
1980	1-4V	7.9	150-3600	245-1600	std. in 98, Custom Cruiser, Toronado; opt. in Cutlass
324 V-8					
1954	1-2V	8.25	170-4000	300-2000	88
1954	1-4V	8.25	185-4000	300-2000	Super 88, 98
1955	1-2V	8.5	185-4000	320-2000	88
1955	1-4V	8.5	202-4000	332-2400	Super 88, 98
1956	1-2V	9.25	230-4400	340-2400	88
1956	1-4V	9.25	240-4400	350-2800	Super 88, 98
330 V-8					
1964	1-4V	10.25	245-4600	345-2400	std. in Jetstar 88
1964	1.2V	9.0	230-4400	325-2400	std. in F-85
1965	1-2V	9.0	250-4800	335-2800	opt. in F-85, Jetstar 88
1965	1-2V	10.25	260-4800	355-2800	std. in Jetstar 88
1965	1-4V	10.25	315-5200	360-3600	std. in Cutlass; opt. in F-85, Jetstar 88

Year	Carb.	Comp. Ratio	HP-RPM	Torque-RPM	Remarks
1966	1.2V	9.0	250-4800	335-2800	opt. in F-85, Jetstar 88
1966	1-2V	10.25	260-4800	355-2800	std. in Jetstar 88
1966	1-4V	10.25	310-5200	335-3600	opt. in Cutlass
1966	1-4V	10.25	320-5200	360-3600	std. in Cutlass; opt. in F-85, Jetstar 88
1967	1-2V	9.0	250-4800	335-2800	std. in Vista-Cruiser; opt. in F-85, Cutlass
1967	1-2V	10.25	260-4800	355-2800	std. in Delmont 88
1967	1-4V	9.0	310-5200	340-3600	opt. in F-85, Cutlass, Vista-Cruiser
1967	1-4V	10.25	320-5200	360-3600	std. in Cutlass Supreme; opt. in F-85, Cutlass, Delmont 88

350 V-8

Year	Carb.	Comp. Ratio	HP-RPM	Torque-RPM	Remarks
1968	1-2V	9.0	250-4400	355-2600	std. in Delmont 88, Vista-Cruiser; opt. in F-85, Cutlass, Cutlass Supreme
1968	1-4V	10.25	310-4800	390-3200	std. in Cutlass Supreme; opt. in F-85, Cutlass Delmont
1968	1-4V	10.44	325-5600	360-3600	opt. in F-85, Cutlass, Cutlass Supreme
1969	1-2V	9.0	250-4400	355-2600	std. in F-85, Cutlass 88, Vista-Cruiser
1969	1-4V	10.5	325-5400	360-3600	opt. in F-85
1970	1-2V	9.0	250-4400	355-2600	std. in F-85, Cutlass V-8, Vista-Cruiser, Delta 88
1970	1-4V	10.25	310-4800	390-3200	opt. in F-85, Cutlass, Vista-Cruiser
1970	1-4V	10.5	325-5400	360-3600	opt. in F-85, Cutlass
1971	1-2V	8.5	240-4200	350-2400	std. in F-85, Cutlass, Vista-Crusier, Delta 88; opt. in Cutlass Supreme
1971	1-4V	8.5	260-4200	360-3200	std. in Cutlass Supreme; opt. in F-85, Cutlass
1972	1-2V	8.5	160-4000	275-2400	std. in Delta 88, F-85, Cutlass, Vista-Cruiser; opt. in Cutlass Supreme
1972	1-4V	8.5	180-4000	275-2600	std. in Cutlass Supreme; opt. in F-85, Cutlass, Delta 88
1973	1-2V	8.5	160-3800	275-2400	std. in Delta 88; opt. in Omega
1973	1-4V	8.5	180-3800	275-2800	std. in Cutlass; opt. in Omega
1974	1-2V	8.5	180-3800	275-2800	std. in Cutlass, Delta 88
1974	1-4V	8.5	200-4200	300-3200	opt. in Cutlass
1975	1-4V	8.5	170-3800	275-2400	std. in Delta 88; opt. in Cutlass
1976	1-4V	8.5	170-3800	275-2400	std. in Cutlass Wagon, Delta 88; opt. in Cutlass
1977	1-4V	8.5	170-3800	275-2000	std. in Cutlass 4-D, Wagon 98, Custom Cruiser; opt. in Omega, Delta 88
1978	1-4V	8.0	170-3800	275-2000	std. in Customer Cruiser
1979	1-4V	8.0	160-3600	270-2000	std. in 98, Custom Cruiser; opt. in Delta 88
1980	1-4V	8.0	160-3600	270-1600	opt. in Cutlass, 88, 98, Toronado, Custom Cruiser

350 V-8 (Chevrolet)

Year	Carb.	Comp. Ratio	HP-RPM	Torque-RPM	Remarks
1975	1-2V	8.0	145-3200	270-2000	opt. in Omega
1975	1-4V	8.0	164-3800	260-2200	opt. in Omega
1976	1-2V	8.0	140-3200	280-1600	opt. in Omega
1976	1-4V	8.0	155-3400	280-1800	opt. in Omega
1977	1-4V	8.5	170-3800	270-2400	opt. in Omega, Delta 88
1978	1-4V	8.5	160-3800	260-2400	opt. in Cutlass

350 V-8 (Diesel)

Year	Carb.	Comp. Ratio	HP-RPM	Torque-RPM	Remarks
1978	Injection	22.5	120-3600	220-1600	opt. in Delta 88, 98, Customer Cruiser
1979	Injection	22.5	125-3600	225-1600	opt. in Cutlass Cruiser Delta 88, 98, Custom Cruiser, Toronado
1980	Injection	22.5	105-3200	205-1600	opt. in Cutlass, Toronado, Delta 88, 98 and Custom Cruiser

371 V-8

Year	Carb.	Comp. Ratio	HP-RPM	Torque-RPM	Remarks
1957	1-4V	9.5	277-4400	400-2800	88, Super 88, 98
1958	1-2V	10.0	265-4400	390-2400	Dynamic 88
1958	1-4V	10.0	305-4600	410-2800	Super 88, 98
1958	3-2V	10.0	312-4600	415-2800	J-2 option
1959	1-2V	9.75	270-4600	390-2400	Dynamic 88
1959	1-4V	9.75	300-4600	410-2800	opt. in Dynamic 88
1960	1-2V	8.75	240-4400	375-2400	std. in Dynamic 88

394 V-8

Year	Carb.	Comp. Ratio	HP-RPM	Torque-RPM	Remarks
1959	1-4V	9.75	315-4600	435-2800	Super 88, 98
1960	1-4V	9.75	315-4600	435-2800	Super 88, 98
1961	1-2V	8.75	250-4400	405-2400	Dynamic 88
1961	1-4V	10.0	325-4600	435-2800	Super 88, 98
1962	1-2V	10.25	280-4400	430-2400	Dynamic 88
1962	1-4V	10.25	330-4600	440-2800	Super 88, 98
1963	1-2V	10.25	280-4400	430-2400	Dynamic 88
1963	1-4V	10.25	330-4600	440-2800	Super 88, 98
1963	1-4V	10.5	345-4800	440-3200	Starfire
1964	1-2V	10.25	280-4400	430-2400	Dynamic 88
1964	1-4V	10.25	330-4600	440-2800	Super 88, 98
1964	1-4V	10.5	345-4800	440-3200	Starfire, Jetstar

400 V-8

Year	Carb.	Comp. Ratio	HP-RPM	Torque-RPM	Remarks
1965	1-4V	10.25	345-4800	440-3200	std. in 4-4-2
1966	1-4V	10.5	350-5000	440-3600	std. in 4-4-2
1966	3-2V	10.5	360-5000	440-3600	opt. in 4-4-2
1967	1-4V	10.5	300-4600	425-2600	opt. in Cutlass Supreme
1967	1-4V	10.5	350-5000	440-3600	opt. in 4-4-2
1968	1-4V	9.0	290-4600	425-2400	opt. in 4-4-2, Vista-Cruiser
1968	1-4V	10.5	325-4600	440-3200	opt. in 4-4-2 Automatic
1968	1-4V	10.5	350-4800	440-3200	std. in 4-4-2
1968	1-4V	10.5	360-5400	440-3600	opt. in 4-4-2

	Carb.	Comp. Ratio	HP-RPM	Torque-RPM	Remarks
1969	1-4V	10.5	325-4600	440-3000	opt. in 4-4-2 Automatic
400 V-8					
1969	1-4V	10.5	350-4800	440-3200	std. in 4-4-2; opt. in 88
1969	1-4V	10.5	360-5400	440-3600	opt. in 4-4-2
1975	1-4V	7.6	185-3600	310-1600	opt. in 98, Custom Cruiser
403 V-8					
1977	1-4V	8.0	200-3600	330-2400	std. in Toronado
1977	1-4V	8.0	185-3600	320-2200	opt. in 98, Delta 88, Cutlass
1978	1-4V	8.0	185-3600	320-2200	opt. in Delta 88, 98
1978	1-4V	8.0	190-3600	325-2000	std. in Toronado
1979	1-4V	7.8	175-3600	310-2000	opt. in 98, Custom Cruiser
425 V-8					
1965	1-2V	9.0	300-4400	430-2400	opt. in Dynamic 88, Delta 88
1965	1-2V	10.25	310-4400	450-2400	std. in Dynamic 88, Delta 88
1965	1-4V	10.25	360-4800	470-2800	std. in 98; opt. in Delta 88, Dynamic 88
1965	1-4V	10.5	370-4800	470-3200	std. in Starfire, Jetstar I; opt. in Dynamic 88, Delta 88, 98
1966	1-2V	9.0	300-4400	430-2400	opt. in Dynamic 88, Delta 88
1966	1-4V	10.25	365-4800	470-3200	std. in 98; opt. in Dynamic 88, Delta 88
1966	1-4V	10.5	375-4800	470-3200	std. in Starfire; opt. in 98, Delta 88, Dynamic 88
1966	1-4V	10.5	385-4800	475-3200	std. in Toronado
1967	1-2V	9.0	300-4400	430-2400	std. in Delta 88, opt. in Delmont 88
1967	1-4V	10.25	365-4800	470-3200	std. in 98; opt. in Delta 88, Delmont 88
1967	1-4V	10.5	375-4800	470-3200	opt. in 98, Delta 88, Delmont 88
1967	1-4V	10.5	385-4800	475-3200	std. in Toronado
425 V-8					
1968	1-2V	9.0	310-4200	490-2400	std. in Delta, Delta Custom; opt. in Delmont
1968	1-2V	10.25	320-4200	500-2400	opt. in Delta, Delta Custom, Delmont
1968	1-4V	10.25	365-4600	510-3000	std. in 98; opt. in Delmont, Delta, Delta Custom
1968	1-4V	10.25	375-4600	510-3000	std. in Toronado
1968	1-4V	10.25	400-4800	500-3200	opt. in Toronado
1969	1-2V	9.0	310-4200	490-2400	std. in Delta 88
1969	1-4V	10.25	365-4600	510-3000	std. in 98
1969	1-4V	10.25	375-4600	510-3000	std. in Toronado; opt. in all 88's
1969	1-4V	10.25	390-5000	500-3200	opt. in all 88's
1969	1-4V	10.25	400-4800	500-3200	opt. in Toronado
1970	1-2V	9.0	310-4200	490-2400	std. in Delta 88
1970	1-4V	10.5	365-4000	500-3600	std. in 4-4-2
1970	1-4V	10.25	365-4600	510-3000	std. in 98; opt. in Delta 88, Vista-Cruiser
1970	1-4V	10.25	320-4200	500-2400	opt. in Cutlass
1970	1-4V	10.5	370-5200	500-3600	opt. in 4-4-2
1970	1-4V	10.25	390-5000	500-3200	opt. in Delta 88
1970	1-4V	10.25	400-4000	500-3200	opt. in Toronado
1971	1-4V	8.5	280-4000	445-2000	std. in Delta 88 Royale, Custom Cruiser; opt. in Vista-Cruiser, Delta 88
1971	1-4V	8.5	320-4400	460-2800	std. in 98; opt. in Delta 88, Cutlass, Custom Cruiser
1971	1-4V	8.5	350-4200	460-3200	std. in 4-4-2
1972	1-4V	8.5	225-3600	360-2600	std. in 98, Custom Cruiser; opt. in Delta 88
1972	1-4V	8.5	265-4200	325-2800	std. in Toronado
1972	1-4V	8.5	270-4400	370-3200	opt. in F-85, Cutlass, Vista-Cruiser
1972	1-4V	8.5	300-4200	410-3200	opt. in Cutlass
1973	1-4V	8.5	225-3600	360-2600	std. in 98, Custom Cruiser; opt. in Delta Royale
1973	1-4V	8.5	250-4000	375-2800	std. in Toronado; opt. in Cutlass, Delta 88
1973	1-4V	8.5	270-4200	370-3200	opt. in Cutlass
1973	1-4V	8.5	210-3600	350-2400	std. in 88, Custom Cruiser; opt. in Delta 88
1974	1-4V	8.5	230-3800	370-2800	std. in Toronado
1974	1-4V	8.5	230-4000	370-2800	opt. in Cutlass, Delta 88
1975	1-4V	8.5	190-3400	350-2000	std. in 98, Custom Cruiser; opt. in Cutlass, Delta 88
1975	1-4V	8.5	215-3600	370-2400	std. in Toronado
1976	1-4V	8.5	190-3400	350-2000	std. in 98, Custom Cruiser; opt. in Cutlass, Delta 88
1976	1-4V	8.5	215-3600	370-2400	std. in Toronado